INFANT OBSERVATION
AT THE HEART OF TRAINING

INFANT OBSERVATION
AT THE HEART OF TRAINING

Janine Sternberg

KARNAC
LONDON   NEW YORK

First published in 2005 by
H. Karnac (Books) Ltd.
6 Pembroke Buildings, London NW10 6RE

British Library Cataloguing in Publication Data

A C.I.P. for this book is available from the British Library

ISBN: 1–85575–360–X

10 9 8 7 6 5 4 3 2 1

Edited, designed, and produced by Communication Crafts

Printed in Great Britain by Hobbs the Printers Ltd, Totton, Hampshire

www.karnacbooks.com

For Rachel, Daniel, and Sarah

CONTENTS

vii

ACKNOWLEDGEMENTS

This book arose out of work I carried out for a doctorate in psychoanalytic psychotherapy at the Tavistock Clinic/ University of East London. I am most grateful to Meira Likierman, who persuaded me to undertake that work, and to Anne Alvarez and Andrew Cooper, who supervised it with unfailing encouragement and enthusiasm. I am deeply touched by how consistently generous they were with their time and their thoughts. I also learned a great deal from my fellow doctoral students, especially Tanya Nesic. The part of this book that concentrates on empirical research could not have taken place without the help and cooperation of many people: I am indebted to the institutions that agreed to my interviewing their students, to the infant observation organizers and seminar leaders who engaged with me on discussions of the task, and, of course, most of all to those students who participated in the research meetings. They have generously agreed to allow me to use their thoughts and words.

I do not know how to thank enough Dilys Daws, who inspired me to consider adapting my doctoral research to a book, and Ann Scott, who then engaged in the editorial task of helping me to do this, with both care for detail and a broad interest, which were of immense assistance. Miranda Passey read the manuscript with attention and care, and Asha Phillips provided creative inspiration for the chapter titles; I am intensely grateful to them for their advice, comments, and enduring friendship.

My passion for infant observation arose from my own experience of it many years ago, and I am profoundly thankful to Alessandra Piontelli for this. I also owe so much to many inspirational teachers during my child psychotherapy training at the Tavistock, and subsequently at the British Association of Psychotherapists. I have so enjoyed teaching the next generation of child psychotherapists and owe so much to them and to the institutions that gave me the opportunity to do so. My colleagues in my work and teaching settings have shown me the value of questioning assumptions, as have those whom I taught, and, of course, my patients, over the years.

Most importantly, heartfelt thanks to Michael and my children, who have had to bear my preoccupation with this work for so many years, as well as to be on hand to make suggestions about phrasing and offer invaluable computer assistance.

PREFACE

The experience of infant observation was a life-changing one for me. Many years ago I embarked on the pre-clinical training for child psychotherapists at the Tavistock Clinic uncertain about my commitment to psychoanalytic work. I found my experience of infant observation challenging, moving, disturbing, exciting—I felt deeply involved in it and in the psychoanalytic formulations that I saw being lived out in front of me. I was thrilled to watch personality being formed and developed, and over time I realized that such experiences helped me to see the distinctiveness and uniqueness of each individual. Later, as a qualified child psychotherapist invited to teach an infant observation seminar, I found great pleasure in trying to create for a new generation something of the experience I had been privileged to have. My enthusiasm for infant observation, shared by many of my colleagues, led to my teaching or organizing infant observation seminars for many different student groups.

Later still, I supervised an adolescent training case for a trainee child psychotherapist. Together, the student and I became aware of how she observed the often silent, withdrawn adolescent on the couch. The observational skills that she had learned through infant observation were, in my view, being put to good use in her meticulous, detailed awareness of the tiniest shifts in her patient's state of mind and body. As in any psychoanalytic psychotherapy, the therapist's use of her countertransference was crucial. We realized that the experience of sitting and being with the patient gave the trainee the space to reflect on her countertransference experience in a way that seemed familiar to her from her experience of infant observation. In that situation the emphasis on tiny body movements, the silence and the excruciating nature of the feelings sometimes experienced were full of resonances from her infant observation experience, while the slow pace of the work also allowed the opportunity for her feelings to be carefully considered, as they had been when she was observing. However, further reflection led me to wonder how much the therapist's experience of attending to the countertransference in all therapeutic situations might be deepened as a result of the infant observation experience.

These seminal experiences led to my wanting to think carefully about the place of infant observation in the training and development of a psychoanalytic psychotherapist, and hence to my research and, eventually, to this book.

Note

Throughout this volume, all the emphases in quotations are as in the original unless otherwise stated. When citing authors, I use the term the original writer has used, so at times clinicians are referred to as therapists and at other times as analysts, depending on the usage of the original author. When I write of practitioners, I refer to therapists. Although I have tried to use ungendered language where possible, where I am referring to ideas stated by a writer, I keep to that writer's use of he or she when referring to the therapist or patient. Otherwise, for clarity, where ungendered language would have been too clumsy, I refer to the therapist as she and the patient as he. When writing of mothers and infants, I have tended to refer to the infant as male, to differentiate the baby clearly from the mother. I have often used "she" for the observer, as this reflects the reality of my teaching experience where the great majority of observational students have been female.

ABOUT THE AUTHOR

JANINE STERNBERG is a Consultant Child Psychotherapist at the Portman Clinic, Tavistock and Portman NHS Trust, having worked for many years at the Tavistock Mulberry Bush Day Unit. She trained originally as a child psychotherapist at the Tavistock Clinic and subsequently as an adult psychotherapist at the BAP. She is very involved in training issues in both institutions and active in the professional body for child psychotherapists, the ACP. She is currently Joint Editor of the *Journal of Child Psychotherapy*.

PART I

PRELUDE

Observation vignette: Elliott at 22 weeks

Elliott was in his baby chair on the kitchen floor, smiling and stretching, with his socks coming off his feet through the movement of one limb against the other. Beth was amused by it, smiling repeatedly at him. He held his hands together firmly. His tongue protruded a lot, and his eyes scrunched up; at one point he almost squinted he seemed so excited. He made quick sounds: "da, da". Beth busied herself with preparing to clean the floor, emptying bins, etc. Elliott wriggled in his chair, with a troubled expression on his face; he seemed to be agitated at the noise. During the silent mopping, Elliot, now calm again, followed her intently with his eyes. They felt peacefully connected. Beth opened the back door, and the air became chillier. Elliott trembled, but stayed patient for a few more minutes. Beth said, "You're getting bored—it's nearly done". He brightened. She scooped him up deftly, holding him above her, nuzzling his face—he beamed down on her, she beamed up at him. Then she walked with him on her hip to the living room; I was behind them and did not see either of their expressions, but there was an ease in their movement down the hall. Still balancing Elliott on her hip, Beth played back a message on the answering machine. Then she sat down to return the call. Sitting in the comfy armchair she propped Elliott on her legs, jigging him up and down while she talked. He held himself up well, and he'd look round at me and smile. Beth talked in an efficient, but tense and somewhat exasperated way, and during the call Elliott became a bit distressed, starting to cry. I became anxious, tense, perturbed at Elliott's crying; I wondered what the call was about. When Beth put the phone down, she said, half to me and half to him, she wondered if he didn't like what she was talking about. She tried putting him in the pram near the armchair, and I could see signs of him wriggling; it seemed he didn't want to lie down. I felt strained and uncomfortable. The light in the room seemed to lessen. Beth volunteered to me that the call had been about something problematic—distressing and stressful. Then she said to Elliott, a bit briskly, even pleadingly: "Do you want a suck?" She lifted him swiftly from the pram and moved across to the sofa, hoisting herself up on it, with Elliott resting across her lap. Elliott didn't want to feed, he strained and arched his back, looking in to the middle of the room and away from Beth. Again I felt awkward and pained. She propped him up and he burped. Beth said, in a friendly way: "Is that what was making you grumpy? Do you want a play?" She put him on the floor and brought the baby gym round to him. He smiled, catching hold of the plastic animals suspended from the frame. He became absorbed in his play and seemed reassured by it. Watching him attentively, Beth said, "You can hold things now, you're growing up." She sounded proud and rueful at the same time. Elliott seemed better coordinated, and bouncier in mood. I began to feel relaxed.

We see Elliott excited on many levels, and his excitement giving pleasure to his mother. He is sensitive to her, following her while she cleans; and sensitive to the change in the environment when he trembles at the open door. Here Beth, as she often did, puts Elliott's feelings into words—on this occasion "You're getting bored"—and it leads to a relaxed, happy response from him, a rather familiar experience. He is responsive to her pleasure in holding him. Equally, when she speaks on the phone, his mood darkens, showing the "exquisite sensitivity to the caregivers' moods" described by Brazelton and Cramer (1991, p. 142). The call initiates a break in the contact between them. In the awkward sequence that follows, in which Beth seeks to breastfeed Elliott, he takes his distance by physically straining away from her. Beth has herself wondered if the conversation has upset him. She returns to being in tune with him when she discovers that the baby gym *is* what would help him; Elliott has helped her to get there. In this sequence, which came near the end of my observation hour, I was aware of becoming quite identified with Elliott. I had felt at peace in myself earlier in the hour, comforted by the closeness between Beth and Elliott. The break in the contact between them made me anxious. I felt Elliott's discomfort acutely and wondered how he made sense of the evident change in his mother's mood. It almost seemed as if they needed a bit of physical separateness—negotiated via Elliott's turn to the baby gym—to return to each other. I was relieved that the connection between them was restored and that they weren't left in the unattuned state for long.

Note

I am indebted to Ann Scott for this observational material.

CHAPTER ONE

Introduction

T he short observational vignette and the observer's thoughts on it with which this part begins display many of the aspects of infant observation that I address in detail throughout this work. We see Elliott, aged five-and-a-half months, in a very ordinary domestic situation: sitting in his chair to begin with, watching his mother engage in domestic tasks. We see the fine detail of observation in the way the observer describes his small movements, noticing excitement, the baby's tracking of his mother with his eyes, his response to being picked up. We see Elliott's reaction to his mother's change of mood with her phone call, and we follow the observer's experience of watching Beth offer Elliott the breast at a point when, we might speculate, she is responding to her own need to feed him. The observer creates for the reader a vivid picture of Elliott's response to this, both through the words she uses to describe him straining, arching his back, and looking away, and through her comments on what she feels at the time. In this way we see the observer showing an awareness of her own feelings, tolerating and processing them— activities to which we return repeatedly in the course of this work. Additional reflection on the experience, putting it into context, noting the familiarity of some aspects, thereby building up a sense of understanding emerging over time are shown. We also see the observer using theoretical concepts to further her understanding when she gathers her thoughts together in her comments on this experience. By the end of the vignette, we see Elliott and Beth again in tune: the observer is aware of the relief that she feels about this. She has had a live experience of seeing the importance of attunement, the infant's capacity to make his needs known, deficit and repair, and many other significant aspects, which will hopefully remain inside her, available to be drawn on in future clinical work.

From this brief look at a small piece of observational material we see the observer engaged in many tasks. She has to be able to look, notice, feel, be aware of how what she sees impacts on her, reflect, remember, process, think, and then write about it all. In the course of this book I shall be looking closely at all these different capacities and skills and considering their relevance for practising as a psychoanalytic psychotherapist.

A brief description of infant observation

The term "infant observation", as used in this work, refers to what Alvarez called "naturalistic infant observation" in the debate between André Green and Daniel Stern (in Sandler, Sandler, & Davies, 2000). This approach, developed initially by Esther Bick, is contrasted in its duration and regularity with observations of infants carried out on an occasional or even one-off basis. An observation student, studying on a course offered by a psychoanalytic or psychoanalytic psychotherapy training institution, is instructed to find a family who are about to have a new baby and who are willing to allow an observer to visit them at home regularly—usually weekly—for a minimum of a year. In child psychotherapy trainings such observations usually take place over a two-year period; for adult psychotherapy or psychoanalytic trainings they often last one year. After a preliminary visit to the family, the student begins regular observations as soon after the infant's birth as possible. When visiting the family, the student tries to take up an unobtrusive, non-interfering position, attempting to concentrate on the infant and to take in as much as possible of what she sees happening—the classic "observational stance". Some training institutions expect the observer to concentrate primarily on the infant, while others pay more attention to the mother–infant dyad, referring to the task as "mother–infant observation". Exposure to the maelstrom of feelings experienced by observing a mother–infant couple is seen as being of use to the development of psychotherapeutic capacities in ways that I discuss in chapter 5. No notes are taken at the time, but the student aims to remember in as much detail as possible what she has experienced and to write this down soon afterwards. The fullest description possible of the baby's actions and about his interactions with others present is recorded. Over time, patterns in the infant's ways of behaving and responding may become apparent. The student may be encouraged to note, while acknowledging that it is separate, what she had felt as she observed what she is now recording. These recorded observations are discussed subsequently in a small seminar group (not usually exceeding six members), which meets on a weekly basis for the duration of the observational assignment. In the seminar group the students also share observations and come to know about the infants and families observed by their colleagues. In the course of this book we shall see both the myriad learning outcomes that are claimed for the infant observation experience and also some empirical evidence that matches this in certain dimensions.

Infant research versus infant observation

It is important to be clear from the beginning that there is a substantial body within the psychoanalytic community who do not value infant observation. Some of them have had the experience of it and did not find it personally useful. Others have concerns that the emphasis on the hypothesized internal experiences of the infant leads to a form of theoretical brainwashing. However, the majority of those who speak against it could be thought of as having their views represented by André Green, who, when he objects to infant observation as not being concerned with the unconscious, unfortunately fails to make a clear distinction between naturalistic infant observation as described and discussed in this work and infant observation research. It is fundamental to clarify the distinctions between these. Infant observation research, described by Elizabeth Spillius (in Sandler, Sandler, & Davies, 2000) as "systematic experimental infant observation", should not be confused with "naturalistic infant observation", although both are observational and both are, or can be, used as a form of research. Tyson (1989) also makes a distinction between longitudinal naturalistic research, where the emphasis is on development and the differentiation of psychic structures, and that carried out in academic psychology, where carefully designed experiments aim to test particular hypotheses. These researches have increased our understanding of the range and complexity of infants' competencies. Although in recent years Stern has brought an interest in the inner life of the child to the more directly observable phenomena that had previously been the only currency of infant observation research, referring to the "inferred subjective life of the observed infant" (1985, p. 14), infant research can still be differentiated from naturalistic infant observation.

Infant observation research includes the many and varied studies that have been carried out to increase our knowledge of the capacities and the development of infants and to try to infer from these studies the development of relationships between the infant and his caretakers. These fascinating studies have included evidence of newborns' ability to recognize their mother by smell and voice (Condon & Sander, 1974; De Casper & Fifer, 1980; MacFarlane, 1974, 1975) and young babies' preference for patterns that follow the configuration of the human face (Bruner, 1977; Fantz, 1961). Work done by Brazelton and others (Brazelton, Koslowski, & Main, 1974; Kimberly, 1970; Sander, 1974; Wolff, 1963) charts the to-and-fro nature of interaction between the infant and his caretaker and shows how infants "learn the rules" and learn how to adjust and adapt their needs to what is available. The term "infant observation research" could also include the more longitudinal studies of researchers such as Lynne Murray (Murray, Fiori-Cowley, Hooper, & Cooper, 1996), which have shown the long-lasting effects of mothers' postnatal depression on their children's later cognitive abilities. Developments in technology, especially the use of video, split–screen, and microsecond analysis, have opened our eyes to knowledge that could not have been available earlier. The last three decades have seen a continuing creative use of this medium, by Beebe with her pioneering application of it for making psychoanalytically informed interventions with mother–infant dyads and, more recently, by Dean and Moore (2001) to aid early recognition of child protection issues.

Naturalistic infant observation—that is, infant observation carried out according to the Esther Bick method—brings different gains. It can also enable the observer to see patterns of behaviour, but it concentrates on those that are specific to each mother–infant dyad rather than those of a whole cohort, where small variations in patterns of behaviour will assume less importance. The weekly contact with the observed infant contrasts with "laboratory" studies of infant research, where the infant observed is likely to be seen less frequently and regularly. Observers have the experience of being exposed to often painful feelings and reflecting on them, as is substantially evidenced in this work. Such experience is of more direct relevance to psychoanalytic practitioners than is grudgingly acknowledged in the "indirect relevance" that André Green (in Sandler, Sandler, & Davies, 2000), Peter Wolff (1996), and others have conceded that infant observation research may have for psychoanalysis. For these writers, the emphasis within infant observation research only on what is observable severely restricts its value. Indeed, the main focus of those who are dismissive of infant observation research is that it has little of relevance to say to psychoanalysis. Wolff says: "Empirical infant observations are of interest as empirical studies on the process of social development, but . . . such observations are irrelevant for psychoanalysis as a psychology of idiosyncratic meanings and hidden motives" (1996, p. 377).

Green goes further in saying that not only are the findings of infant research, albeit interesting in themselves, ultimately irrelevant, but additionally, the emphasis on what can be observed may in the end be damaging to psychoanalysis. He makes an impassioned plea for keeping the emphasis of psychoanalytic work on things that cannot be seen. In his famous debate between with Stern, he states that "Its relevance or irrelevance depends on whether its object is the specific objective of psychoanalysis: That is, neither the infant nor the child, but the unconscious" (in Sandler, Sandler, & Davies, 2000, p. 51).

It is my contention that naturalistic infant observation uses both that which can be seen and that which can only be deduced or inferred, largely through awareness of the observer's countertransference, to enhance the practitioner's clinical skills. There is much to be learned simply from what can be observed, and I value what infant research can teach us. The work on making links between infant research and psychoanalysis with adults (Dowling & Rothstein, 1989)

is fascinating. However, I want to emphasize again that infant observation, unlike infant research, goes far beyond what can be seen.
Green argues with the view that infant research/observation can help
the clinician better to understand the patient—a view put forward by
Brenman-Pick in the dialogue between Stern and Green (in Sandler,
Sandler, & Davies, 2000)—by quoting Winnicott, acknowledged as
having vast "hands-on" experience of infants, as saying that the
consulting-room may well be the most fertile ground for understanding more about infantile states: "My experiences have led me to
recognise that depressed or deeply regressed patients can teach the
analyst more about early infancy than can be learned from direct
observation of infants, and more than can be learned from contact
with mothers with infants" (Winnicott, 1960, p. 141). While this may
be true, I will show that naturalistic infant observation has a value
that goes far beyond teaching prospective clinicians about early infancy, although I would argue that to an extent it can do that very
effectively.

Benefits of naturalistic infant observation

By conflating naturalistic infant observation and infant observation
research, Green and others largely miss the point. Naturalistic infant
observation is *not* only about what can be observed. The student of
infant observation learns much more than child development: the
observer learns much to do with herself, and such learning correlates
closely with the development of capacities and skills that a psychoanalytic psychotherapist will need. The observer who experiences
difficulty—as most do—in where to position herself, often quite literally in terms of where to sit in the room, is learning so much: perhaps
she is experiencing the pain of feeling unwanted, excluded; perhaps
she is feeling anxious at receiving attention that, she feels, the baby is
lacking. She may be struggling to be a figure who is viewed in a
benign way but who is not actively being helpful in a centre-stage
manner. She will also be gaining an awareness that what you see
depends on where you are seeing it from and what you are looking at.
And all of this has happened within moments of arriving at the home.

In considering again the observation vignette of Beth and Elliott,
we can note how the observer, now familiar with this family, is aware

of and struggles with making sense of the ebb and flow of her emotional reactions to what she is witnessing. The core of learning is formed from what the observer experiences and the ability to reflect on that experience. This reflection is carried out with the help of the seminar group. If the student is in therapy at the same time, it is likely that the analytic space will offer opportunities for her to think about aspects of herself that have been stirred up by the experience, so that she can begin to make distinctions between what is personal and what belongs to the mother and baby.

The importance of experiential learning

While it is true that other forms of learning to be a psychoanalytic psychotherapist also use experiential learning—indeed, one might argue that it is only the theoretical seminars that do not engage in this manner—it is striking that infant observation is usually offered right at the beginning of the training experience. I believe that observation is used by training schools because learning psychoanalytic skills from books is impossible, and it offers a direct experience. Indeed, at this beginner stage of the process there is no other way that allows the would-be therapist to have such a complex experience, one in which the observer is both deeply involved and yet not expected to "do" anything, and which thus provides very fertile ground for learning. Additionally, I think the placement of infant observation at the beginning of training is influenced by the commonly shared theoretical view that the adult mind is formed through the earliest experiences and that understanding the therapeutic process is influenced by appreciation of the mother–infant dyad.

The thinking behind the research

I valued the opportunity of teaching infant observation and often looked forward eagerly to the seminars. However, as someone involved in the teaching of infant observation and in the training of both child and adult psychotherapists, I was concerned that many of our teaching practices seemed to have evolved over time in a way that seemed to preclude questioning their value. Over the years, the context in which infant observation is taught has altered significantly. From originally being undertaken only by those who had been accepted for clinical training and offered within the context of that training, it now often takes place on courses that have been academically validated and are offered by a training institution linked to an academic institution. Psychotherapy training, which was originally outside the world of academia, is increasingly connected to it, as is having to think about and frame its teaching practices in the language and terms used by institutions who have put much thought into the learning process, as Ann Scott (personal communication, 2003) has commented. Many psychoanalytic therapists may balk at thinking of the way they work within a session being described in terms of "competencies", but those involved in trying to evaluate in a serious way what clinicians do and how they do it in order to consider how to engender and enhance the abilities of the next generation of practitioners are currently using such terms.

Observation courses are now available to a wider constituency of students, not all of whom are interested in undertaking clinical training. While this has the advantage of offering a valuable sensitizing experience to a much wider cohort of students, many of whom are involved in working with people, often in distress, in a variety of settings, it inevitably alters the balance of what can and should be done within the seminar: the fact that many observers are not in analysis or therapy while they are conducting the observation alters both the way the seminar leader conducts herself and what the observer gets from the experience. Additionally, the academic requirements of the courses, demanding essays of an adequate standard on the experience, can at times lead to a different emphasis on the task of the seminar group. While I believe that much of value can be gained from the experience of formulating one's thoughts in an organized and disciplined way and that the act of writing a paper clarifies and deepens the experience for many participants, nevertheless, if the papers required are discussed within the seminars, this inevitably takes time and attention that would otherwise be focused on the infant and his relationships.

Why do we teach what we teach in the way we do? Not surprisingly, this proved to be far too extensive a topic to tackle in its entirety, but because of my particular enthusiasm for infant observation, when I came to undertake research for a doctoral programme, I chose to concentrate on trying to discover whether it was possible to evaluate whether—and if so, in what ways—the experience of infant observation contributes to the development of a psychoanalytic psychotherapist. As a teacher within this field, I wanted to conduct an enquiry into why, along with many of my colleagues, I feel so enthusiastic about teaching and engaging in infant observation. I hoped to identify the specific learning outcomes that arise from engaging in it: our practice should be informed by evidence. I was also interested in investigating whether the relevance differed for adult and child psychotherapists—for example, whether those involved with child patients are more aware of the continuing presence of infantile feelings (Bick, 1964), although obviously psychoanalytic psychotherapists with adult patients hold an awareness of the infant within the adult. Certainly child psychotherapists may have a greater interest in the "normal" child development aspects of infant observation. As a child psychotherapist, I am aware that I have an interest in the concept of developmental thrust, which is not always seen in work with adults, where a retrospective perspective is taken. Additionally, I had an impressionistic view that infant observation is more valued by certain theoretical orientations, and I wondered, if this was the case, why it might be so.

In designing my research project, I realized that in order to establish whether and how infant observation contributes to the capacities and skills needed by the psychoanalytic psychotherapist, I first had to work out what those were. This was a challenging enterprise: little has been written overtly about this, although, of course, case examples show how practitioners work and what they consider to be important in the work. The conceptual research that this involved is described in chapter 2, on the design of the research. Having detailed these capacities and skills, I also examined those said by practitioners and within the literature to be gained from engaging in infant observation. It was then possible to "map" these in a way that illustrated that some areas matched and others did not. In order to see whether it could be shown that the experience of carrying out an infant observation led to an increase in relevant capacities in the participants, I also engaged in empirical research, interviewing small groups of students who were involved in infant observation both at the beginning of their observation experience and again at the end. As is described in detail in chapters 2 and 6, on the design of the research and introducing the empirical research, respectively, I conducted a close analysis of the texts of these interviews. Through the use of grounded theory I was able to identify a number of categories and to see whether there were any differences in the way these categories were talked about in the pre- and post-observation interviews. I then examined how these categories related to my previous conceptual mapping.

I hoped to discover from these interviews whether something substantive happens in this learning process. By interviewing the trainees both near the beginning and near the end of their observation training, it became possible to hypothesize about their use of the infant observation experience. I expected that for some it would form the beginning of a capacity to be built on, while for others it might represent something that could not be sufficiently used at the time. In the latter case, I wondered whether the capacities we would hope to gain from infant observation could be acquired from elsewhere as the training continued, or whether this might in itself indicate some lack of corresponding ability to develop into an effective psychoanalytic psychotherapist. For example, Elizabeth Spillius's 1998 statement (cited in Davids, Miles, Paton, & Trowell, 1999) about the predictive use of "success" in infant observation for the Institute of Psycho-analysis suggests that "doing well" at infant observation is the most accurate predictor of future development as an effective psychoana-lyst. I hypothesized that this concept might illuminate why training institutions prefer infant observation to be the initial experience on psychoanalytic psychotherapy training. Is it the best way of learning capacities that are built on later? Is it the foundation for later capaci-ties, and if so, can they develop without it?

From all this I hoped to find evidence to test my hypothesis that the experience of infant observation makes a contribution to essential aspects of development that are part of the training to become a psychoanalytic psychotherapist. However, I was aware that it was likely to be impossible to *prove* that the infant observation experience is central. Any positive views expressed by students could simply be seen as showing that they have taken on board the dominant ideology of their institutions. I was looking for and found evidence of change over the course of the observation period; in chapter 11, I discuss my contention that this change arose within and so probably from the infant observation experience.

It is not my intention to judge the experience of the observers by suggesting that one training institute "did better" than another: that would be invidious and of uncertain value based on the single sample and the nature of the free-flowing discussion. However, there are differences to be seen in the way the participants responded, in the issues that interested them, and in the distance that they seemed to have travelled. As we will see when looking closely at the different groups of participants used for the research, they varied considerably in terms of experience, with not all of them committed to future clinical training. We cannot help but be aware that different training institutions have different theoretical biases and that this may influence what the participants are encouraged to focus on. Additionally, individual seminar leaders undeniably have their own interests and even hobbyhorses. Just as we acknowledge that some clinicians are more gifted than others, at least with certain types of patient, so it seems reasonable to assume that some teachers enable their students to get more from the experience. Traditionally psychotherapy training institutions use senior and respected clinicians to lead their seminars, and, depending on other circumstances, there may or may not be some guidance to those clinicians on aspects of teaching.

I had originally hoped to look closely at the whole of a training in psychoanalytic psychotherapy and to consider what an institution thought it wanted to convey and how it used its curriculum—in the widest sense of the word—to achieve this result. Not surprisingly, this turned out to be a much wider task than the one in which I was engaged. I am left hoping that the work I have done in delineating capacities and skills needed for psychoanalytic psychotherapy could form a useful building block to such an endeavour. If the capacities and skills that I have attempted to produce are accepted as those understood by the community of practitioners as needed for the work, then perhaps future researchers can look into the ways in which the psychotherapy trainings encourage and enhance these—or not.

Presentation of the material

Readers will notice that in the course of the book I use the terms "psychoanalysis" and "psychoanalytic psychotherapy" interchangeably. Without entering the debate about the difference between them, I feel that the points made are equally valid for both. The chapters on the capacities and skills needed for the work are intended to show those that nearly all practitioners would agree on. Naturally, certain theoretical schools would privilege some attributes over others, and it may be that certain practitioners would want to add attributes I have neglected, having found them particularly useful in their work. However, this is intended as a broad sweep, an attempt to find a wide consensus. It is only when we can say that a psychoanalytic psychotherapist needs, for example, the capacity to wait for meaning to emerge that we can then question whether the infant observation experience helps to develop this capacity. Similarly, in examining skills—or, to put it in a more familiar way, the technique we use within a session—when we consider the usefulness of the clinician using words from the patient's narrative, we can then wonder in what, if any, way the experience of infant observation has contributed to this.

Chapter 2 looks at my research methodology. It gives the reader the opportunity to follow in detail the thinking that I was engaged in when setting up the research project and locates the research firmly in the qualitative research domain.

Part II then takes the reader through the conceptual research, showing in chapters 3 and 4 which capacities and skills are cited in the literature as being of relevance for working as a psychoanalytic psychotherapist. When thinking about those capacities that the therapist must have within him or herself and then considering how they are used in a psychotherapy session to further the psychotherapeutic work, I found myself describing these as feeling similar to a musical instrument that the therapist has within the self, with the way that they are then used within a session being resonant of the way that when an instrument is played, a harmonious sound is produced. I have therefore called chapter 3, on therapist's capacities, "The Therapist's Inner Instruments" and chapter 4, on the skills used within the session, "From Instrument to Melody", illustrating the way the capacities are used and the discipline and careful technique that is required in the service of creating the melody. Throughout the book I have used the term "skills"—familiar to those fluent in the language of learning aims and objectives but less familiar to those engaged in psychotherapeutic work—in order to bring concepts with which we are comfortable from clinical work into a closer match with the rigour of a different academic discipline, one in which much infant observation and psychotherapy training is now taking place. I use the term "skills" to refer to the technique that the clinician employs within a therapy session, the activities engaged in to advance the therapeutic aims. This attempt to map the capacities and skills needed for clinical work is the precursor to seeing whether we can match them with those said to be gained from infant observation. This is summed up in Table 4.1, which shows how a capacity may show itself in technique.

In chapter 5, "Feel the Music", attention is given to the capacities and skills that are said to be engendered through the experience of observation, as garnered from references in the literature that may not necessarily concentrate on that point but do show the author's attitude from, for example, descriptions of the task, and from the private communications of colleagues involved in teaching infant observation. This chapter is called "Feel the Music" to imply the conjunction of feeling and experiencing within a structured framework that is suggested to result from the experience by the writing on infant observation. Table 4.1 reappears here, in a modified form, as Table 5.1: it adds to the former what the literature says about the capacities and skills gained from infant observation and again shows how these skills and capacities map onto each other.

Part III introduces the empirical research and details how the categories were derived (chapter 6). Table 6.1 shows whether those areas were evidenced in the pre- and post-observation interviews. The interviews conducted at the beginning of the research are considered in the light of the categories that later emerged, and the lack of depth and richness in these early interviews is noted. The significant themes that emerged form the basis of chapter 7, which delineates the categories and notes the way that each group mentions (or not) each particular issue. Chapter 8 gives a full account of the interviews conducted at the end of the year. Using the principles of grounded theory (see chapter 2), various themes and issues emerged. There were differences between the groups with regard to the importance they accorded to each issue and the various ways they discussed it.

Chapter 9 looks at how frequently statements on specific topics, which were then gathered together as concepts, were made by each of the groups, both in the initial and the end interviews. This chapter draws together the findings, mapping to see in what way the capacities and skills matched and whether the interviews showed evidence of the participants having greater access to areas that would be seen as being of importance. The table of capacities and skills is presented again as Table 9.1, now showing whether those areas were evidenced in the pre- and post-interviews, whether there was an increase in the attention they were given, and thus what impact the experience of infant observation has had on the development of capacities and skills said to be necessary for psychotherapeutic practice.

Finally, Part IV brings the previous two strands of the work together. At this point the issues are considered from a different perspective. Rather than deconstructing the way a clinician works to find all the separate activities, as was done in earlier stages of the research, I now look at the mind of a clinician at work in a more integrated way. Using some clinical material provided by Ogden (2001), in which he carefully guides the reader through what is going on in his mind in part of a session with a patient, I both examine what skills and capacities we see in operation at the time and also emphasize the way the whole adds up to more than the sum of its parts. Just as, with successful poetry, when the words used become imbued with a quality because of the way they have been put together, so in creative clinical work what is formed takes on an additional depth from the way it fits together. The way aspects—both capacities and skills—are used within a session, woven together and informing each other, lifts the work to a different level. I follow this with looking at the mind of the observer as evidenced in extracts from the interviews, to see whether it is possible to find there the same complex interweaving of capacities and skills. Chapter 11 highlights the meaning and significance of the findings and some of the conclusions, also pointing out some aspects of research methodology that might be questioned and drawing attention to areas that merit further research.

It was possible through the analysis of the participants' responses to show considerable increase in certain dimensions, which had already been identified as being important for therapeutic work. There is naturally the difficulty of separating out one influence from all the others. Much that has been taken in may only be understood at an unconscious level, and evidence of the influence of infant observation may be inferred from some responses. Developments in capacities are likely to be due to many interwoven influences, including personal analysis, theoretical learning, and supervision, as well as, where relevant, learning from ongoing clinical work. However, I am of the opinion that the following chapters do give evidence of the way that infant observation contributes to the development of capacities and skills deemed necessary for effective psychoanalytic psychotherapy.

CHAPTER TWO

Design of the research

This research project contains both empirical research and what is described by Dreher (2000) as "conceptual research": "Conceptual investigations in psychoanalysis are just as important as are the various forms of empirical research" (p. 4). Michael Rustin (2002) also addresses the particular link between psychoanalysis and the modelling and mapping devices developed in work on complexity theory and chaos theory. The empirical component in this study may be more familiar to the research community, as, although it certainly falls within the heading of qualitative research, it uses interviews with groups to generate data through recorded texts of the interviews. As is detailed further on (chapter 6), the texts of the interviews were then examined using the principles of grounded theory to see what categories emerged. The groups were interviewed twice—first when they were beginning the experience of infant observation and again after they had completed an academic year of it—in order to make a comparison possible. However, it was necessary first to have engaged in a conceptual mapping exercise to generate a systematic taxonomy of the skills and capacities that are held to be important, implicitly or explicitly, by the community of practitioners for the practice of psychoanalytic psychotherapy.

Dreher (2000) points out how important it is to have a "systematic clarification of psychoanalytic concepts". She shows the way the meaning and nuances of concepts used by psychoanalytic practitioners has in some cases altered so substantially that the words have become almost meaningless, and she discusses the need for "evidence as to the explicit as well as the implicit use of a concept in clinical practice" (2000, p. 76).

Little can be found in the psychoanalytic literature specifying explicitly the capacities and skills practitioners are using. More frequently, this is revealed through the way practitioners write about the interaction between themselves and their patients. Dreher makes a cogent case for research into concepts, with an investigation of the changes from their original usage to be considered as equally valid and important as empirical research. While, for reasons of space and emphasis, I can only make passing reference here to the way certain concepts have changed, the systematic gathering in of views from a wide number of authors is in the tradition of conceptual research. The need to discover both consensual and dissensual aspects of a concept is discussed by Dreher, who describes how non-prescriptive descriptions of concepts can be found while emphasizing that the rules governing the use of a concept can and do change: "There hardly seems to be a concept about the meaning of which there is a high degree of consensus in our scientific community—which, on the one hand, points to the lively character of an empirical science but, on the other, clearly shows a great need of concept-reflecting discourses" (2000, p. 164). Once a moderate level of consensus about a concept has been achieved, it is then possible to engage in discourse about its use. The literature review that follows is intended as the beginning of this task—conceptual mapping to explore the ways in which infant observation might enhance the capacities and skills needed for psychotherapeutic work.

Conceptual research: literature review

Capacities and skills needed
by the psychoanalytic psychotherapist

In designing the research project, it was clear that in order to establish whether and how infant observation contributes to the capacities and skills needed by the psychoanalytic psychotherapist, it was first necessary to find out what, within the professional community, the latter were considered to be. This was a challenging enterprise because of the relative dearth of written material on the subject. Moreover, it seemed very important to gather a "theoretical-orientation-neutral" spectrum of capacities and skills. Obviously no activity is ever theory-neutral. Conscious and preconscious theory influences all that we do. Inevitably, ideas about the purpose of psychoanalytic psychotherapy must alter the capacities and skills that are deemed to be important for the task, and I consider this in later chapters. However, it is possible to envisage a range of views, at least within the United Kingdom and to some extent North America, that could be thought of as lying along a spectrum: ideas at the far ends of the line would be those that individual practitioners would privilege according to their personalities and theoretical views, but in the centre there might well be a cluster of shared views, and it is those on which I concentrate.

Rather than proffering a Contemporary Freudian, Independent, or Kleinian approach to psychoanalytic psychotherapy, the task was systematically to map a broad view of the capacities and skills needed and then examine the contribution made by infant observation. Interestingly, research revealed less disagreement about the basic range of capacities and skills than might have been anticipated. Certain theoretical differences led to a differentiation of technique with particular patients, and, as is discussed, the changing views about the way of conducting a psychotherapeutic treatment have led to changes in emphasis on qualities needed.

Hewison's (2004) research into the influence of theoretical concepts on the clinical practice of marital therapists is in the tradition of conceptual mapping, as is Hamilton's (1996) work on the influence of analysts' preconscious theories, which discovered that at times analysts of different theoretical orientations shared an interest in theories that influenced their approach to their patients in some very interesting, and often unexpected ways. Hewison, using questionnaires to learn from respondents working in the field of marital therapy which ideas they used in their work, was able both to map each individual's stated use of the core concepts under discussion and to see whether respondents who favoured certain concepts tended to cluster together or whether respondents favoured concepts in totally individual ways. While it was not the focus of my research to look at how and in what way practitioners use the concepts that emerged from the literature, these examples show the usefulness of mixing conceptual and empirical research methods.

In order to have a broad sweep and offer a consensus view, I have not had space to evaluate the authors cited. Because I was aiming for such an inclusive approach, writers from different theoretical schools sit cheek-by-jowl; practitioners from the early years of psychoanalysis are cited next to excerpts from the most recent papers. While I do refer to changes in accepted practice or highlight how certain concepts have altered, this is not the thrust of those chapters. This is partly to do with my eclectic approach, a belief shared in the Independent tradition that eclecticism does not in and of itself reflect intellectual laziness or a lack of rigour. However, within the context of this work it is also because I was aiming to produce a description of capacities and skills that would be acceptable to at least those psychoanalytically informed practitioners whom I viewed as being in my "cluster", as defined above.

The book contains substantial sections on both capacities and skills. I have chosen to use these particular terms, not normally very familiar to practising clinicians, in an attempt to formulate the rather imprecise way of thinking about psychoanalytic psychotherapy in the more restricted language of learning objectives and outcomes. The term "skills" is used to describe the actions engaged in—what the community of practitioners usually refers to as the technique that the clinician uses within the therapy session. I have attempted to generate a set of descriptions of the cognitive/intellectual capacities needed by a psychoanalytic psychotherapist in a comparatively specific theoretical-orientation–neutral manner that would be acceptable to most theoretical orientations. By looking closely at the technique employed within a session, I have been able to identify skills needed for the psychotherapeutic task. As part of this, I have also noted the different emphases that writers of different theoretical orientations place on certain attributes (for a further consideration of this, see M. J. Rustin, 1997a). I have mostly written about capacities and skills in general, but I give brief consideration to whether some of the capacities and skills specifically needed by child psychotherapists would make infant observation particularly useful to them.

Capacities and skills said to derive from infant observation

In order to test the relevance of infant observation to the training of psychoanalytic psychotherapists, it was necessary first to examine what it is believed it contributes, and whether it does what it is held to do. Much has been written about this from a psychodynamic perspective, and I looked at what people claim the experience of infant observation contributes to the development of an effective psychotherapist. The research carried out by Trowell, Paton, Davids, and Miles (1998) into the usefulness of infant observation investigates the effects on a wide group of professionals. They are interested in capacities gained that could be of value, for example, for social work practitioners, whereas I am interested in the place of infant observation in psychoanalytic psychotherapy trainings.

As well as conducting the mapping exercise, I also interviewed colleagues involved in organizing the infant observation component of courses or teaching it. In a group interview with senior members of the child psychotherapy discipline at the Tavistock, those present spoke of their experiences of carrying out infant observation, of teaching it, and of what they viewed it as offering to students. I also met with the organizer of the Anna Freud Centre MSc infant observation component and with the person responsible for organizing infant observation for BAP (British Association of Psychotherapists) MSc students. I spoke with the member of the Institute of Psychoanalysis who organized the infant observation seminars there, and also, briefly, with each of the three current seminar leaders. I had a lengthy meeting with one of the seminar leaders from the AFC MSc. These interviews were used to inform me further about the capacities and skills thought to be engendered or enhanced by the experience of infant observation and, as such, were part of the mapping exercise.

As well as hearing their views about the capacities necessary to be an effective psychoanalytic psychotherapist, I was alert to noting different theoretical views about the purpose and value of the infant observation experience. Those responsible for selecting trainees were also a source of information about what capacities they would expect trainees to have at the outset of their training, which they expected would be developed during training. Those responsible for judging candidates to be ready for qualification were also able to contribute their views as to what qualities, capacities, and skills should be in evidence by that stage. I also noted that outside the United Kingdom infant observation is not necessarily thought to be relevant for psychoanalytic or psychoanalytic psychotherapy trainings, although, as described in the introduction, frequently its critics conflate naturalistic infant observation and infant research.

Areas of overlap and areas of difference

The information having been gathered, it was now possible to map it in a way that showed where areas matched and where they did not. Some capacities gained from the experience of infant observation might not seem central to the skills needed by a psychotherapist, and some capacities needed to be an effective psychotherapist often can only be gained through other avenues, such as theoretical seminars, supervised work, personal analysis, and aspects of clinical work. As the reader will see, it has been possible to create a clear and careful picture of where these areas match and where they do not: Figure 2.1 is a diagrammatic representation of this and of its relationship to the empirical component of this research.

Empirical research

Having examined the literature, I conducted a small-scale study to see whether such capacities could be found in students who had undertaken an observation experience. Together with my supervisors, I considered how best to do this. Although the idea of showing videoed material of infant observation or of clinical work to people who had not experienced infant observation—whether experienced clinicians or beginners—and to those who had, has some appeal as a way of testing for discrepancies between their capacities, it seemed to have too many other variables that could make any findings unreliable. Clearly in conducting qualitative research it is not possible to control the variables in the way experimental research aims to do; nevertheless, it would be apparent that differences in responses to the stimulus—the videoed material—could be accounted for in so many ways (e.g. the theoretical orientations of the practitioners, their own analytic experience, their clinical experience since qualifying) that it would be impossible to evaluate whether the previous infant observation experience had any part to play in any discrepancies seen. Similarly, discussing written infant observation presentations did not seem likely to show up anything other than that those who had done infant observation had learned to approach "the text" in a certain way.

While it seemed very likely that any sort of interviews ran the risk of only discussing conscious views and that the deeper, more meaningful contribution of the infant observation experience might go unrecognized, interviews were chosen as an approach in which some opportunities for assessing views would be available. While any interviewing is limited to verbal behaviour and self-reported data (Morgan, 1997), it was hoped that the use of grounded theory to access levels of meaning beyond that which could be instantly noted in the discourse would mediate the fact that participants were ostensibly only talking about what was consciously available to them.

The idea of interviewing students as they were beginning their observation experience and then again after one year was adopted as the most fruitful approach, hoping that treating the transcripts of the interviews as texts that could be analysed using grounded theory would yield data of depth and substance about the developmental process of training to be a clinician, which is held to entail the gradual deepening of specific emotional, cognitive, and reflective capacities. The constructs—the development over time of qualities that linked with those that became apparent in the mapping—could be studied through their emergence in the texts using the grounded theory method. It seemed important to use a methodology that would leave

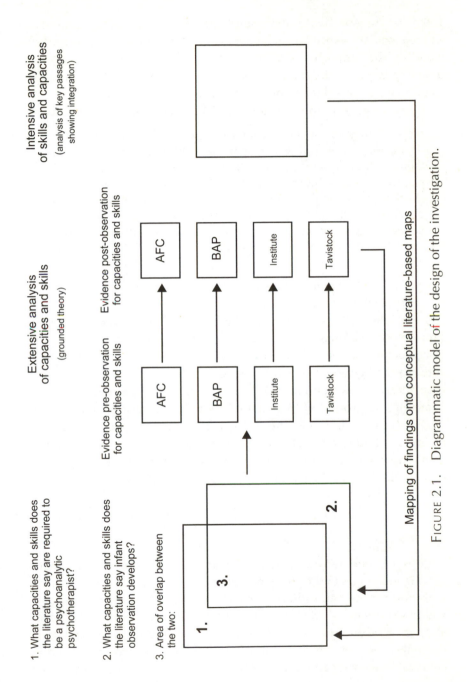

FIGURE 2.1. Diagrammatic model of the design of the investigation.

Intensive analysis
of skills and capacities
(analysis of key passages
showing integration)

Extensive analysis
of capacities and skills
(grounded theory)

Evidence pre-observation   Evidence post-observation
for capacities and skills   for capacities and skills

AFC   AFC

BAP   BAP

Institute   Institute

Tavistock   Tavistock

1. What capacities and skills does
the literature say are required to
be a psychoanalytic
psychotherapist?

2. What capacities and skills does
the literature say infant
observation develops?

3. Area of overlap between
the two:

1.

3.

2.

Mapping of findings onto conceptual literature-based maps

room for the specificity and complexity of the process. Qualitative approaches are especially relevant when the emphasis is on understanding the individual's own thoughts, experiences, or use of language in depth and detail. The data of qualitative research are most often language—documents, interviews, observations—and, as Midgley points out, the psychotherapist is well placed for this, as

> the skills needed for good qualitative interviewing overlap a great deal (though not completely) with the skills we learn as psychotherapists: building rapport, sensitive listening, eliciting people's stories, gradually building up an understanding of a phenomena, checking it out with the other person and attending to complex, provisional and incomplete knowledge. All of these skills are necessary to produce the kind of interview-based data that is central to many qualitative approaches to research. [2004, pp. 94–95]

My primary focus being on participants' experience as they described it, I approached the transcripts using grounded theory (Atkinson & Coffey, 1996; Glaser & Strauss, 1967; Pidgeon & Henwood, 1996). From close examination of the transcripts an extensive list of the issues being discussed was produced, and these were grouped into coherent categories. When I found that some features did not fit, I then returned to examine the text once more. Thus, following the principles of grounded theory, there was a constant to and fro between the raw data and the emerging themes. As new categories emerged, I had to return to the original data to test out, refine, and in some cases abandon my earlier attempts at categorizing. The section on data analysis and chapter 6 give further details of this.

Method

Groups of students were interviewed to elicit information about what is gained from the study of infant observation. As it was important for one of my subsidiary research questions ("is the infant observation experience differently valued by different theoretical schools and/or by adult and child psychotherapists?") to have research participants who were studying at different institutions and on different courses, I interviewed students on the following trainings: the Anna

Freud Centre (AFC) MSc course, the Tavistock MA in Psychoanalytic Observation (M7, the "gateway" to the Tavistock child psychotherapy training), the British Association of Psychotherapists MSc, and the Institute of Psychoanalysis. The interviews were conducted in groups. All trainees from one institution were interviewed together, and the four sets of interviews were conducted on two separate occasions. The groups ended up being uneven in size, but as statistical significance was not being sought, this difference was not thought to affect the results. From these interviews I hoped to have a representative sample of the three main theoretical groupings in British psychoanalysis (Contemporary Freudian, Kleinian and Independent), and of differences between child and adult trainings.

Although the decision to interview participants in groups was partly made on pragmatic grounds, there were also important advantages in the use of these groups. In focus groups, the interaction between group members is important as it produces "data and insights that would be less accessible without the interaction found in a group" (Morgan, 1997). Of course, inevitably there is less time for each participant than there would be in individual interviews, and there are risks that participants may tend to conformity or, indeed, offer extreme views in an attempt at polarization (Fern, 2001). Writers on focus groups also acknowledge ways in which group interviews can be less useful. Fern (2001) writes of "production blocks": waiting for the opportunity to speak can lead to participants forgetting or abandoning what they had intended to say. He and others (Bloor, Frankland, Thomas, & Robson, 2001) also write of participants holding back for fear of the evaluation of others, or putting themselves in the "normalized" position of others. Nevertheless, as Morgan (1997) points out, the comparisons the participants make between each other's experiences and opinions are a valuable source of insight into complex behaviours and motivations, as the "share and compare" culture within groups can enhance the level of discussion, and it is generally agreed (Bloor et al., 2001; Morgan, 1997) that discussions within focus groups tend to produce data related to actual experience, going into greater depth than simply talking about opinions or perspectives.

The literature on the setting up of focus groups gives considerable attention to methods. Much of this was not of direct relevance to this study, as there was no question of creating heterogeneous groups or of attempting either to match groups according to various factors, such as age and gender, or to form segmented samples along those lines. I could not choose my research participants but relied on those who had volunteered. It was important that the groups interviewed were representative of the training institutions—what Maher refers to as a "sample of subjects that is representative of the population in question" (1998, p. 135). As such, the participants were in nearly all cases known to each other. Only the Tavistock M7 course, being a very large one with over 50 students per year, all in small seminar groups, gave the opportunity for the research group to be composed of people with a common interest—in infant observation—who were not already known to each other. Of the other three groups, the AFC and BAP MSc groups were in fact composed of existing seminar groups who worked together on infant observation, and the Institute group participants were part of a relatively small training group all of whom worked—away from the training—in the same large institution, although in different departments. In fact, as will be seen in the section on setting up the interviews, the way the participants were recruited had, of necessity, to be left to contacts in the training institutions. However, there are many instances of focus groups in organizations and other situations in which acquaintance is unavoidable (Fern, 2001; Morgan, 1997). Fern (2001) writes of group cohesion being important, and Bloor and colleagues (2001) suggest that there are advantages to using pre-existing social groups, as their prior knowledge of each other can help the way the discussion is generated.

Obviously, the composition of a group generates different group dynamics, but authors emphasize that it is important that the group can discuss the issues comfortably: "Small groups . . . work best when the participants are likely to be both interested in the topic and respectful of each other" (Morgan, 1997, p. 40). Indeed, while much of the literature on focus groups advises a group size of 8–10 participants per group, there is also a suggestion that smaller groups can in certain circumstances be more useful because there is more time for each member to talk and it is possible to make more sense of each participant's reactions (Bloor et al., 2001). Fern (2001) emphasizes the moderator's role in providing time and an atmosphere that allows individuals to express their views. I was not able to control how many people attended the research group interviews. Two of my groups had three members each, with five and six members, respectively, in the other groups. Since the mode of interview was that of free-flowing discussion, with myself as the moderator, there to use prompts if certain topics were not addressed, inevitably, topics came up in some groups and not in others. I address these differences when analysing the data generated by the interviews.

However, it is important to remember that it was not the primary purpose to compare and contrast the experiences between the groups. Rather, the main focus of the research was to determine whether, and if so in what ways, the experience of infant observation added to the skills needed by a psychoanalytic psychotherapist. As such, the emphasis was on changes *across* the groups, using each as an additional source of data rather than primarily looking for differences between them, although when these were apparent, they were noted, and possible reasons for these differences were suggested. Bloor and colleagues (2001) point out that focus groups are not the best means of mapping differences in *individual* behaviour and behaviour change. As the research was not designed to look for any individual changes, this was in accord with its purpose.

Fern (2001) states that the researcher can generalize from the specific if their sample of respondents recruited for the focus group project is representative of the relevant population of respondents, while Bloor and colleagues say that "The generalisability of findings needs to be assured . . . by ensuring that the different groups when taken together cover the *complete* range *of the study population*" (2001, p. 91; emphasis in original). While a smaller number of respondents has some limiting effect on the generalizability, the representative nature is most important. The participants in this study represented first-year observation students at the training institutions approached.

The topic of the recruitment of focus group members is given much attention in the literature. Obviously this is partly to do with the purpose of such groups, many of which are commercially driven, and so writers discuss issues to do with appropriate payment for attendance. It is clearly important that any participants in research do so in an informed and voluntary way. Kazdin (1998) suggests that it is easier to involve volunteers with research when they see the research as important and worth while.

Setting up the interviews

The decision was made to interview students on these academic courses, realizing that not all of them would be going on to clinical training. This meant that the three Institute candidates were in a very different position from the others, all being at a more developed stage in their professional careers; in fact, as it turned out, all three had carried out infant observations previously. Within the other three groups, there were significant differences in the experiences of the observers in terms of familiarity with therapeutic concepts, sophistication of thinking, and evidence of familiarity with the language of the unconscious.

I wrote to the person responsible for organizing the infant observation component of their training, as described above. I had meetings and discussions with those people and in some cases with infant observation seminar leaders who had an interest in research. In one institution I notified infant observation seminar leaders and asked them to bring my request for volunteers to meet for research purposes to the attention of their seminar members. I also put up notices telling students of my research and asking them to contact me if they were willing to participate. In another institution with only five students on the relevant course, their infant observation seminar leader discussed participation with them, and they all agreed. A similar approach was taken in another institution, where the three participants in one seminar group were invited by their seminar leader to take part. With the fourth training, having gained the agreement of the individual seminar leaders and been given the names of their trainees, I approached one of the students, who then undertook to gather together those of his peers who were willing or able to meet at a certain time. Three trainees turned up for the meeting, although others had been expected. There are important issues to be considered in the fact that two of the groups were composed of members who only came together for the purposes of the research, while the other two groups met regularly for infant observation seminars—and in one case for theoretical seminars too—throughout the year. While this may not have had much impact on the initial interviews, when the on-going groups were not well established, by the end of the academic year it had significant implications. Fern (2001) writes of the concept of shared and unshared information within a group. The more group members know each other and an item of information, the more likely it is that that item will be mentioned and discussed. However, he states that this is more common in heterogeneous groups who are searching for any common ground. The groups that had been learning together were able to think about issues that were common to the group as a whole, compare their experiences across the group, and refer to how they had felt about episodes then being spoken of in the meeting, which they had previously heard about within the seminar group. This clearly created a situation in which there were further discrepancies between the groups. However, since the research was primarily concerned with the impact of the observation experience as a whole on the participants, it is likely that these issues did not undermine the findings in relation to that.

It is also worth noting that at the time I had a clear and public role within two of the training institutions, and this may have affected the willingness of my colleagues to agree to the research and may have influenced the responses of the participants, who might have imagined that I would in some way be influential if they wished to progress with their training. It is also possible that although I had explained the purpose of the research and my wish to generalize from their particular experiences, the participants might have thought that I would discuss their responses with their seminar leaders or other influential people. Bloor and colleagues (2001) state that when researchers are involved in an organization, this may "limit open and honest debate and discussion within the group". Issues of power may result in participants being stubbornly silent or bland. Silence was certainly not an issue within the groups I conducted, where all participants contributed freely. However, a wish to offer bland responses or statements that it was presumed I would want to hear could have influenced certain responses, although the depth of the responses, especially when looked at using the principles of grounded theory, somewhat negates this view.

I had prepared a sheet explaining the purpose and method of the research and assuring students of confidentiality with regard to their comments. There were consent forms for them to sign and an understanding that they were free to leave at any point if they wished to do so. The interviews took place in the training institutions of three of the four groups. The fourth, the Institute group, met at the institution where they all worked—a very familiar setting to them. Bloor and colleagues state that "there is no such thing as a neutral venue for a focus group" (2001, p. 39)—all venues have their difficulties. Meeting the participants in a place familiar to them, a place associated with the topic under discussion—either infant observation or for the Institute group its link with their professional practice—offered a setting in which the purpose of the research was uppermost in the participants' minds was well as being most convenient for them in a practical way.

The group meetings lasted one hour—a length of time chosen in order not to over-extend the good will of the volunteers while being sufficient to gather the required information. Given the relatively small number of participants, the time allowed was sufficient for each participant to speak individually as well as to engender discussion between them.

The interviews

Merton, Fiske, and Kendall (1990) delineate four broad criteria for effective focus group interviewing:

1. *Range:*   covering a range of relevant topics;
2. *Specificity:*   providing data that are as specific as possible;
3. *Depth:*   fostering interactions that explore particular feelings in some depth;
4. *Personal context:*   taking account of the personal context of the participants in generating responses to the topic.

When discussing range, they suggest that interviews should cover issues known to be important as well as issues the researcher had not anticipated. They also write of the importance of "concrete and detailed accounts of experiences", not generalizations. The interviews should not be moderator-dominated (in Bloor et al., 2001, the person conducting the interview is called a facilitator). With these ideas in mind, I carried out my interviews.

The group format was intended to facilitate ideas being taken up and expanded by the members of the small group. We were very aware that direct questioning would probably elicit answers largely only on a conscious level and that there was a likelihood that these would be heavily influenced by the training institutions' explicit expectations. However, in a fairly unstructured free-ranging discussion it would be possible to notice underlying issues and, through the use of grounded theory (Atkinson & Coffey, 1996; Taylor & Bogdan, 1998), as discussed above, to extrapolate themes that would go beyond the supposedly "correct answers".

Trainees were first interviewed at the beginning of their training prior to starting infant observation. In some of the trainings mentioned, students' infant observation experience occurs before acceptance to the clinical training. In such instances I asked for volunteers from among those who wanted to proceed to the clinical training, but obviously those students were still in a very different position from those on the Institute training, who were experienced clinicians, already accepted as candidates for training. I then interviewed the same students again at the end of one year of the observation experience, as this was the end point for two of the four groups.

At the first interviews I asked each group two questions: "What do you expect to learn from undertaking an infant observation that might be relevant to you as future clinicians in training?" with a subsidiary question: "Did the fact that the course that you're on has an observation component attract you to the course or not?" In the second set of interviews, at the end of an academic year, participants were invited to talk about aspects of the observation experience that seemed important to them.

Both sets of interviews were fairly discursive—those interviewed could talk freely. They were semi-structured interviews that covered a number of defined thematic areas resulting from the literature searches and discussions with senior staff responsible for training. I had in reserve a number of "prompts", which could be used if areas I had identified were not addressed in the free-flowing discussion. In a wide-ranging discussion, students talked at the beginning about their hopes and expectations; at the end, they looked back and described experiences, obviously influenced by their continuing development. I expected that during the post-observation interviews participants might think about how they themselves understood any connection between these experiences and their own current or future development as psychotherapists, and that the influence of infant observation would still be consciously available to the interviewees, rather than having become deeply embedded in the overall way of thinking about and responding to the patient, which would be the situation with more experienced practitioners. The interviews were tape-recorded and transcribed, so that they could be coded for thematic analysis and the data contained in them treated in a systematic way. I analysed these interviews as texts and used a systematic form of textual analysis to order and code responses.

Analysis of data and interpretation of findings

The term "data analysis" refers to the systematic evaluation of the information that has been collected. I went through the transcripts and, using the ideas of grounded theory, took each statement in turn and extracted from it the many complex issues it contained, moving from the particular to the general. Chapter 6 shows this in detail. The issues were grouped in clusters, and aspects that did not fit within that framework were noted. Following the principles of grounded theory, I then returned to my raw data, the transcripts, examined them further to see how the emerging categories needed to be refined, and noted the concerns raised by each group in turn. Having identified a number of themes that emerged in the post-observation interviews, I then returned to the pre-observation interviews and noted the presence or absence of these themes there. In examining the data through the use of grounded theory and thus creating categories, I was able to relate surface observations to deeper levels of theoretical explanation (M. J. Rustin, 1997b), as becomes apparent when we look at the categories of "awareness of feelings, tolerating feelings, and reflecting on feelings", where the participants' responses relating to such experiences were then examined in the light of psychoanalytic theory about projection and the use of the countertransference. Although Bloor and colleagues point out that "The interactive nature of focus groups, which leads to some uncertainty in the data, resulting from contradiction and unfinished speech, causes problems for systematic approaches to analysis" (2001, p. 70), the grounded theory approach allows for the emergence of themes.

In coding data from focus groups it is agreed that the fundamental unit of analysis is the group, not the individual (Morgan, 1997). Although discussion in the group depends on both the individuals in the group and the dynamics of the group as a whole, nevertheless, in terms of addressing the data, it is accepted that statements are treated as a group response. According to Fern (2001), focus groups can be used to generate theoretical constructs and hypotheses, and these can be identified and defined from discussion transcripts. Through a process of aggregation, what the respondents say can be creatively structured into higher-order theoretical constructs. Starting from the statements made, these were then grouped and seen as second-order constructs, which were, in turn, used to create generalizations. Similarities and differences between the groups were noted. These are described at the end of chapters 7 and 8, which give the narratives of the interviews.

Questions of validity and generalizability

The research was undertaken in a naturalistic setting, using descriptive methods, a form well established in the social sciences (M. J. Rustin, 1997b, 2002). The use of groups can be considered as equivalent to the single case study—a view accepted by Kratochwill, Mott, and Dodson (1984) and by Kazdin (1998). It is acknowledged that the use of a single case study may achieve "an important knowledge base that is unobtainable through traditional large quantitative research" (Kratochwill et al., 1984, p. 55). Kazdin writes of the focus of the case study often having been on the individual with a "reliance on anecdotal information" (1998, p. 405). While making it clear that he views anecdotal reports about changes as unreliable, Kazdin accepts that where there is what he terms "objective information"—that is, clear measures that show that change has actually occurred—such research should be considered valid.

Bellack and Hersen (1984) specify that even in the most "hard" research it is often not possible to show cause and effect—two or more variables may be related, but it may be impossible, beyond this, to show that *A* causes *B*. Similarly, researchers, even those conducting experiments in laboratories, often have problems with variables over which they have no control (Gayle Beck, Andrasik, & Arena, 1984): "In any research however stringent multiple influences are likely to affect one another as well as the outcome" (Kazdin, 1998, p. 17).

Clearly, as I acknowledge in later chapters, there are likely to have been many factors that caused the changes seen in the participants. As Kimble says: "Almost nothing in behaviour results from a single environmental influence" (1998, p. 22). Indeed, not only can there be other *separate* causes, but these then will also influence the cause under discussion. The impact of something depends on multiple factors—that is, it is moderated by or interacts with those other factors, making it difficult, if not impossible, to isolate the factors that have influenced change. Kazdin (1998) states that the degree to which inferences can be drawn about the causal agent in the treatment of a clinical case also depends on the *kinds* of changes that occur. Maher (1998) emphasizes that it is what happens *in* the sample that is of importance and that it is not necessary to generalize. In the research under discussion it is sufficient to say that the observed changes took place in the context of carrying out infant observation and in taking part in discourse about it. Michael Rustin (2002) writes of the problems of applying principles of causality to mental life and suggests that psychoanalytic research should instead have an interest in "mapping changes and development over time", identifying patterns. Using the ideas of complexity theory, he refers to "binding conceptions" so that "the interest and value of these models lies in their capacity to give definition to many differentiated kinds of pattern. . . . This is why its preferred style of thinking is in terms of multi-dimensional narratives, rather than by the correlation of discrete variables" (2002, p. 138).

Sechrest (1984) states that the measurement of change—i.e. differential change—"is one of the most problematic tasks faced by social science researchers". Through looking at the increased frequency of certain dimensions, I was able to show that the participants gave more thought to certain areas after the infant observation experience than they had before. Clearly those committed to quantitative research see multiple problems in generalizing from qualitative research. Fern (2001) states that by using focus groups, individual particular characteristics and group composition *do* pose a threat to generalizability, because groups with those members cannot be reproduced, but that the qualitative knowledge they generate is more important. Descriptive counting is especially useful in research projects that compare distinctively different groups to determine how often various topics are mentioned (Morgan, 1997). As the groups in the research sample were not structured, it was more difficult to compare group with group because topics arose in some groups and not in others. As the main hypothesis related to the influence of the infant observation experience for all practitioners, with only a secondary interest in whether this varied between theoretical groups or in adult/child trainings, this was less important; nevertheless, it was possible to make some comparisons between the groups, noting differences between them.

Aims of empirical research

The research was designed to establish whether something substantive, relating to the *assumed* contribution of infant observation to psychotherapy training, actually happens in this learning process. By interviewing trainees near the beginning and again near the end of their observation training, it became possible to hypothesize about their use of the infant observation experience for the purposes of training. From the literature and from discussions with colleagues it seemed likely that for some it would form the beginning of a capacity to be built on, while for others it might represent something that could not be sufficiently used at the time.

The empirical research looked for evidence to test the hypothesis that the experience of infant observation plays a definite and definable role in the development of specified capacities and skills necessary to become a psychoanalytic psychotherapist. While acknowledging that it was likely to be impossible to establish that infant observation was a necessary condition for those developments, the following work demonstrates that the participants' responses showed evidence of considerable development and deepening along certain dimensions of learning, which I had already identified as being important for therapeutic work. Much that has been taken in may only be understood on an unconscious level, and evidence of the influence of infant observation may be inferred from some responses. Developments in capacities are likely to be due to many interwoven influences, including personal analysis, theoretical learning, and supervision, as well as, where relevant, learning from ongoing clinical work.

PART **II**

CONCEPTUAL RESEARCH

CHAPTER THREE

The therapist's inner instruments

In order to examine what the experience of infant observation might contribute to the equipment of a psychoanalytic psycho-therapist, it is necessary first to examine which capacities and skills are considered to be relevant for a therapist. However, these issues are not well addressed in the literature, which makes it all the more important to draw a distinction between capacities and skills. I understand "capacities" to refer to the qualities of the personality, the generalized approach of the practitioner; "skills" (I am using "skills" and technique as synonymous), on the other hand, could be translated as the individual tools that are used within the session. Skills may on occasion exist without the underlying capacities, and skills can certainly be practised and honed. Obviously there are ways in which the two interact: for example, the capacity to bear uncertainty and wait for something to emerge may display itself in the session in the therapist's silence and lack of questioning. However, I think we can be clear that being silent and not questioning may not in itself mean that the practitioner has the capacity to bear uncertainty. Because technique arises from and is closely interwoven with capacities, it is difficult to write about them separately in a cogent way. Some skills are readily understandable applications of capacities, whereas others

43

are not. We might question whether, for example, a particular way of listening is a skill or a capacity. In this chapter I have concentrated on capacities and note the technique that arises directly out of them; in chapter 4 I address those aspects of technique that seem less closely tied up with capacities.

Remarkably few writers have discussed capacities in an overt way. On the whole, psychotherapeutic practitioners address ideas or issues that interest them, and from their description of the work the reader can pick up implications of the capacities needed or techniques that were helpful in that instance. There are, of course, exceptions to this, and some writers (Greenson, 1974; Langs, 1973; Schafer, 1983) are wonderfully clear about how to proceed. While some capacities are innate, there is no suggestion that they could not be improved upon through practice and supervision. Similarly, some areas of difficulty would be addressed in personal analysis/therapy. A trawl through the literature revealed a collection of capacities that I detail below. I do not believe that it is intended that all qualities reside within all practitioners, but perhaps most aspiring psychotherapists would want to acquire such capacities.

Different authors give different weight to differing capacities, and in some cases we can see a theoretical bias affecting what is valued or thought to be necessary. Many are simply mentioned in passing, without further description of why or in what way they are useful or necessary, while some are given considerable attention. Using terms from operational research (Cooper & Payne, 1980; O'Brien, 1986), we could divide these capacities into those practitioners may have had, to a greater or lesser degree, as a feature of their personality, a way of interacting with the world around them, prior to beginning training as a psychotherapist, and those that are only brought into play in the therapeutic situation. The former may well be enhanced and refined considerably by training, but they nevertheless exist from the start and may even, to an extent, be the qualities that led the practitioner into a career in psychoanalytic psychotherapy in the first place. O'Brien (1986) points out the interactional nature of work and personality and looks at ways in which the work carried out affects the personality of the person doing it. While I think this may well be so for many people who spend their working lives engaged in psychotherapeutic work, it seems important here to be able to make a distinction for ease of discussion.

The capacities necessary for effective functioning in the consulting-room are not—or, at least, should not be—the way the psychotherapist relates when not in working mode. Guy (1978) shows how unhelpful and dysfunctional it can be for the psychotherapist to relate to spouse and children as if they were her patients. The model proposed by Schafer suggests that the analyst "operates through what may be called the organisation and presentation of a *second self*" (1983, p. 43): "The analytic second self is a way of conducting an analysis. It does not refer to an essence that lies behind the actions and expresses itself through them" (p. 52). While some object to this idea, feeling that being real and genuine is a necessary part of the analytic relationship, it is useful to be aware that, of course, therapeutic practitioners offer or bring to the fore certain aspects of themselves for use in the professional encounter that inevitably and rightly causes them to behave differently from the way that they would with their friends or in other situations. I later look briefly at some ideas about the "real" person of the therapist and the "real relationship". However, despite the considerable emphasis in contemporary psychoanalysis on the therapist's use of self, it is important, I think, to be aware of the professional self that is being used in the consulting-room. Certain capacities are being deployed in the service of a task—the psychotherapeutic work—purposefully, discriminatingly, with attention to an end in mind, and in a way that thus separates out the therapist's way of behaving in working mode from that used at other times, even if the same capacities are evidenced.

Personal characteristics

The question of which personal characteristics are necessary for becoming an effective clinician, while very interesting, is not strictly relevant when thinking about the contribution infant observation might make to psychotherapy training, as these capacities, although they could be honed by training, would already be in evidence without any particular aspects of the training curriculum. There is an implicit assumption in the literature that candidates entering training come with a personality that is essentially suitable for training: as Andrew Cooper (personal communication, 2004) comments, there is no expectation that training could turn a psychopath into a psycho-therapist. However, the trainee is expected to develop substantially on the personal journey that takes place in the course of the training. Whatever the personal aptitude and disposition of "the man in the street", we would not expect him to be effective in the consulting-room without training in the task of psychoanalytic psychotherapy.

Writers refer to intelligence, curiosity, and an interest in the emotional life of the self and others; more deeply, a willingness to be taken by surprise, some wish for introspection and imagination (which, it is suggested, could be fed by literature) are privileged. Therapists need to be flexible, patient, and have a need to repair. A certain wish to be private, which may or may not be connected to an avoidance of narcissism, is also recommended. It is also suggested that the would-be therapist needs to have independence of mind, integrity, and a love of truth, and be compassionate and warm—although it is also noted that if the therapist is too "giving", it stunts the patient's opportunity to explore certain negative aspects of himself. It is also clear that too much emphasis by the therapist on these qualities may make for all sorts of difficulties, for the patient cannot express a negative transference if the therapist cannot bear the "injustice" of hearing it. If the therapist is too keen to be appreciated by the patient, the work will be seriously impeded. We will see that different theoretical groupings place different emphases both on the importance of the negative transference and on how to use it. As will be seen when looking at technique, a therapist has to have a certain ease with communication and a way of listening that has an interest in the space between words and the underlying texture. The strains of analytic work call for stamina and resilience, and therapists need to have an awareness of their own limitations.

The analytic attitude

- *The analytic attitude and the therapeutic stance*

This is an overarching concept, which includes all those detailed below, but also has additional qualities. It involves a readiness to participate imaginatively in the patient's inner and outer life rather than doing so by direct involvement (Rayner, 1991). It is an approach in which feelings can be recognized by a reflective part of the mind (M. E. Rustin, 1988). Coltart (1993) writes of being a detached observer and involved at the same time. The state of mind in which the therapist can feel but does not have a non-analytic response is one in which, as Dryden (1990) puts it, the therapist's own personality has been "subordinated to the analytic attitude". King (1978) uses the Buddhist term "non-attachment" to go some way towards describing this elusive quality.

- *Attitude to the patient*

Aveline (1990) says that the therapist's relationship with the patient needs to be both passionate and ethical. While some writers (Greenson, 1978) suggest that therapists need to like their patients, for others the important thing is to be willing to be engaged and involved with them. Perhaps again we see a theoretical difference with therapists in the Contemporary Freudian group being more keen to see qualities in their patients that they can respect and so like, while Kleinians may find it sufficient to be interested in why they feel dislike for a patient. Many writers (Greben, 1975; Nelson-Jones, 1982; Schafer, 1983; Strupp, 1973) emphasize that the therapist needs to have a respectful, accepting attitude to the patient, one that is non-valuative and non-condemning. However, Parsons (1986) suggests that this is something to which lip service may be paid: there is often an implicit hierarchical attitude within the therapeutic relationship which assumes the analyst's reality as the norm by which the patient's reality has to be modified. He says that it is difficult *genuinely* to enter the patient's viewpoint but emphasizes how important it is for therapists not to impose their viewpoints on patients but to let them arrive at their own truth.

The suspending of judgement is also deemed to be important. Bion (1962) writes about the need for receptive observation, not judgement on what is observed. Greenson (1974) goes further, to say that the therapist should suspend judgement even to the point of gullibility, as this enables empathy to develop. However, Langs (1973) warns of the need for a balance between a non-judgemental, tolerant approach and one that fosters acting out. The difference in emphasis may in part be due to the authors having in mind different patient populations— after all, with a more psychopathic patient it would be important not to foster a climate in which the patient believed the therapist to be unaware of the perversity and pathology evidenced. Goldberg (1999) has stated that judgement is inevitable: the therapist cannot—and should not—only see things from the patient's perspective. He writes of the eye of "the other"—this other has preconceptions, theories, and their own perspective, which affect what is seen and how it is thought about.

- *Realistic hopefulness and a wish to help the patient*

As with other capacities mentioned, this is one where there is a "Goldilocks view": not too much and not too little, with an idea that there *is* an—unspecified—amount that is "just right". Hamilton (1996) quotes Bowlby as saying that a psychotherapeutic practitioner must have faith and hope, and that such qualities are therapeutic. Margaret Rustin (2001) writes of her work with two very damaged children:

> For the task, courage and some hopefulness about human beings' capacity for change and development are needed, but, since we are expecting our patients to have at least a small store of those qualities of mind (it takes a lot of guts for such children to begin therapy), it does not seem unreasonable to draw attention to what we need in ourselves. [2001, p. 274]

Studies cited by Strupp (1973) show that where therapists viewed the patient favourably, they had strongest expectations of success, and that this situation, which engenders a warm attitude in the therapist, then affects the way the therapist approaches the work and, in a circular way, tends to lead to success. While we may have questions about what seems a rather naive approach, apparently relying on conscious motivation, nevertheless the recent emphasis on the interactional nature of a therapeutic encounter must alert us to how strongly unconscious expectations in the therapist can affect the spirit of the meeting.

There are, of course, occasions on which the therapist *needs*, for whatever unconscious reasons, to succeed with a certain patient, and in such circumstances the urgency of the need is likely to "vitiate" the work itself (Wheelis, 1956). Allied to this, Greenson (1974) alerts us to the quality within the therapist that must be capable of inflicting pain, if necessary. The therapist who is too anxious about this cannot be sufficiently helpful.

- *Emotional attention, observation, and reverie*

Again there is a consensus about the need for the therapist to give a considerable degree of attention to the patient. This attention needs to take place with the therapist being emotionally available. Buechler (1997) says that therapy demands the "full presence" of the analyst at every working moment. Therapists need to have all their emotional resources at the ready, so that they can be in touch with the minute shifts both in their own and in the patient's emotions that need to be noted. Hanna Segal also stresses the quality of attention, the importance of detail. She contrasts her own technique with that of Klein, her analyst, commenting that nowadays "we pay more attention to minutes of silence, tone of voice and things like that" (in Hunter, 1994, p. 50). Such attention to detail needs to take place with the therapist also paying attention to the context within which something is taking place.

This ability to notice has, of course, always been present in and valued by psychoanalysts. Describing the case of Dora, Freud shows how noticing the way Dora fiddled with her reticule informed his understanding of the case (1905e [1901]). It is, of course, important to think about both what is observed and the way it is observed. It is acknowledged that everything is inevitably seen through the eyes of the observer and so cannot be deemed objective. The therapist's countertransference influences what she sees. Renik (1993) says that actually it is what is observed at the level of micro-activity that influences the countertransference: observed data of such a minute nature that we are not even aware that we are observing them then influence what we feel. This emphasis on the therapist's feelings being inevitably influenced by what they have noticed links closely to the importance of emotional receptivity (Gordon, 1997).

Green (1975) links Bion's (1970) statement about the absence of memory and desire with the therapist's willingness to be "permeated" by the patient's state as fully as possible. Since Bion (1970), there has been a view that the primary task of the analyst is to be available for the patient and to open her mind to receive the patient's communications with as little interference as possible. This idea about giving the patient a place inside us has also been written about by Eigen (Molino, 1997) and Ferro (1999), among others. James Fisher (2002) points out that the self that is willing to go out towards another and to take that other into the self must, of necessity, return different from the self that had set out. Etchegoyen (1991) suggests that it is only our own anxiety that prevents us from "receiving" the patient in this way. Perhaps we can see some roots of this anxiety when we add in Parsons' (1986) idea that therapists must let the patient's illness be lodged in themselves so that it can then be processed. Ferro (1999) also writes of the importance of being willing to give the patient a place inside oneself but suggests that what is left inside the therapist is toxic, and the therapist then needs to devote personal time, outside the session, to detoxifying it.

- *Empathy*

The concept of the therapist being "permeated by the patient" very much connects with the idea of empathy, suggesting the patient and the therapist "in tune" with each other, perhaps in some way identified with each other—although then the risks of identification are great. Many writers, most famously Kohut (1959), consider empathy to be a precondition for therapeutic work. It is referred to by numerous others, even if they then go on to express concerns about the "right amount" (Aveline, 1990; Emde, 1988; Green, 1975; Greenson, 1974; Guy, 1978; Lampl-De Groot, 1979; Nelson-Jones, 1982; Symington, 1996). It seems that writers often use the term as if it were synonymous with countertransference, which is questionable—empathy, or an experience of feeling as someone else does—is surely only part of a countertransference experience. Indeed, we could view empathy as something that goes from the therapist to the patient, whereas countertransference is composed of all the feelings the therapist experiences within him/herself as a result of the experience of being with the patient.

Writers warn of over-identification with the patient, and Symington shows the need for another perspective: "I am quite sure that no therapy can succeed, unless the psychotherapist manages to see things from the patient's point of view, but if he sees things *only* from the patient's point of view, the therapy will lack an essential ingredient—the experience of the Other" (1996, p. 131).

Clearly, empathy alone is not enough. The therapist needs to experience the patient's experience and also to make the unconscious connections that are there but are not experienced (Goldberg, 1994). For a considerable time—perhaps following what was viewed as the excesses of Alexander's ideas about the "corrective emotional experi-ence" (Alexander & French, 1946)—there was concern about what was seen as an overvaluation of empathy. Heimann wrote that there was "a widespread tendency to see nothing but good qualities in empathy, whilst I would maintain that empathy too needs careful watching" (1962, p. 229). Unfortunately she does not expand on this statement, which was part of a discussant's response to papers given at an International Psychoanalytic Congress looking at curative fac-tors in psychoanalysis, but it followed statements about tact, honesty, and kindness not being enough: "there is plenty of that outside analysis". Meissner adds another dimension, saying that "empathy has its limits. The current over-emphasis on empathy in psychoanaly-sis puts the analyst at risk of over-estimating the capacity to know and understand the inner mind of the patient empathically and under-valuing other sources of information about the patient" (1996, p. 161).

Indeed, an emphasis on empathy can be intrusive: during analysis the patient, as well as being and feeling understood, needs to experi-ence what Modell (in Hunter, 1994) calls "a kind of protected soli-tude".

- *Neutrality*

Ideas about the therapist's neutrality seem mostly to refer to the idea that the therapist should show as little of him or herself as possible, in the words of Freud's famous dictum: "The doctor should be opaque to his patients and, like a mirror, show nothing but what is shown to him" (1912e, p. 118). Certainly over the years it has become an ac-cepted part of therapeutic technique that therapists should never be in a position of giving their own opinions or showing too much of themselves. Strupp (1973) states that if the therapist is too much himself, spontaneous and relaxed, then he is not in a favourable position to be an objective and dispassionate observer; if, on the other hand, he is too much of a "scientist", this interferes with the free "give-and-take" of interaction. This highlights an important theoreti-cal issue: the question of what theoretical model of the mind the therapist is intending to use. Neutrality was especially valued when the drive model theory was in the ascendant (Greenberg & Mitchell, 1983). Using that model, the—traditionally male—therapist needed to be in a position to put his mind to the productions of his patient's mind. However, once a more interactional approach is being privileged, then there is an expectation that the therapist can never be neutral (Sandler & Dreher, 1996) and that, at the least, one's own pathology must be part of the analytic process, in what Langs (1982) termed "the bi-personal field". More far-reachingly, the whole analytic encounter is seen as one of to and fro movement.

Coltart writes more forcefully: "Whatever analysts say about being non-judgemental, or being neutral on matters of morality is, of course, absolute bunkum: Analysts are making judgements all the time" (in Molino, 1997, p. 203). She elaborates that while one's whole moral outlook is there all the time, it is important not to impose one's own judgements on the patient, but that we need to acknowledge that we cannot help expressing them indirectly, so that patients hear "echoes of that morality" (p. 203). However, the therapist can still aim to bring as little of herself as possible into the therapeutic encounter, because, as Rayner (1991) says, there is a risk that the patient will try to "be" what the therapist is presumed to want, and such impingements on the patient are conducive to false-self perpetuation.

The idea of solitude in therapy—perhaps Winnicott's picture of a child playing in the presence of another—connects with Bollas's (1987) idea about the importance of the therapist's neutrality to facilitate the patient's reverie, untroubled by demands from the analyst. There is an intermediate space in which analyst and patient can have the experience of each other as both of the self and yet other. This links with Matte Blanco's ideas on symmetrical and asymmetrical relationships, as expounded by Rayner (1991); the other is self (symmetrical) and not self (asymmetrical) concurrently: "To maintain neutrality, the analyst must always have available a capacity to be identified with the patient, and yet separate, to feel the same as, and different from, to be together and apart, in sympathy and antipathy, and so on" (1991, p. 248).

We should note how the capacity to contain apparently contradictory experiences simultaneously is emphasized here; I return to this subject later.

• *Authenticity*

While adopting aspects of neutrality just mentioned, authors make clear that it is also important for patients to feel they are in the presence of what Bollas (1989), using Winnicott's term, refers to as the therapist's true self. In 1936 Glover had suggested that therapeutic effects came about, not only through interpretation, but also through the unconscious attitude of the analyst. He viewed the analyst's "true unconscious attitude" as very important and believed the patient could perceive it. Winnicott (cited by Klauber, 1986) says that it is important for the patient to experience the analyst as a person capable of a genuine emotional response to him.

This emphasis on the patient experiencing the human qualities of the analyst has arisen both from an interest in the interactional aspects of the work and from the earlier position of the "therapeutic alliance". As can be seen in the discussion of the influence of theory, when practitioners became more interested in the interactional nature of the work, they felt that it was time to give up the historical withholding of human relationships and increase the sense of mutuality (Modell, in Hunter, 1994; Sandler, 1988). Stern and colleagues (1998) have approached this topic in a new way, looking at what they call the importance of "moments of meeting" that occur rarely but significantly within therapeutic encounters. Using a developmental perspective applied to clinical material, they write of procedural knowledge of relationships that operates outside both focal attention and conscious verbal expression. This implicit knowledge remains outside awareness but is very influential, and they link it to Bollas's (1987) "unthought known" and Sandler's "past unconscious". In these "now moments" each partner actively contributes something unique and authentic of his or herself. They emphasize that these moments are rare but therapeutically very significant. Clearly the theoretical model in use is very different from Freud's (1912e) when he suggested the analyst use the model of a surgeon and wrote of "emotional coldness" serving as a protection for the analyst.

- *The capacity to hold on to opposing states,*
  and the capacity to shift

Bearing in mind these demands to be both neutral and authentic, both involved and detached (Cooper, 1990), it is clear that the therapist needs to be able to hold on to these seemingly opposed states within herself. The ability to maintain positions, to experience and observe at the same time, demands a certain flexibility, and the need for this ability to feel and to think at the same time is, I believe, central to becoming a psychoanalytic psychotherapist. The emphasis on the "living relationship" in Nacht's work (1962) seems to prefigure more contemporary interest in the interactional aspects of therapeutic work.

* *Waiting for meaning to emerge*

This attribute has been famously described by Bion (1970) using the poet Keats's term "negative capability". Psychotherapeutic work aims, *inter alia*, towards understanding. Schafer (1983) writes of the use of narrative as a way of *creating* meaning. Yet the therapist also has to wait for this meaning to emerge; it takes time for patterns to become clear. The analyst has to be patient and to tolerate periods of non-understanding (Joseph, 1985; Kernberg, 1993). An attempt to understand can be an avoidance of this process. The pain of waiting for this meaning is vividly described by Slade (1994). Although Slade clearly manages to hold on to her own feelings, we might speculate that she has insufficient outward passivity (Cooper, 1990; Dryden, 1990) and receptivity to find this a comfortable experience. According to Parsons: "The waiting is as central a part of the analysis as any voicing of insight which may come out of it" (1984, p. 459).

In his 1986 paper, Parsons writes about "suddenly finding something matters". Here he emphasizes that not clinging to what one is used to involves a certain loss—a sacrifice—and that this attitude to the unconscious allows meaning that had not previously been seen. Understanding can develop only if we are not anxious to hold on to it.

* *Capacity to tolerate anxiety, uncertainty, and a sense of bombardment*

This quality was specified by Margaret Rustin (1988) but emerges in other writings in various implicit and explicit ways. The therapist will be in the presence of some very distressing experiences—both those reported and experienced by the patient and those that the therapist may be "asked" to experience on the patient's behalf. We also have to think about all the aspects of the patient that the therapist is asked to contain, frequently bearing the unbearable feelings of the patient (Symington, 1996). Unconscious repudiation of certain feelings will not be helpful. How very painful and disturbing this may be is shown in Sorensen's (1997) honest description of her inability to be open to and contain projective identification in a situation where there was a dreadful history of loss and deprivation. As Buechler (1997) makes clear, all therapists enter therapeutic work having a different familiarity with, and internal acceptance of, different feelings. We cannot be equally comfortable or familiar with all. Analysis can increase sensitivity to these emotions, but even with this there is an inevitable personal orientation.

The "real" person

There is the question of whether a collection of capacities can be considered separately from the personality of the therapist. For some time, especially because of the emphasis on analytic neutrality and analytic anonymity, there was an idea that an analysis would somehow be the same—that is, have the same result—regardless of who the analyst was. While lip-service may have been paid to this idea, it is obvious that different therapists have different successes, or failures, with different kinds of patients—not to mention the far more commonsense view that some therapists are better than others. But is it a matter of "better" in an overall sense, or one of having more of some capacities—such as tolerance of aggression, spontaneity—than others that make a therapist more suited to treat a certain sort of patient? Sandler and Dreher (1996) view the idea of a patient–therapist "match" as important: they make it clear that the personality fit between analyst and patient is a crucial factor in determining the outcome of treatment (p. 118) and that the analyst's conscious and unconscious value systems are an integral part of the analytic system.

Parsons is talking at a far more "meta" level when he says: "I am suggesting that who we are and the analysis we do are not just linked, but are actually the same thing" (1984, p. 456). This is more than saying that to do good analysis the therapist needs to have certain qualities or be a certain sort of person: the analysis is in some way an embodiment of who the analyst is—a point also made by Virginia Hunter in her book, *Psychoanalysts Talk* (1994). Trying to see whether events in their earlier lives influenced analysts' theoretical approach to psychoanalytic work, Hunter interviewed a number of leading British and American analysts, showed all of them the same piece of reported clinical material, and recorded a range of different responses to it. Her research shows very clearly that the interests of a reader can affect what is noticed in the material. Klauber (1986) takes Freud's famous dictum about the analyst holding up a mirror to the patient and points out that what one sees depends on where and in what way the analyst is holding the mirror. Indeed, in considering the importance of the "real" person, Freud's (1910d) statement "Each analyst's achievement is limited by what his own complexes and resistances permit" (p. 145) is often cited. Klauber also states that the direction of an analysis must be affected by the psychotherapist's value system, and wonders to what extent value systems are tied up with psychoanalytic schools. Following on from his idea that what interpretation the analyst makes and what path he follows will vary considerably according to his personality and culture, Klauber concludes that the outcome of an analysis depends on a successful interaction between persons.

The real relationship is, of course, close to, but not the same as, the present relationship, a concept that has been of interest to certain theoretical groups more recently and is considered further on in this chapter. Emde (1988), emphasizing the interactional nature of the analytic process, applies recent findings from infant observation and infant research to psychoanalytic theory and therapy and writes on the importance of the function of affects in the development of relations between self and object. He says that changes arising from therapy are more dependent on the patient–analyst relationship than had been previously considered, although it should be noted that in 1963 Truax had stated that the personality and approach of the therapist are of considerable importance in producing improvement, irrespective of the theoretical position of the therapist.

Although the word "real" is being used, this attention has arisen from contemporary interest in the analyst's *countertransference* and owes little to the earlier emphasis on the "real relationship" by certain classical Freudian analysts. In that model there seemed to be an idea of a "real relationship" around the margins of therapeutic work, shown in the way the analyst greeted the patient or, for example, heard news of a patient's injury (Greenson, 1974), and which then fed into the working alliance and made the pain and privations of the analytic work possible.

An issue of *Contemporary Psychoanalysis* in 1988 (Vol. 24, No. 3) includes a number of articles addressing the issues of the analyst's "real" self. Certainly there seem to be aspects of the external reality of the therapist—such as race, age, and gender—that are known to the patient, however much analytic anonymity there is. Additionally, many case studies indicate how much the patient assumes, often rightly, about the "real" therapist from such clues as, for example, the décor of the consulting-room (for the example of a patient who refused to engage in therapy with "someone who decorated his consulting-room with such bad art", see Klauber, 1986, p. 130). Greenson (1974) shares with the reader his experience of a patient pointing out to him the way his (Greenson's) tone and mode of questioning altered according to which political party was mentioned by the patient. I am sure that it is of no surprise to the reader to regard the personality of the therapist as influential, and consideration is given to what may have motivated the therapist's original interest in this work (Carvahlo, 1990; Farber, 1995; Greenson, 1974; Guy, 1978). Various dysfunctional aspects of earlier life may be put to good use in this way, as, according to Parsons (1984), the analyst needs to be someone who is to some extent disturbed and then has been successfully analysed. Of course, it is now generally acknowledged that the analyst is inevitably an integral part of the therapeutic system. In "Farewell to the Objective Analyst" (1994), Goldberg, influenced by contemporary thinking in other creative disciplines, takes a hermeneutic approach. He makes it clear that the idea of a continuous feedback loop also begins to break the boundary between subject and object.

We shall see, when looking at interpretations and moments of meaningful contact between therapist and patient, how there is an emphasis on the therapist being able to offer something authentic. While acknowledging the usefulness of the therapist's professional or—as Schafer (1983) terms it—"second self" as a way of shaping his or her responsiveness to the patient, the true and meaningful activity in therapeutic work arises from genuine contact.

Theory and psychoanalytic practice

The concept of the *purpose* of psychoanalytic psychotherapy—the question of what psychoanalytic psychotherapy was aiming to do and particularly the types of patients it was thought possible to treat—has altered considerably over the last century, as have, correspondingly, the capacities considered necessary and ideas about technique. The "widening scope" of psychoanalysis was discussed at the Twenty-Ninth International Psychoanalytic Congress on "Changes in Psycho-analytic Practice and Experience", and, according to Shengold and McLaughlin's report on the plenary sessions, it was acknowledged that for work with borderline patients "Freud's models are not enough . . . new concepts and terms are needed" (1975, p. 261). From various historical approaches to psychoanalysis (Hedges, 1983; Sandler & Dreher, 1996) it is apparent that the more distant, aloof analyst is a suitable professional to carry out a form of therapy in which the on-going current relationship with the therapist is of little concern. "Freud's view of the 'neutral' psychoanalyst as epitomized in contemporary accounts of the American 'classical' analyst, ac-counts to be sure, that are often carried to the level of caricature" (Hamilton, 1996, p. 23) is contrasted with a more "human" ap-proach—one concerned with the "real relationship" between analyst and patient. Greenberg and Mitchell (1983) say succinctly that the drive model demands neutrality and the relational model participa-tion. The emphasis on the patient's conflicts has led the analyst to create an atmosphere of non-interference, which was integrated into a technique that encourages silence, careful listening, and a disinclina-tion to interrupt the patient. They contrast this with the relational model, which urges on the clinician attentiveness to ways in which he and the patient are mutually influencing each other and increases ability to use the countertransference.

Currently there is an emphasis on the emotional experience of the therapist—the countertransference—and on the analytic relationship. According to Fisher (2002), there is a move away from seeing the analytic process as an explanatory enterprise, towards seeing its pri-mary task as descriptive. We no longer try to explain *why* someone does or feels this or that; instead, we describe *what* someone is doing or feeling. This aspect of change in technique is less explored than the increase in interest in countertransference, but Fisher sees it as inte-gral. Using concepts from T. S. Eliot, he describes the need to think with our feelings, to think feelingly, and he speaks of understanding through "imaginative identification".

The Boston Process of Change group (Stern et al., 1998) takes this emphasis on the importance of the analyst further. They use a wealth of material from infancy research studies to illustrate the interactional nature of any dialogue. As discussed in the section on interpretation in chapter 4, they state the need for "something more" than interpretation. The therapist needs to be able and willing to work in this way, leading to the privileging of different capacities and skills.

Importance of the countertransference

Greater emphasis on analysts' use of the countertransference has led to a corresponding emphasis on their sensitivity to experiences and allowing their countertransference feelings to inform them. Indeed, recent research into the workings of the brain evidences the profound significance of what happens at a preconscious, unnoticed level in any dialogue between two people. The importance of the "to and fro", the unrecognized projection and introjection in any encounter, also has significance for what we then believe happens in the analytic encounter. Greenberg and Mitchell are very clear about the change in theory that has led to this. With the abandonment of the drive theory model, the analyst is no longer seen as outside a process that is unfolding from within the mind of the patient. Instead, the "theoretical assumption is that he will engage the patient, intervene and participate in and transform pathogenic patterns of the relationship" (1983, p. 390). It is not interpretation alone that brings about change, but the nature and quality of the analytic relationship. The influence of developmentalists who show that cognition and emotion cannot be separated is important here. Following this idea, the intervention that takes place within the therapy session between patient and therapist assumes an importance, and everything the therapist does is seen to have an effect. The therapist's need to think carefully about how she is feeling and behaving is vital. These ideas then lead back to the importance of the therapist being able to be aware of, evaluate, and respond to the countertransference. Fonagy says: "Psychoanalytic treatment no longer works primarily by addressing conflict. Instead, particularly through interpretations of transference and countertransference, the analyst recreates an intersubjective process which enhances the patient's reflective self this time in the safety of a benign relationship" (1993, p. 483).

Relationship with the therapist

Influenced by infancy research studies, many analysts have noted the "to and fro" of interactions between the patient and analyst within the session. Familiarity with the interaction between mothers and their infants can increase the clinician's sensitivity to aspects of patient–therapist contact. Awareness of the work that has been done by Stern (1985) and others on the matching of contours both within vocalizations and across different modalities can help to increase the practitioner's careful responsiveness to the patient.

This emphasis on the patient–therapist relationship has considerable implications both for how the therapist conducts herself and for the qualities that she brings to therapeutic work. This approach brings together the intellectual and emotional/empathic aspects of the therapist, which have traditionally been viewed as being separate. In this model the therapist has to be affectively in tune with the patient *and* be able to show it. Of course, some thinkers view this emphasis on attunement as going too far—the emphasis on it can lead to something closer to the excesses of the "corrective emotional experience" (Alexander & French, 1946), a belief that it is the work of the therapy to repair the deficits of the patient's previous experiences, rather than primarily to help him to recognize and think about their influence. However, even among those who are less interested in the intersubjective approach, there is still an increased emphasis on the clinician's use of him or herself.

CHAPTER FOUR

From instrument to melody

A s seen in the previous chapter, separating capacities and skills can at times be an artificial manoeuvre. In this chapter I give attention to those skills that seem less closely interwoven with the capacities described in chapter 3. In considering what skills or techniques the psychoanalytic psychotherapist employs in her working life, it is, of course, immediately apparent that theory influences practice: the model of what psychoanalytic psychotherapy is for and the underlying beliefs about how the human mind operates inevitably alter how the practitioner works. In this chapter I briefly acknowledge the various theoretical views that lead to different emphases on certain techniques or, more specifically, ways of applying those techniques. Similarly, although the way a child analysis is conducted, with the child's use of play material and correspondingly more physical activity on the part of the therapist, differs from traditional adult psychotherapy, both the theoretical underpinning and the basic techniques employed—interpretation, use of transference and countertransference—are the same and can be considered together.

So what is happening within a psychoanalytic psychotherapy session that we could describe as technique? I begin by outlining this in a very flat and bald statement, which I have produced to give a framework for looking at these actions more closely.

From the beginning, the therapist creates a setting within which the work can take place. Once there, the therapist pays close attention to all that the patient does within the session and the atmosphere of the session, as well as to what is noticed and experienced through the workings of the countertransference. A theoretical framework may help in understanding or ordering this material. At a moment the therapist judges to be right, she will then say something to the patient—perhaps simply a question or a clarification or perhaps an "interpretation". From the patient's response to this, the therapist receives further information, which is then used to evaluate what the patient has done with what has been said. Different emphases can be put on how interactional the process is then perceived as being. As well as the technique used within the session, the clinician will also go on thinking, both consciously and unconsciously, about the session and these thoughts will influence the on-going work.

It will be apparent from chapter 3 that certain aspects to which I have just drawn attention closely match the capacities addressed there. Table 4.1 shows how some of the capacities manifest themselves in technique, whereas others are less closely related.

The rest of this chapter delineates those aspects where the technical skill needs to arise from the capacity but where there is some considerable difference between the two. Other aspects, such as the need to pay close attention or tolerate anxiety, being closer to the personal capacities, are not revisited further.

Creating a setting

We can think of this heading as referring to both the physicality of the setting and the emotional atmosphere created within it: both the analytic attitude discussed in chapter 3 and the technique employed are significant. Since Freud, psychotherapists have become familiar with the idea of the separate consulting-room with the use of the couch and an uninterrupted 50-minute session. While some innovators have changed the framework at times—probably the best-known being Lacan with his alteration to the length of sessions—this is a model most analysts use. Many psychotherapists' patients do not use the couch, as the task engaged in does not privilege free association and the abrogation of reality (Klauber, 1972). In child work a very different physical setting is created, with a robust space and play material, but the underlying intention to create a reflective space is the same.

Apart from the physical characteristics, what constitutes this reflective space? It is undeniably the atmosphere that therapists create through their presentation of themselves in working mode, their view of the task and the patient. The setting operates as a secure base within which the patient can begin to face and "narrativize" past pain (Holmes, 1998), helped in the process by the therapist's presence, but with the therapist creating enough space for the patient to experience a kind of "protective solitude" (Modell, in Hunter, 1994), following Winnicott's seminal (1958a) concept of being alone in the presence of another. As we have seen when discussing the therapist's need to have an "analytic attitude", a capacity for neutrality and self-denial are necessary. Many writers (Greenson, 1974; Langs, 1978; Rangell, 1975; Strupp, 1973) make it clear that the therapist needs to safeguard against imposing his own needs and conflicts onto the patient and must avoid self-revelation and off-hand comments. It is acknowledged that the patient will pick up all sorts of ideas about the analyst, some of which are bound to be accurate, but the less the patient knows, the easier it is for the analyst to show the patient when reactions are displacements and projections. Rangell writes that while the therapist should not act as a model for the patient in terms of specific choices, he should embody for the patient "ego values of rationality, and the timeless moral values of civilisation" (1975, p. 95). Many therapists would be uncomfortable with the concept of being any sort of role model for the patient and view such an idea as non-analytic, but it has been acknowledged for many years (e.g. Strachey, 1933) that the patient's identification with the therapist is an important factor. The difference perhaps is what the therapist is setting out to create.

A way of thinking about this analytic attitude may be helped by the idea of *where* the analyst is in relation to the patient: she needs to be near enough for connection but far enough away for the objectivity necessary for thinking. There needs to be an intermediate space between analyst and patient so that there is commonality, but they are separate. It is in this intermediate space that the serious "play" of analysis must occur (Rayner, 1991). There are implications here that I address further when considering the importance of countertransference. The analyst must be able to experience whatever the patient is projecting but also to think about what she is experiencing.

Much analytic writing about "the setting" looks at the therapist's attitude to the patient. The patient has to be able to accept a sense of responsibility for how he has approached things, bearing in mind the "script" (McDougall, 1986) with which he started. An attitude of respect and acceptance is emphasized (Etchegoyen, 1991; Greenson, 1974; Strupp, 1973), but it must be clear that acceptance is not the same as approval. Similar human abilities are being recommended, although from rather different perspectives. The observer and the therapist need to be able to see things from the other's point of view without losing their own viewpoint. Parsons (1986) points out how frequently we fail to respect the patient's reality: we frequently assume the analyst's view of reality as the norm by which the patient's reality is to be modified.

It is important to be aware of Bion's (1962) statement that it is necessary for the analyst to *receive* the patient. The therapist has to accept all aspects of the patient in order to enable the latter to accept these aspects of himself (Symington, 1996), although in interpreting conflict the therapist has to show both an understanding of the need to struggle *against* the unacceptable and respect and understanding *for* the unacceptable parts of the self to be defended against (Sandler, 1988, p. 344). The modern Kleinian approach, which sees an aim of therapy as reintegrating parts of the self that have been lost through projective identification is relevant here.

The analyst must be tolerant of, but not foster, acting out and be comfortable at times of regression and chaos (Langs, 1973), accepting but not satisfying the patient's unreasonable demands (Strupp, 1973)—we should, however, note that he does not look into who it is that characterizes these as unreasonable—and indicate acceptance of all of the patient's material by adopting a straightforward approach to even "the most delicate subjects" (Greenson, 1974).

The therapist should be aware of how she is being used by the patient. The patient's need to repeat can push the therapist into being what the patient is familiar with (Sandler, 1981), although Anne

Alvarez has pointed out (personal communication, 2000) that patients also need to rewrite the past. Schafer says that analytic work should not be unconsciously subverted into a repetition of that which must be analysed; any neutral activity on the therapist's part, including appropriate listening, is bound to be represented in the analysand's psychic reality as a confrontation and a provocation, "for it introduces a way of seeing things and experiencing them emotionally which, try as the analysand might, does not adequately conform to his or her desperate attempts to repeat the past over and over again" (1983, pp. 155–156).

Acknowledging the infantile rage and destructiveness that lies within patients, Kernberg (1993) writes of the analyst's need to protect the analytic setting from the patient's attempts to destroy it. He states that some severely regressed patients will go on until they have provoked the analyst, and this may lead to the temporary abandonment of analytic neutrality. The analyst must tolerate becoming provoked without abandoning a sense of responsibility or concern for the patient, but this concern may take the form of anger. The analyst should never use non-interpretative ways of dealing with the countertransference, but there might occasionally be unavoidable acting out of the countertransference.

Boundaries need to be maintained enough to contain healthy protest (Holmes, 1998). The analytic atmosphere must be sufficiently safe for painful feelings to be experienced, although there is a question as to how "benign" this atmosphere should be. This question links with the idea of the "treatment alliance", "therapeutic alliance", or "working alliance", as it has been variously called. This view sees the analyst's non-interpretative interventions and spontaneous human reactions (Greenson, 1978) as important, but Greenberg and Mitchell (1983) point out that what, for example, Greenson considers prerequisites to the interpretative function of the analysis are seen as curative in the relational model. Whatever view is being taken of "analysis proper", there is agreement that insight alone is insufficient; therapy must be an emotional experience for the patient. Intellectual understanding in itself does not produce therapeutic change; certain sorts of interpretations—especially "here-and-now" interpretations—create an emotional experience for the patient. Stern and colleagues (1998) take this idea further in their description of "now moments".

Attention and a particular way of listening

As well as noticing all non-verbal activity, the therapist must have a very particular way of listening. This includes, again, close attention to detail and listening at a more meta level. The analyst must be sensitive to the intonational, syntactical, and linguistic habits of others and to hear the meanings "between and behind words"(Rayner, 1991), paying attention to procedures such as speech rate, timing, stress of utterances, and silence (Nelson-Jones, 1982). We need to listen both to content and context, being aware of when something is said and in what way.

This way of listening has marked differences from the way we listen conversationally, and Schlesinger (1994) argues that the therapist must unlearn the accustomed ways of listening conversationally. He points out that in conversational mode we often listen "too closely" and lapse into identification with the speaker. When listening socially, we assume that the speaker means to make sense, and we fill in the elisions—both in our minds and literally through nods and additions—and ignore pauses, but this is not helpful in analysis. This surely connects with Freud's well-known idea of free-floating attention, according to which the analyst should turn his own unconscious like a receptive organ towards the transmitting unconscious of the patient (1912e, p. 115).

Schafer's (1983) idea of narrative has profound implications for the way the therapist listens. Within the framework of "narrative" in which there is no "out-there" reality, what the patient says is treated as "narrative performance"; there is no final or definitive version, experience is always being constructed or reconstructed. The way of telling then becomes central: telling is not "an indifferent medium or transparent medium for imparting information" (1983, p. 228)—rather, the analyst is interested in the how, when, and why of telling and pays close attention to gaps, evasions, and non-sequiturs. The analyst is, of course, attending to the analysand's selection and arrangement of what they are talking about and thinking about the context and timing, the style of telling, and why this topic has been chosen. Schafer warns that there is no purely figurative speech in the unconscious: in some ways the therapeutic listener must always listen literally. Although Schafer uses a more hermeneutic and interactional model that suggests that what the patient says cannot be separated from what the therapist then feels and his response, for the moment I think that it is useful to try to think about what is coming *into* the therapist and how it needs to be held and processed inside, before we move on to how it is then used to further the therapeutic process.

Awareness and the use of transference and countertransference

I am assuming a certain familiarity on the part of the reader of the basic concepts of transference and countertransference and also of the history of how these concepts have been treated in analytic circles. Since Heimann's seminal paper, clinicians have realized that "the analyst's emotional response to his patient within the analytic situation represents one of the most important tools for his work. The analyst's countertransference is an instrument of research into the patient's unconscious" (1950, p. 74). The analyst needs to have "a freely roused emotional sensibility so as to perceive and follow closely his patient's emotional movements and unconscious phantasies" (p. 75). We can see that the therapist must not be defended too strongly against these experiences; she must allow herself to experience them but not be so overwhelmed by them so as to be unable to think about why she is experiencing them.

In doing this, the therapist must be able to create space to think about her feelings. In the first place, the therapist must try to think about what aspects of what she is feeling belong to the patient and which are what Heimann calls "pathological phenomena"—that is, those fitting the way countertransference was thought of in the years leading up to her paper. It is important to note that since Heimann's introduction of the concept, the term has been rather over-extended. It is now often used to include the clinician's intuitive, empathic response to the patient in a way that elides the distinction between what the clinician has had projected into her by the patient and what she is aware of from other sources. Anticipating issues I develop further on, I would point out that from the experience of infant observation it is hoped that the clinician can distinguish between feelings in the countertransference, such as those of tension that she might experience when a baby screws his face up and resolutely keeps his eyes shut, and others she might feel, such as concern when she observes that the mother and baby are depressed. The countertransference feeling may enter the observer in a strongly experienced, almost visceral way the reason for which the observer would probably not appreciate without further thought, while the more conscious empathic response would be informed by a number of stimuli, often visual, which could be readily understood. Despite our current position of valuing working with the countertransference, nevertheless it is worth bearing in mind that Bion, one of the most influential psychoanalytic writers, argued against it:

> There is only one thing to do with counter-transference and that is to have it analysed. One cannot make use of one's counter-transference in the consulting room; it is a contradiction in terms. . . . It is one's *unconscious* feelings about the patient, and since it is unconscious there is nothing we can do about it. If the counter-transference *is* operating in the analytic session the analyzand is unlucky—and so is the analyst. [1974, p. 88]

The ability to tolerate the often intense countertransference feelings is important. Through countertransference, through affective internal response to the patient, the analyst is compelled to relive elements of the patient's infantile history (Bollas, 1987): Symington writes of the analyst being "lassooed into the patient's illusory world" (1983, p. 287). According to Hanna Segal, the analyst's task is to enable the mentalization of the process: "You must understand what patients are projecting and show them how they are doing it, and then gradually *why* they're doing it" (in Hunter, 1994, p. 58).

Over the years, the approach has changed. Previously it was considered helpful, where possible, to refuse to accept patients' projections and to give them back. With the notion of containment, the therapist is now concerned with what to do with the projections she has received. The ability to keep on thinking is vital, although this is often difficult because of the strength of what is being aroused or projected (King, 1978). Having noticed the usefulness of countertransference experiences, Heimann specifies that while the analyst must be receptive, he must not act on the feelings but use them to understand and help formulate interpretations. Current thinking suggests that often it is impossible for the therapist not to act out a countertransference response in some way (Carpy, 1989; Renik, 1993), because the therapist often only becomes aware of the countertransference reaction as a result of her behaviour, which then feels uncomfortable or out of character. *Awareness* of countertransference is an asset that contributes to analytic work, while any substantial expression of countertransference in *action* is a liability that limits analytic work. Again we see the importance of a reflective space within which the therapist must hold on to feelings and think. In Chapter 10 I revisit this in greater depth when I discuss Ogden's (2001) description of a part of a therapy session that shows him attending to his countertransference. Ogden shows how his attention to all he thinks and feels within a session, which, adapting Bion's famous term, he calls "reverie", enables him to respond to the patient in a creative and meaningful way.

Noticing, feeling, thinking, interpreting

The process in which a feeling is recognized by a reflective part of the mind (M. E. Rustin, 1988) seems to me to be very much at the heart of effective therapy. We have addressed noticing and feeling and can now, briefly, think about thinking. An important part of thinking is the theoretical framework that underpins understanding. The therapist needs to know theory and know how to apply it; Symington (1996) gives the analogy of a workman knowing which tool to use for which job. However, as Steiner (1993) states, theory should be in the background, not the foreground of our minds when engaged in clinical work. Schafer (1983) connects this use of theory with experience to write of what he calls "anticipation". He uses the analogy of a tennis player, involved in a game that is each time new and fresh, using his experience of previous games and his understanding of how certain strokes operate to save himself from running all over the court.

Even without being heavily theory-laden, the therapist must use cognitive skills to organize the patient's associations correctly and in meaningful patterns (Kernberg, 1993; Langs, 1973). Such gathering-in communicates the analyst's containing function to the patient and helps to increase the patient's sense of containment. In order to carry out the cognitive aspects of this complex process of holding on to feelings, the therapist needs a certain detachment, an ability to think, evaluate, remember, and anticipate. The capacity to become temporarily and partially detached is a prerequisite of analytic work

(Greenson, 1974), but its temporary nature is essential. We have already seen how vital it is not to be detached but be intimately involved in order to have the necessary countertransference experiences.

This ability to hold on to ideas and feelings, often uncomfortable ones, is an essential therapeutic tool. Tolerating periods of not understanding is essential and unavoidable: the therapist must tolerate ambiguities and not necessarily use questions to resolve them (Bion, 1962; Langs, 1973). We must not foreclose by understanding too soon. Ella Freeman Sharpe (1930) points out that we only see fragments of a pattern at one time: it takes the entire analysis to see the pattern as a whole, so the therapist must not rush to assumptions. "Understanding" is often grabbed at and interpretations made to deny the anxiety aroused in the analyst; true understanding "can only develop if we are not anxious to hold on to it" (Parsons, 1986, p. 487).

Timing

We have seen that sometimes as therapists we *do* something because we cannot bear to do otherwise. An important therapeutic skill lies in finding the right time to do something, but it is difficult to exercise this judgement under pressure. We need to distinguish between the therapist not yet knowing and easing *her* pain about this and the therapist feeling that she understands the material and then communicating it inappropriately to the patient. Ferro also suggests that at times, as therapists, we interpret as a defence against allowing ourselves to know more primitive parts of our own minds (1999, p. 43). Naturally the issue of timing also includes waiting too long as well as rushing. Aveline (1990) writes of when and when not to intervene, and many writers from Freud onwards warn against premature interpretation (Greenson, 1974; Langs, 1973; Rayner, 1991; Sharpe, 1947). Freud himself said that "One must be careful not to give a patient the solution of a symptom or the translation of a wish until he is already so close to it that he has only one short step more to make in order to get hold of the explanation for himself" (1913c, p. 140).

Hanna Segal (1962) states that the analyst should communicate her understanding when the analysand is most ready to receive it, but how to judge this moment is never stated explicitly and perhaps never could be, given the myriad microinteractions that make up a therapeutic moment.

Verbal communication

Before looking closely at interpretation, it is necessary to say something about verbal communication as a whole. Recent work by Schore (1994, 2000) highlights that the right brain is non-verbal and the left brain is verbal, although the use of a few words with deep emotional resonance, such as curse words, is governed by the right brain. Schore explains that within a therapy session there is a time at the beginning when the left brain is dominant, but in the middle of the session the right brain comes into dominance, with all that that implies for the patient's non-verbal communications. He stated (2000) that the left and right brain come together at the close of the session. This knowledge means that as well as paying attention to the verbal content, clinicians should now be aware of and thinking about which levels of the self are to the fore.

The way the therapist talks is of vital importance. The therapist's tone of voice, verbal nuance, cadence, and intonation can convey something genuine to the patient in a way that words may not (Rayner, 1991), and the musicality of the therapist's voice may, according to Asha Phillips (personal communication, 2004) and Maria Rhode (2004), have an immense unrecognized impact on the patient's way of receiving what is said. Schafer (1983) suggests adopting a tactful, tentative, circuitous style. He specifies that the analyst should never use "don't", as the analysand may mishear this as a criticism. He also outlaws demands: "exhortation has no place in the analyst's interventions" (p. 232). In terms of the actual words used, therapists develop with patients "a shared language of personal meaning" (Aveline, 1990), drawing on key words and phrases from the patient's own associations. This use of appropriate language is something to which child psychotherapists are very sensitive, having to be aware of the chronological age and development of their patients.

Words should match the affect. Greenson (1974) gives the example of talking of the patient being "scared" rather than "apprehensive" if childlike feelings are being addressed. He also advocates avoiding technical terms—for example, saying "you're turning away from or avoiding" rather than mentioning resisting. Langs (1973), advocating the use of the patient's language and idiom, writes of the need to avoid technical language in interpretations so that intellectualization and rationalization are minimized. The long and complex interpretations will hinder self-analytic capacity in the patient (Rayner, 1991). According to Strupp (1973), the therapist should be sparing in verbally communicating his interest and understanding as the patient must work things out for himself, feel the achievements as his own. It is noted (Langs, 1973) that the therapist may talk too much for his own narcissistic reasons, and this overactivity is a reflection of his own problems and pathology.

Although interpretation is a pivotal part of verbal communication, we must also consider the therapist's use of aspects of verbal communication that are not strictly interpretative. These would include the therapist asking questions and seeking clarification. This may be in the service of a future interpretation, gathering in sufficient evidence or perhaps checking out that something has been accurately understood, but it may also be sufficient in itself. Observations and descriptions that are not interpretations may, because of coming from a different viewpoint, present something new and previously unthought about to the patient (Guy, 1978). However, Langs (1973) points out that questions and clarifications deal with manifest content, and although they can be used to get to deeper levels in the hope that the patient will realize the latent content, there is a risk that such questions can prevent the material from deepening and avoid unconscious fantasies.

Silence

There are many times when silence is an appropriate tool for the therapist. According to Langs, silence is not used enough: unless the therapist has clear and good reason to speak, he should remain silent, as by doing so he does not interfere with material that is moving in a meaningful direction. He states that the therapist should remain silent when he does not understand and "respect the value of silence as the primary therapeutic tool for understanding the patient" (1973, p. 369). Additionally, the therapist's silence creates pressure for the patient to search consciously and unconsciously for further associations and to communicate more meaningfully. Although he says that such silence must be accompanied by warmth to indicate acceptance of the patient, he later acknowledges that certain patients would find such silence persecuting and would leave therapy prematurely. Clearly different patients and at different times in their analysis will experience silence differently. Late on in analysis, a patient may use silence as a space to develop his own feelings and thoughts in his own way. In this space the patient can recover contact with lost original objects (Stewart, 1987). When the analyst remains quiet while the patient finds his voice in the analytic situation, this offers the patient the opportunity for "self-generated insights" (Bollas, 1987). Lanyado (2004) has written most interestingly about the quality of communication that can take place within silence. It is perhaps easier for a child psychotherapist to remain silent while a child plays in their presence than it is when with a silent adult, but the healing and creative moments that can take place within silence are respected by all practitioners.

So silence can be used to facilitate the patient's reverie, untroubled by demands from the analyst. Bion, in his usual provocative way, says that he replied to the question "Do you ever do anything except talk?" with the answer "Yes, we are silent." He talks about the importance of silence, which he likens to the rests in music, and says that they are used for observing (1974, p. 70).

Interpretation

Interpretation, at its simplest, is the therapist conveying to the patient her understanding of what is happening at that moment in therapy, referring to unconscious processes and perhaps linking it to the patient's past experiences and/or her relationship with the therapist—in fact, as Freud said, "making the unconscious conscious". Clearly many skills are necessary for creating an interpretation, including what Inge Pretorius (personal communication, 2003) called "clarity of thought and fluency of tongue", together with an attunement to the patient to realize what he can bear and attention to the countertransference to understand the patient's situation. In my review of the literature for this section I came across a number of fascinating ideas, including thoughts about the number of levels at which an interpretation could be made (Roth, 2001), the privileging of the transference interpretation, and the idea of interpreting "when the iron is cold" (Pine, 1985). From this wealth of material it seems important to highlight the aspect of the connection between therapist and patient.

A successful interpretation brings patient and therapist together emotionally. There are at least two dimensions to a successful "interpretive event": the information conveyed and the fact that in the act of conveying the information, the relationship between the patient and the therapist is deepened or altered. "A correct interpretation implies a deep and empathic form of relatedness" (Greenberg & Mitchell, 1983, p. 392). This connects with the view of Elizabeth Bradley (personal communication, 2001) that what makes a difference in therapeutic work is being able to make *contact* with the patient. It is this experience of contact that then leads to change. Pine (1985), however, also pays attention to the cognitive aspects of an interpretation, distinguishing between an empathic statement that describes and explains but does not link and an interpretation. Interpretation promotes *understanding*, whereas the empathic statement promotes a feeling of *being understood*. Steiner's work on patient-centred and analyst-centred interpretations also addresses how to describe what is happening in a way that the patient can hear and make use of. If the patient is made too anxious and persecuted by what he feels to be the blame implied in a patient-centred interpretation, he may not be able to "develop an interest in understanding no matter how small or fleeting" (1993, p. 141) that is a purpose of the therapeutic encounter.

Different authors privilege certain aspects of the purpose and style of interpretations, with all emphasizing that the patient has not previously consciously known about certain aspects of himself and his internal objects (Langs, 1973; Roth, 2001). These may not be welcome to the patient who needs to have the capacity to realize that while the therapist is pointing out unpleasant inner or life-history realities, he is *not* doing so to condemn, humiliate, provoke or ultimately abandon the patient (Pine, 1985). He says that an interpretation needs "soil on which it can fall and take root" (p. 149). However, not all patients have this capacity: some may need to operate defences so that they do not feel overwhelmed by feeling flooded or disorganized by the interpretation. With this in mind he advises alterations in technique to minimize this possibility. He states that classical psychoanalytic interpretations are left open-ended, through either vocal tone or sentence structure, as this is thought to leave the patient room to react, but he thinks that more fragile patients can feel panic and rage at this, and so he suggests that the therapist should use phrases that emphasize the working-together aspects. He also advises that the therapist should "strike while the iron is cold", in contrast to the usual expectation of addressing a feeling in the heat of the moment, so that the patient can have available adequate control structure to receive the interpretation (p. 153).

Strachey (1933) famously wrote of the "mutative interpretation", which, he said, analysts see as a sort of "magic weapon". Mutative interpretations are always transference interpretations. This view of transference interpretations being the most, if not the only, effective form of interpretation continues. However, not all writers privilege transference interpretations for all patients. Meltzer (1992) suggests that patients living in the claustrum have avoided the pains of infantile feelings and have no infantile transference, and that for them transference interpretations have no therapeutic value. Although one hears about successful mutative interpretations, usually psychic change comes about in a series of small steps rather than through one amazing, magically "mutative" interpretation. Even when apparently dealing with some aspect of the past, interpretations are always concerned with the relationship between the patient and the therapist. In thinking of the here-and-now transference, we can see that the patient has the opportunity to check how he is experiencing the therapist and to an extent evaluate how much he is influenced by unconscious processes in forming this view. This links with Fonagy's (2001) concept of reflective self-functioning.

Few writers specify how to make an interpretation. Aspiring psychotherapists can gather how interpretations are made from reading accounts of cases, but often few interpretations are given verbatim; those that are frequently seem to be a number of interventions put together, but they hardly sound like the words that were actually used at the time. Suggestions about how and when to interpret are relatively rare. Margaret Rustin talks about the pacing of language in describing work with a very passive and depressed boy whose traumatic history had caused a "massive closing down of his mind": "I saw that I had to investigate the imbalance between my sense of desperate effort to make contact and his mute retreatism. I struggled to slow down my words, to simplify sentences, to leave great amounts of time for a possible response from him" (2001, p. 282).

Anne Alvarez's (1997) work also emphasizes the vital importance of the therapist being aware of the need for choosing her words carefully. She draws attention to the "grammar of interpretations", distinguishing "between the grammar of wishes in neurotic patients and the grammar of imperative needs in borderline patients" (p. 753). She describes how her thinking on this issue has changed: she now realizes that what she had previously thought of as manic, omnipotent, and paranoid defences "were desperate attempts to *overcome* and *recover from* states of despair and terror" (p. 754). She carefully explains how this viewpoint then calls upon the therapist to interpret in a different way: "Where there is little ego to start with and perhaps a cruel depriving superego, the interpretive grammar of wishes may carry all too cruel implications; rather than help the child to think about deprivation, it actually succeeds in depriving him or her further" (1997, p. 766). This approach suggests that the clinician must be aware of the effect of interpretations and consider carefully not only when but also in what way to make them.

It is important to think about the purpose of what the patient has just said. If a patient's motive for projective identification is evacuation rather than communication, then a verbal interpretation will make him feel that something unwanted is being pushed back into him (Ferro, 1999; Meltzer, 1967; Rosenfeld, 1971). The practice of some child psychotherapists of "interpreting in the displacement"—that is, commenting on the actions shown in a child's play, talking of, for example, what the lamb had done and thinking about how the lamb might have felt about things but not overtly linking it up with how the patient had experienced similar things—can be helpful in allowing reflection on very painful issues.

The Boston Process of Change group (Stern et al., 1998) applied a developmental perspective to clinical work, using the concepts of declarative knowledge and procedural knowledge to formulate their idea of a "now moment" and "moments of meeting". The actions that make up a now moment are *not* routine or habitual; other aspects of the relationship must be accessed: "now moments" are much more than a technical manoeuvre, "the therapist must use a specific aspect of his or her individuality that carries a personal signature" (p. 913).

In a moment of meeting transference and countertransference aspects are at a minimum, as "the personhood of the interactants, relatively denuded of role trappings, is brought into play" (p. 914). From moments of meeting, something new is created in the relationship, which alters the intersubjective environment. Stern and colleagues clearly have a different conceptualization of what is happening within a therapeutic session, and this means that different clinical procedures may be required.

Again we see how the concept of what the therapist is doing and is aiming to do in psychotherapeutic work alters the technique(s) used and the skills that are thought to be needed for the task. Monica Lanyado (personal communication, 2002) drew a distinction between "heart-to-heart" and "head-to-head" communications, seeing "now moments" as clearly "heart-to-heart". Rather than privilege one over the other, it is important to have both together. She also pointed out that statements of any sort made by the therapist tend to have significance for the patient, tend to "get in", because it is the therapist who has said it, regardless of their externally validated qualities.

Differences between child and adult psychotherapy

It could be argued that the skills needed for child work are no different from those needed for adult work, since, as Winnicott said, "Psychoanalysis of children is not different from that of adults. The basis of all psychoanalysis is a complex theory of the emotional development of the infant and child" (1958b, p. 116). However, it may be that there are some differences in emphasis. Anne Alvarez (personal communication, 2004) points out that psychotherapeutic work with children pays more attention to both bodies and development than does work with adults. Of course, psychoanalytic work with children and adults has to be conducted in a different way: "The very nature of analytic work with children, dependent largely on action rather than words, demands real technical differences" (Joseph, 1998, p. 359), and the alterations in technique call upon different technical skills. Looking at such differences and the capacities they require is too wide a topic for be addressed properly here, but I highlight some of the more obvious issues.

Play

Children express themselves far less through language than do adults. Although over recent years we have become more alert to the *unspoken* parts of the dialogue between patient and therapist, still in our work with adults we expect much of the emphasis in the work to be on what is said—and not said. With children, especially younger children, there is a different form of communication: that of play. Play is at the centre of child psychotherapy, but what sort of play and how it is understood will vary between theoretical groups as well as from practitioner to practitioner. Child psychotherapists provide specific limited play material, designed primarily to be used as an aid to symbolic expression. In the setting of the consulting-room, the child psychotherapist makes this play material available and observes what, if anything, is done with it. The amount of active engagement in the child's play, as opposed to watching but not participating, will vary according to the therapist's personal and theoretical views. Child psychotherapists do not automatically assume that all play is necessarily symbolic and expressive of underlying phantasies. From recent work with children on the autistic spectrum we have become painfully aware of the meaninglessness of certain play, and even with very different children play can be used in a repetitive, mind-numbing, defensive way, reminiscent of the "chuntering" of which Joseph (1982) writes. The ability to observe closely and to be alert and responsive to the countertransference aroused within us from what we are seeing is surely crucial here.

Interpretation

It is in the area of interpreting that we can perhaps see the other major technical difference between child and adult work. Many important aspects of interpretation have been addressed above, and issues to do with timing or the tone of voice used are as vital with children as they are with adults. Adult therapists need to think about the impact of their interpretation and phrase it in a way that will be most helpful, but when a child reacts to interpretations as attacks or criticism and feels he must fight them off, the need for care in offering interpretations may be even more essential. Often children object to the therapist talking to them as they play. For some this is because it interrupts their sense of being immersed in the play: they cannot simultaneously both "live" it and stand outside it to answer questions about it.

The way children use toys allows the child a certain degree of displacement or externalization of self and object relationships and of the interaction between them. The therapist may make an interpretation in the form of a comment about a toy figure or character in the story without obviously linking it to the child himself. In this way the therapist hopes to make the interpretation more internalizable by the patient. The interpretation in the displacement acts as a spur to thinking, offered in a way that can be received, when a more overt interpretation could lead to resistance and a pulling down of the emotional shutters.

Management of boundaries

Therapists working with children also have to contend with issues to do with the management of boundaries. In circumstances where a child is doing something dangerous, the need to address both the activity, whatever it is, and the underlying communication it contains *simultaneously* calls upon particular skills that may be less necessary for a therapist working with adults who has more space to address the underlying communication with less sense of need to alter the activity *immediately*.

Sooner or later in a child analysis the therapist will be called upon to set limits. It is likely to be an important and necessary part of the therapeutic work that a child will test any limits to assess the therapist's tolerance for and acceptance of them. While the therapist must interpret what the child is trying to do, she must also stop the child when necessary. This is different from adult work, when fantasies or thoughts are being expressed verbally. As Sandler, Kennedy, and Tyson say: "In adult analysis there are no limits to free association, whereas in child analysis there are limits to action" (1990, p. 190).

Betty Joseph is adamant that the child psychotherapist must provide a setting in which the child is able, with few limitations, to express his aggression and actual destructiveness. A therapist who is worrying about protecting the room or herself can all too easily get caught up in rushing about and then is unable to observe the child and think about him. In such situations the analyst can become like the child, "violent, difficult and out of control" (1998, p. 361), and the child has been able to force his desperate, violent self into the analyst, who has become a suitable receptacle for it. It is essential for the analyst to go on thinking and talking, and not just defending or retaliating. While, as we have seen before, this is essential for any therapist, the additional strain that is imposed when the violence is physical is immense. Child psychotherapists need to process their reactions very fast and hold on tight to their own feelings until they have had the opportunity to do so. Leading writers suggest that it is possible to make effective interpretations while physically restraining a child, but the need for the capacity to observe, process, and be involved simultaneously is surely very great.

Transference and countertransference and the impact of the external world

According to Esther Bick, "the countertransference stresses on the child analyst are more severe than those on the analyst of adults, at any rate of non psychotic adults" (1961, p. 107). She understands this as being due both to the unconscious conflicts that arise in relation to the child's parents and to the nature of the child's material, for her the intensity of the child's dependence and the primitive nature of his phantasies tend to arouse the analyst's own unconscious anxieties. Bick comments that it is difficult to contain the violent and concrete projections and that the child's material is more difficult to understand, since it is primitive in its sources and mode of expression. Because of this, the child analyst has to depend more on his unconscious to provide him with clues to the meaning of a child's play and non-verbal communication. While other theoretical schools might argue that this reliance on the therapist's unconscious is a double-edged sword, we can see an emphasis on the child psychotherapist's need to have free access to countertransference feelings. Transference also needs thinking about differently: "Children have a continuing dependent relationship with the parents in the present. This complicates the task of distinguishing between a fixed pattern of behaviour used with parents and adults in general and the specific revival of a past experience within the context of the treatment situation" (Sandler, Kennedy, & Tyson, 1990, p. 81).

Child therapists have to tread very delicately—a suggestion that life at home is unsatisfactory may challenge a child's loyalty, and references to, for example, an unreliable mother figure could inhibit the play. Harris refers to certain sorts of interpretations as "conversation stoppers" and contrasts these with the sort that "lead on to further enquiry" (1977, p. 279).

The reality of a child's parents impacts in many different ways upon child analytic treatment. It is not possible—and, I would argue, not desirable—to avoid contact with parents. Especially with younger child patients, the parents must be seen to ensure that they provide the continuing emotional and practical support that is needed for the child to continue in treatment. Moreover, there may be many circumstances in which without changes in the child's family, the treatment for the child can only be partially successful. Sandler, Kennedy, and Tyson (1990) point out that while an adult can remove himself from a particular situation once he has understood why it is appealing or feels necessary, a young child has relatively little control over his environment. Child psychotherapists may also find themselves more actively involved in trying to influence the external world of the child by attending Review meetings or liaising with concerned professionals. Although traditionally some of this has been done by other colleagues, there may be times when it is the child's therapist herself who engages in this work. Obviously such contact potentially poses problems about confidentiality, and the therapist needs to be very aware of these. Monica Lanyado has written (2004) about the need to keep a child "in her pocket" and be very active in the network on their behalf at times of transition or entering adoption. She makes a cogent case for the value of this work. This may then lead to tension between the need to communicate and the need for privacy. The child psychotherapist's awareness of the child's helplessness in the situation may lead to identification with that helplessness, or an omnipotent "busyness", neither of which are helpful.

Esther Bick (1961) suggests that the child psychotherapist inevitably experiences unconscious conflicts in relation to the child's parents and tends to identify either with the child against the parents or with the parents against the child. It often happens that therapists experi-

Table 4.1. The interrelationship of capacities and skills (technique)

Capacity	Technique
analytic attitude: absence of narcissism	creating a setting; neutral, objective, suspension of judgement
bearing humbling experience	keeping oneself back
respect for patient	respect for patient
open oneself to the experience of shock	find something new
tolerate anxiety & uncertainty	manage strong feelings
wait for meaning to emerge	wait for meaning to emerge
	attitude to patient, hold patient inside self, receive all aspects of patient, reverie
empathy	thoughts about how patient uses therapist, avoid acting-out responses
realistic hopefulness	
retain apparently contradictory experiences simultaneously	
close attention	close attention, non-verbal, sensitivity to infantile modes of communication
cognitive abilities	using cognitive skills to organize into patterns
	think, evaluate, remember, anticipate
	think about what experiencing
	hold onto ideas & uncomfortable feelings, don't grab at understanding
	create space to think about feelings
	awareness of transference & countertransference
knowledge of theory	background use of theory
	feelings recognized by a reflective part of the mind
listening & skill in communication	verbal communication: how to talk to the patient, silence, questions, clarifications
	interpretation

ence rivalry with parents or a desire to be a better parent to the child, and such feelings need to be recognized, well managed, and used appropriately.

The question of how much, if at all, a child consents to having therapy may in many, although not all, cases be very different for adult and child patients. Usually with adults the problem is much simpler, because if the treatment alliance sinks below a specific level, the patient stops treatment. If the patient continues to attend, the analyst tries to find out what brings him, but with the child all this is obscured by the fact that the child is not necessarily coming of his own volition. Indeed, parents are encouraged to bring the child at times when he does not want to come. Sutton (2001) and Daws (1986) both explore the question of *what* the child has consented to and how this must fluctuate during the course of the treatment. Anna Freud bluntly suggests that if for one week children only came to therapy if they *really* wanted to "without any pressure from anybody else I don't say there would be none, but you'd be surprised by how few there *would* be" (in Sandler, Kennedy, & Tyson, 1990, pp. 18–19).

Summary

From this examination of the technique that the therapist adopts within the session we have laid out the sorts of skills we are expecting the clinician to possess and noted in a few instances the slightly enhanced skills that child psychotherapists might need. Now we can look at whether we might anticipate, from the literature, that the experience of infant observation would engender those skills. Table 4.1 shows the interrelationship of capacities and skills. This table is added to in chapter 5 (Table 5.1) to show how the capacities and skills outlined here map onto those said to be engendered from infant observation, and then, in due course, Table 6.1 shows whether and in what ways the interviews showed evidence of the anticipated capacities and skills being enhanced.

CHAPTER FIVE

Feel the music:
how infant observation develops
the equipment for clinical practice

Historical background

Infant observation began to be used as part of a formal curriculum in psychoanalytic psychotherapy training when introduced to the Tavistock Child Psychotherapy course by Esther Bick in 1948. It was added to the Institute of Psychoanalysis course, as an option, in the 1960s. The Anna Freud Centre also began what they call "mother–baby" observation at home in 1962, although their students had been observing in the well-baby clinic from the late 1940s. Of course, other people, not only psychoanalytic psychotherapists, had been observing babies and young children for much longer. Freud's famous observation of his grandson with the cotton reel shows the observation of precise details, with an emphasis on the total context within which it occurred, which were to become the hallmarks of psychoanalytically informed observation. Charlotte Bühler in Vienna is also credited with being an important early observer. Infant and young child observations were thought to be important for work with children in order to understand the way non-verbal communication is predominantly used by very young patients. However, we also see during the Controversial Discussions that reported observations of infants and young children were used to provide evidence for Klein's radical theories. In some wonderfully detailed observations she notes infants' behaviour and then extrapolates from this concepts with which we may now be familiar but which at the time were thought by many in the psychoanalytic community to be outrageous and unfounded (Klein, 1944). This problem of whether what is seen can be "fact" or is always altered by theoretical preconceptions may be thought in some part to have contributed to resistance to acknowledging the usefulness of infant observation in certain theoretical quarters.

To begin with, the emphasis was on gaining an understanding of young children, and it is only over the years that other, more fundamental learning experiences have been attributed to it. Esther Bick, in her seminal "Notes on Infant Observation in Psychoanalytic Training" (1964), suggests that infant observation will help students to conceive vividly the infantile experience of child patients, increase the student's understanding of non-verbal behaviour and play and of the behaviour of the child who neither speaks nor plays, help the student get a better history from the mother when engaged in clinical work; increase knowledge of infants through being able to compare and contrast them in seminars, and give students a unique opportunity to find out for themselves how relationships within a family emerge. Although her paper goes on to acknowledge the "intense emotional impact" of being close to a new mother and baby, the importance of this aspect is not flagged at the beginning of her paper. Wittenberg (1998) states that the "enormous richness" of infant observation in fact dawned only gradually on its practitioners. The view of infant observation as an opportunity to know more about infants and children, with some attention to early relationships, may account for why many adult psychoanalytic psychotherapists do not view it as having important relevance for them.

Current views

Although these aspects of learning are still deemed to be important, it seems to me that there is another aspect that makes infant observation such a central part of a psychoanalytic psychotherapy training: the way that infant observation stirs up powerful feeling in the observer.

The observational vignette at the front of this book shows the observer experiencing a number of intense, varied feelings in a relatively short time span. That particular extract is of a very ordinary, relatively uncomplicated interchange between mother and an infant aged almost six months. If we can see such intensity of feeling experienced in a generally good setting, with a slightly older baby, how much greater is the strength and depth of feeling of many observers with younger infants or in more disturbing circumstances? The feelings experienced by all of us in the presence of a newborn are extremely intense. Birth and death are major life crises. While trainees on some courses undertake observations of older children, in newborns we see a human in the rawest, most undefended state. This can make infant observation painful, but also valuable, because it is the task of the psychoanalytic psychotherapist to be prepared to engage with the most primitive levels of life. Having experienced extreme feelings, the observer then has to find a reflective space in which to think about and process such feelings.

What goes on within the observer during observation

Although the components of the task are tightly interwoven I have tried to separate them in order to delineate the different qualities thought to be gained from carrying out an infant observation.

Looking without preconceptions

At its simplest, we could say that the observer needs to watch and think, to be reflective, not active, within the setting. Clearly the task of watching or looking is a very particular one. It is important to acknowledge that "observation is never neutral. Observation is always contextual, based on assumptions, values, constructions of experience" (Mitchell, 1995, p. 83), and "It is an epistemological fallacy to think that we can stand outside what we observe, or observe without distortion, what is alien to our experience" (Levenson, 1972, p. 8). The observer's part in what they see is looked at in greater detail when considering the subjective experience of observation, but here I want to concentrate on the risk of the student seeing things through the potentially distorting lens of a particular theory. Sue Reid says: "The student is encouraged and supported to *see what is there to be seen* and not to look for what they think should be there" (1997, p. 1). Awareness of the distortion that can arise is the first stage in the development of the possibility of "objective evaluation" (Trowell, 2002).

The infant observation teaching on which this research is based is taking place in institutions operating within a psychoanalytic framework, and it seems very likely that what is seen is thought about and used to clarify and enliven theoretical concepts. The different theoretical schools will privilege certain concepts, but from a fundamental interest in unconscious processes. The infant observation experience can endow "with profound emotional meaning some rather intellectually understood aspects of theory" (Sandelson, 1999). Steiner (lecture, M18 Course, Tavistock, 2000) spoke of how infant observation enhanced his understanding of the paranoid–schizoid and depressive positions when he realized that depressive-position functioning, moments of integration, had been becoming longer and more sustained over many months. He saw moments of integration and disintegration in the baby he observed, and he recalled how he saw the disintegrating baby "come together" when able to focus on something such as a rattle, or observed how being undressed caused the baby to disintegrate. He stated that this concept of integration and disintegration is very important to his clinical work, and he felt that he had understood it through his infant observation experience.

This very fact, however, gives ammunition to some writers who feel that what is seen and reported on is too influenced by certain theories. Trevarthen (1998), in reviewing Briggs's book, *Growth and Risk in Infancy* (1997), points out that the way one does an observation will reinforce expectations (for Klein's followers having been particularly accused of this, see chapter 11). Bick (1964) writes of students finding evidence of splitting, and Harris (1976) says that observation of the early months brings home to the observer the reality that emotion is rooted in bodily states. These concepts are being noted because the writers believe passionately in the importance of them. However, while Klein's theories about infant capacities were initially derided because it was thought that she attributed to infants capacities they could not have, Fonagy points out that "More sophisticated methods of observations of infant behaviour revealed that the human infant possesses relatively complex mental capacities, even at birth, in some cases exceeding what was presupposed by Kleinian theory" (2001, p. 159).

A particular way of observing

Waddell describes infant observation as "a method with no claims to impartiality or objectivity. Rather the reverse: it is one that is rooted in subjectivity of a particular kind" (1988, p. 313). Observers are encouraged to note detail of a very particular sort. Infant observation does not simply chart that which can be seen on video or by micro-analysis. Some psychoanalytic thinkers, such as Beatrice Beebe, as well as Mary Sue Moore and Janet Dean (Dean & Moore, 2001), do use these techniques and show to us how much the naked eye must miss, but Moore and Dean also describe the experience of having physically observed in families where it was suspected that abuse had taken place, with filming going on simultaneously. Using these videos in a teaching situation, they talk of having had feelings of disquiet at the time, the source of which they could not consciously identify; these feelings were then confirmed by being able to slow down the film. It seems that these experienced and gifted practitioners felt something, and then the examination of the film was used to demonstrate what they had known intuitively. Nevertheless, if we accept that "seeing" alone could be done better by mechanical means, it becomes apparent that observing involves attending to the emotionality surrounding that data. This concentration on the emotional content enables the observer, in turn, to understand more about the emotional life of infants and young children and to begin to think about relationships and how they are formed.

Houzel (1999) outlines three aspects of what he calls "receptivity". He describes (1) receptivity at a perceptual level, of things that can be objectively noted, such as gestures, vocalizations, and changes in muscle tone, and (2) emotional and empathic receptivity, which allows the observer to experience what the infant and others around him may be experiencing. He then writes about (3) "unconscious receptivity", which, he says, manifests itself in the countertransference. In my opinion it is this third aspect that has come to be seen as of paramount importance.

It is of immense value that psychoanalytic observation depends on introspection. Students have to learn to look within and become aware of their own states of mind, studying themselves in response to what they are seeing. "It is a method which requires the observer to be as minutely cognisant of his or her internal processes as of those of the subject of the observation" (Waddell, 1988, pp. 313–314). This emphasis on being able to reflect on what is happening within the self is cited by many writers (e.g. Canham, McFadyen, & Youell, 1997; Green & Miller, 2001) and crosses theoretical boundaries. As Ruth Robinson writes (1992): "For me as an observer it was an important part of my development to learn to be aware of my feelings. This allowed me to use them as a source of information about what was going on in the observation but also to think about how they might distort my observation."

"The issues raised by the observer's response are a vital part of the training of potential therapists for clinical work" (Alison Cantle, 1995). The observer is encouraged to notice his or her own experiences and to use them to understand what is being communicated. Many writers warn that, as in psychotherapeutic work, it is important to try to think about what is causing these feelings; there can be a readiness to label them countertransference in an inappropriate way. In describing her teaching approach, Ruth Robinson (personal communication, 2001) explained that she encourages her students to think very carefully about their own behaviour, emphasizing the importance of distinguishing between their feelings and what the other might be doing, and Harris views many of the feelings as deriving from the observer's past: "most people who undertake this exercise find that the closeness to the infant and mother arouses in them extremely intense feelings deriving from their own infancy" (1977, p. 266). These may include envy of the mother–baby relationship or be the experience of projective identification received from mother and infant.

Intensity of emotions and the capacity to think about them

The intensity of the experience is acknowledged by all who write about it. Some writers (Bard, 1997; Crick, 1997; Magagna, 1987) refer to the manoeuvres that the observer may use in the face of unbearable pain, such as recourse to defensive use of theoretical and intellectual understanding, and Magagna (1987) writes movingly of working to keep herself fully present, "keeping feelings intensely alive and simultaneously thinking about them" and when unable to do this, tending to cut herself off "from emotional involvement" to become "a video camera". Margaret Rustin (1988) describes vividly how extreme the emotions felt can be: "The exposure to intense feelings, the impact of feeling oneself drawn into an emotional force-field and struggling to hold one's balance and sense of self, the encounter with the probably unfamiliar confusion and power of infantile emotional life, are especially valuable aspects of infant observation for beginning therapists" (1988, p. 8).

Rustin sees exposure to these feelings as an opportunity for growth, in line with Bion's (1976) concept of turbulence, in which, provided one has the capacity to tolerate doubt in the face of the unknown, growth can follow. Wittenberg parallels the students' experience with that of the new baby: "Being born into the role of observer is invariably traumatic. We have all defended against deep infantile anxieties by idealising babies and babyhood. To actually experience the baby's frequent falling apart . . . what agonies babies, mothers and fathers go through is always a shocking discovery for the inexperienced observer" (1993, p. 23). She points out that the observer may attempt to evade the catastrophic anxiety aroused by this by blaming the parents or idealizing the baby.

Despite the main focus on the family, most observers are encouraged in their final papers to show some awareness of the impact on them of the experience. From the many I have read, a few examples stand out. Sandelson (1999) writes of finding herself choking after she had observed the baby's attempt to spit out an unwanted dummy. Warin (1996) describes "struggling to hold onto my balance and sense of self". McFadyen (1991), in writing about infant observation as part of a child psychiatry training programme, gives the example of feeling that she has abandoned the mother as the mother feels she has abandoned the baby. This is an example of projective identification, which many writers feel they often see and experience within infant observation.

> When the feelings involved are often very powerful, and probably communicated on a pre-verbal basis, the work on transfer-

ence and countertransference is fundamental, and is connected with another valuable aspect of studying infants, namely the sensitivity to infantile modes of communication which can develop. Students can learn to perceive normal projective identification, to understand some of the body language of infants, and to struggle towards a language for describing pre-linguistic experience which will serve them well in work with patients if the infantile transference is to be tackled. [M. E. Rustin, 1988, p. 20]

However, it is not only the receptivity to these emotions that is important, but also how they are managed. Harris thinks of this in terms of a position:

If one does not come close enough for the relationship to have an impact, many details will be missed and the quality of learning impaired. On the other hand, in order not to be drawn into action—into acting out the anxieties evoked instead of containing them by reflection—one must find a sufficiently distanced position to create a mental state for observing what is happening in oneself as well as in the mother and baby. [1976, p. 227]

Bick (1964) counsels a certain "detachment", meaning that the observer's behaviour must not, wherever possible, be influenced by whatever she is feeling. Crick expands this idea:

The "detachment" that Bick advises is, I think, the position from which the observer is able not only to be aware of what is going on in herself, but also able to see what is happening between the mother and the baby, able to be in identification with each of them, but also free to dis-identify enough to retain the observer's point of view. [1997, p. 252]

Crick likens this—which she calls the "third position"—to the position of the analyst when analytic work is going well, and she says that it is lost in both analysis and observation when the therapist/observer is being projected into with great force. In order to achieve this position, the observer has to find within her own mind a space in which to think about the felt feelings. This, it seems to me, is at the heart of the learning experience, and it is easy to see how it correlates with psychoanalytic psychotherapy. The observer has to note, experience, and think about what she is experiencing, just as a therapist does. Refusal to open oneself up to the feelings may seem like a tempting option, but is one that then prevents the observer from having the experience and the therapy from being effective.

Maiello (1997) writes of how the observer is inevitably an other, a third, and how painful this can feel. Using Britton's (1989) description of the development of the oedipal configuration, the third position, for young children, Maiello states:

> If he (the observer) resists the urge to avoid feelings that are difficult to bear, he will widen and develop his internal emotional and thinking space. In other words, if he tolerates remaining in the third position, he maintains an awareness of his separateness with his painful corollary of feelings of abandonment, exclusion, helplessness and solitude. [1997, p. 49]

She cites Britton: "This provides us with the capacity for seeing ourselves in interaction with others and for entertaining another point of view whilst retaining our own, for reflecting on ourselves whilst being ourselves" (p. 49). She explains that the observer who enters into contact with himself as an other develops "negative capacity". It enhances his ability to bear not knowing, to be the other in relation to knowledge and predictability, helping him to renounce the impulse to control events. "This quality is at the very basis of the capacity of both genuine listening and creative thought" (p. 50). It is the reflective space and the work that is done within it that is crucial, and Maiello gives us a very helpful theoretical framework for thinking about this.

Other writers have talked of "getting on with the task" (Waddell, 2002), "the ability to carry on when an emotional storm is eroding all the ability to think" (Graham, 1999, p. 59), and "the contained management of themselves while all this is going on" (M. J. Rustin, 1997b). From these we can see the clear link with the therapist's ability to keep reflecting and thinking while under the impact of all the projections flying about in a consulting-room—what Schafer (1983) calls the "direct experience of the force field of emotions". Margaret Rustin (1988) talks of the need for the observer to think about feelings:

> This requires space in the mind where thoughts can take shape and where confused experiences can be held in an inchoate form until their meaning becomes clearer. This kind of mental functioning requires a capacity to tolerate anxiety, uncertainties, discomfort, helplessness, a sense of bombardment. It is the personal

equipment needed by a psychoanalytic psychotherapist. [1988, pp. 20–21]

Some students seem able to do much of this painful work by themselves. Sorensen, Foster, Jarrell, Mack, Presberg, and Weeks (1997) give an example of an observer who is able with searing personal honesty to examine the uncomfortable envious feelings stirred up within her while watching a nursing couple and then to see how the same processes interferes with her clinical work.

Green and Miller summarize the immeasurable gains in this when they say: "Those who acquire observation skills and insights have also made progress in becoming further acquainted with themselves" (2001, p. 12). I think it is worth noting here that we expect a lot from students in being able to process their feelings in this way. Brenman-Pick writes of infant observation giving the students an "enhanced capacity to observe and experience something of the intensity of the relationship between infant and mother—and to experience *whilst in analysis* the intense feelings this stirs up in the observer—is an invaluable introduction to clinical work" (2000, pp. 109–110; italics added). However, given the emphasis that I have placed in this work on the central importance of this capacity to experience and reflect, I wonder what are the implications of the fact that students are *not* necessarily in analysis while engaged in this task. Might they, without the support and safety of the analytic session, feel unable to feel sufficiently or think about what has been felt? Such defensive manoeuvres would be very understandable, but would then potentially undermine the far-reaching effects of the most vital aspects of the task.

Tanner views the ability to reflect on action, to think about an experience after it has occurred, as necessary for professional growth. She acknowledges that it can be difficult when the mind is flooded to think at all, and she writes of the painful experience of confronting "the unrecognised assumptions and stereotypes that pervade our thinking" (1999, p. 22). I wonder if we could make a link between the capacity to *think about* the painful experience and what I understand to be a key feature of the Adult Attachment Interview rating. For AAI raters it is not the original quality of the experience that is the prognostic indicator of mental health, but the ability to reflect on it, to have integrated it in some way, of which sense can then be made.

Indeed, there may be some observational circumstances that feel impossible to think about at the time but can, with the help of the seminar, be processed in some way. Lazar (1998), in describing observing a premature baby, writes of the impossibility of thinking at the time and the acute pain of thinking about it afterwards, which was then shown in the observer's struggle to write about it. The seminar, and in some cases the observer's own therapy, can help the student to bear to think, to stay within the necessary reflective space. Lanyado (1994) suggests that it can be helpful to the family as well as to the future clinician to see the "value of standing still and being receptive in the midst of painful feelings and general mayhem" (pp. 6–7).

The pain of abstinence

The pain of the observation is made more acute because the observer is asked not to take any action: "The emotional proximity of the observer to the rawness of infantile anxieties, without the option of intervention, makes the task more complex" (Segal, 2003, p. 13). "Doing nothing" means the observer cannot use her usual mechanisms for coping with feelings (Trowell et al., 1998), since "doing" precludes the opportunity to be and reflect (Tanner, 1999). It is acknowledged (Davids et al., 1999) how very difficult it can be in certain circumstances to refrain from action, but Brafman (1988), thinking about an observer having to watch a baby crying while mother is unavailable, points out that from this the observer can realize that the baby can manage discomfort. This part of infant observation, often excruciating when first experienced, is frequently noted by those questioned about their experiences afterwards. Miles and Trowell's research (1991) on social work trainees' response to infant observation gives many examples of practitioners valuing the "space for thinking rather than acting" and noting their increased ability to contain the urge to do so. However, the giving up of one's professional identity can be painful, although the purpose of it is to create a space in which the intense emotions can be felt more keenly.

How the observer relates to the family is always a preoccupation of new observers. The need to have a human response can be overlooked by observers being so determined to do it "properly" that they create in their minds a parody of a distant analyst. This wish for distance may also be a response to the observer's anxieties about being intrusive, such feelings often being exacerbated by being confronted with the intimacy of the mother–baby relationship. Brafman writes that there is always a point when the parent asks the observer whether she wants to hold the baby, and in his view, although one cannot see it until later, "this sequence can summarise much of what follows in the course of the visits" (1988, p. 80). Miriam Steele (personal communication, 2001) spoke of how the essence of the work of infant observation was for the observer to develop an observational stance and acknowledged ideas about how other training schools would have much "stricter" or more distant "rules" about how this was done. Ruth Robinson (1992) wrote of feeling at times during her observation experience that the idea that there was a "proper" way observation should be done was conveyed. Questioning the validity of this, she states that the negotiation of the boundaries of the role is in itself a major task of observation, and that it would be better to acknowledge this than convey the idea of an ideal observation as one where boundaries are effortlessly maintained. W. Ernest Freud (1975) sees a major part of the seminar leader's work as fostering, in an unobtrusive way, "desirable attributes", especially those thought to be assets for later analytic technique, in the students. For him the injunctions against moralizing, criticizing, and advising would fit into this pattern, while he also felt that the patience needed for the "slower pace" of the mother–infant observation could be good training for psychoanalytic work.

This capacity to wait and not use activity to mask uncertainty and anxiety is very important. There are particular and additional difficulties for male observers (see Jackson, 1998) that, though not the focus of this study, deserve attention. Borensztejn, Kohen de Abdata, Dimant, Nemas de Urman, and Ungar, following their infant observation experiences, saw that interpretation in a session could be used as a comfort: "This has made us stronger in our own belief, in clinical practice, that observation and description of transferential evidence in the session must prevail over the need to attribute quick meaning" (1998, p. 81). Reid also writes most movingly of how looking in a new way, without preconceptions or one's professional self, can be an alarming experience. The observer is "exposed to a whole new level of perception of human relationships. This is both disturbing and exciting" (1997, p. 1). She writes of the shock of realizing "how little we see usually of what is going on." This need to be shocked and disturbed is echoed in other writings about psychoanalytic capacities. Tuters states that

> It was the experience of Bick (1964) E. Freud (1975) and Harris (1977) that all students have difficulty with infant observation no matter what the background or how much experience they have had with infants. This difficulty appears related to unconscious emotional conflicts that stem from one's own childhood that are reactivated by observing an infant and mother. [1988, p. 96]

Interestingly, in the same paper Tuters writes of her experience of teaching two groups for infant observation: one doing it for general professional development, the other embarking on a child psychotherapy training. She found the group going in for training resistant to the experience at first, viewing it as an imposition and a diversion from their main task. However, as the experience progressed, views changed, and by their second-year essay the participants were able to identify and recognize what individual difficulties in observing infants had evoked in terms of their own unresolved emotional conflicts from the past. Indeed—although writing about a very different cohort—Bridge and Miles state: "In none of the observations were the observers untouched by raw personal issues brought to the surface by what they were seeing" (1996, p. 128).

This ability to experience emotion and then to contain it is at the heart of the observational experience. "Learning to recognize and contain anxieties generated within the observational setting and within oneself is a universally underlined benefit of infant observation" (L. R. Miller, 2001, p. 12). Moreover, the ability to use those feelings in the service of understanding oneself and the observed family—and in future patients—better is also central. Alison Cantle's dissertation on transference and countertransference reactions within infant observation and then clinical work concludes: "It is clear that my own feelings, however they be named, in response to the mother and baby *do* increase my understanding of their experience when coupled with the evidence of close observation" (1995, p. 40). In short, psychoanalytically informed infant observation, where the observer is learning, through experience, develops one of the central tools of the analyst's work. Crick writes:

> The particular potency of mother–baby observation as part of psychoanalytic training lies not so much in what is learnt about babies, as in the work that has to go on in the analytic candidate to find internally "the position of the observer". This is an essential part of what is involved in eventually acquiring a psychoanalytic identity. [1997, p. 245]

Waiting for meaning to emerge

In writing about infant observation, many writers (Miller, 1992; Reid, 1997; M. E. Rustin, 1988) refer to the fact that observers are strongly discouraged from rushing to premature conclusions—that observation, like clinical work, can generate hypotheses that can then be tested over time. The need to wait and see and to be prepared to find that one's hypothesis was not quite right is emphasized. Silver (1999) writes at the end of a two-year observation that some thoughts she had had about the baby's style of relating at the end of the first year were not confirmed in the second year, causing her to re-evaluate her original thoughts. Looking back on old material can make one reflect in another way (Abrahamsen, personal communication: research workshop at Third Tavistock Infant Observation Conference, March 2002). In both these examples some understanding *has* been reached over time. It seems to be the general view that if the observer can wait, then understanding of a sort will emerge from the pattern of the material. As Bick describes it: "The experience of the seminar is that one may see an apparent pattern emerging in infant observation, but one can only accept it as significant if it is repeated in the same, or a similar, situation in many subsequent observations" (1964, p. 250), and she warns about the need to watch before creating theories. Similarly, Ruth Robinson writes that

> One needs to be aware of the temptation to look for theories which provide total closure in relation to the other. This is connected with the development of the ability to tolerate not knowing what is happening and being able to wait and to revise one's

theories in the light of new information. This information will only be available for us if we keep an open mind. [1992, p. 19]

However, we are very well aware of how hard it is to "develop the capacity not to know". As Harris writes: "It is more painful to wait, to remain receptive and not cut off, to bear the pain that is being projected, including pain of one's own uncertainty, than it is to have recourse to precipitate action designed to evacuate that pain and to gain the relief of feeling that one is doing something" (1976, p. 233). She states that we can see such defensive activity when the mother busies herself with the infant's bodily needs out of anxiety and inadequacy, and also in therapeutic work. Tuters (1988) also describes her students, when prevented from using action as a defence against anxiety, feeling anger towards the seminar leader, later displaced onto the families, who were seen as "pathological". Much work has to be done within the seminar to disentangle these processes.

Processing through writing

Making notes can be a first step in being able to process the experience. According to Anthony Cantle, writing up the observations had the effect of helping him to

> hold on to the experience in a more thought out way. . . . through the experience of recording it, some kind of opportunity to metabolise and think about what had happened . . . rather than feeling too burdened by my own reaction . . . served to help me recover what I felt to be too much under attack at the time of being with this family, namely the capacity to think. [2000, pp. 21–22]

This is "stage two of the observation process": although a tape recorder could record the same sounds, it could not do the necessary sorting out. "The student's mind is a place where mental processes are active: the experience of the recent observation needs examining, shaping, putting into words and committing to paper" (Green & Miller, 2001, p. 7).

Scott (2002) also draws attention to the work that takes place during the process of writing about an experience. Although referring to experiential group experiences, her statement that "the readiness to stay with the unsettling—may be as much in reflection, in writing, as in the face-to-face work of the group" has relevance for other situations. These descriptions of writing up notes show that this activity also calls on the working capacities of the adult part of the observer (M. E. Rustin, 1988), which, together with the seminar, can help when the observer is feeling painfully disturbed. It is not my purpose here to address what should be in the notes, but it is worth talking about the difficulty of finding adequate language for pre-verbal experiences as well as finding the right language for emotions. Sandelson states:

> I have found great difficulty in describing the states of bliss I "observed" whilst in the presence of the breastfeeding mother and infant couple. To use the word "observe" is in itself inadequately meaningful because, while I can describe the gestures and comments made in a particular interaction, such a description alone cannot fully convey the rapturous affective ambience I so frequently experienced. . . . I had a tendency to confuse the names of mother and baby as if in their involvement with each other I could not easily perceive them as two separate beings but as one. Poetry, rather than prose, in its combination of words and music, seems the more apt medium. [1999, p. 8]

Bick states that because facts "have to be described in language we find that every word is loaded with a penumbra of implication" (1964, p. 254). She points out that when during a feed the nipple has gone from the baby's mouth, the observer might use any of the following words about it—dropped, fell, pushed, released, escaped. She explains that realizing the different implications of the way that the observer has thought about this "fact" teaches the student caution and reliance on the consecutive observations for confirmation. Ruth Robinson (personal communication, 2001), in describing her teaching methods, says that she advises her students that if they have strong feelings about something at the time, they should include it in the narrative, but if those feelings were experienced later, they should be put at the end. Robinson also spoke of how students are reluctant to say what they cannot remember, but they have a tendency to "gloss over" this, although it is a most important source of information. Bridge and Miles also acknowledge the way "The need to tidy things up, make it simple, keep it straightforward, can also undermine our understanding and ability to hear what we are being told" (1996,

p. 109). Martelli and Pilo di Boyl, having considered the quality of the way observations were reported in the early weeks of an observation experience, report: "Many sequences were forgotten and the content of the observations became . . . incomprehensible. In many cases the defences of the observer made it impossible to understand the observation of the child because the observer protected herself from understanding parts of her own self" (1997, p. 6). However, they note that following group discussion, the reports became richer and more detailed.

The ability to remember and to record will always be clouded by emotional issues—see Lazar's (1998) description of "failure" to record an observation of a premature baby—but the ability to do so becomes an important tool for future therapeutic work. Youell (2002) links the need to be able to talk clearly about what has been seen in infant observation to the clarity required for the Court assessments in which she was involved. W. Ernest Freud views the experience of attending with free-floating attention without note-taking as helpful: "The procedure serves as an excellent preparation for the next stage of training when the student will have to listen to his patients and write reports for his supervisors after sessions" (1975, p. 77). Of course, we need to be aware, especially when reading infant observation papers, that some observers have a facility with language, but this does not mean that they necessarily have a superior ability in observing or thinking about their observations. Being able to write well does not mean, in and of itself, that the student was able to observe well, but it would not be possible to write a good paper—that is, a paper that showed careful and delicate observation, together with the impact of the experience on the observer—without having had and integrated the experience productively. Moreover, the act of drafting and redrafting the language used to describe what was seen and felt can help the student to further her understanding of the experience.

The use of the seminar

The importance of the seminar in making infant observation a meaningful experience is fully acknowledged. Many writers view the seminar as a safe place within which the painful work of "untangling" can take place and felt experiences can be named: "The seminar takes on a crucial role of holding the observer's anxieties so as to allow for space in which the overall pattern of events can be thought about, and to represent the importance of reflection over time and thus diminish the anxious observer's impulse to take premature action" (M. E. Rustin, 1988, pp. 12–13).

Davids and colleagues (1999) describe the seminar as enabling the student to go on thinking and to stay in touch emotionally, with Coll (2000) adding the opportunity to discuss class and culture and relevant literature. In an unpublished paper, Jane Parrot (1998) contrasts her experience of infant observation with that of her medical training, where she felt there was an expectation "of being able to master tasks in the absence of an appropriate learning experience and an emphasis on the responsibility of decision making which sets limits on further exploration." She compares this with her observation seminars, which "allowed for sharing and reflection on possibilities of uncertainty . . . it was as if I had been allowed some freedom to play". The seminar is valued as somewhere where the observer might show vulnerability and realize mistakes made in a safe environment. Harris (1976) makes it clear that she welcomes muddle, not a polished performance, again drawing parallels with the later experience of clinical work and supervision.

Of course, this does not always happen. Writing of her experience of infant observation with Esther Bick, Magagna makes clear her anxieties that if she "disrupted the peaceful conformity" of the group, she could end up being the "unwanted baby": "Group passivity in which members assume infantile dependence on being nourished by the expert is perhaps one of the most daunting initial issues with which infant observation seminar leaders have to contend" (1987, p. 25).

Seminar leaders struggle in other ways too. I have previously drawn attention to the way seminar group members or seminar leaders may find it difficult to address certain aspects of the material (Sternberg, 1998), and Wittenberg (1993) also acknowledges that a seminar leader may "give" too much, preventing students from discovering things in their own time.

Davids and co-workers (1999) helpfully delineate the different tasks of the seminar. They write of the *didactic* task (teaching theory as demonstrated in the observations in an emotionally alive way, and referring to literature once the observational stance is established), *containing* (helping the observer keep on when the task is difficult), and the *developmental* task (developing in the trainee the capacity to cope with the demands of observation), together with *evaluating* their progress (having in mind that such development is an important indicator of suitability for training): "If, as we suggest, observational training is both a profound experience for the students and a useful indicator of the capacity to work sensitively and thoughtfully, and to tolerate the pain and uncertainty of clinical practice, then the seminars are crucial for this learning to take place" (1999, pp. 25–26).

The central task of the seminar group could be seen as that of holding the anxieties in such a way that the observer is able to go on thinking. Wittenberg (1999) writes that by raising questions, by wanting to know more precisely what occurred, the seminar group helps the observer to look more closely and become more accurate in descriptions, becoming more in touch with the infant's experience. Students get better at remembering and writing, partly through experience, but also because they are becoming able to tolerate what there is to see, hear, and feel. She warns that the naming of psychoanalytic concepts should not take place until they have been observed, described, and come to form part of the "felt experience" of the students. Barbara Segal (2003) looks at how important the seminar is in helping students to understand their personal reaction to the observations. She sees the delicate responsibility of the seminar leader where links are uncovered between the observational material and the student's own personal internal conflicts. In the past, when infant observation was more closely linked with the training of psychoanalytic psychotherapists, the observer was very likely to be in analysis, but this is no longer the case and makes this an especially difficult area. Jackson expresses her concerns: "with the proliferation of infant observation into many different courses, many students . . . may be without the internal work of ongoing psychoanalytic help which would enable them to gain personal insight and support in undertaking or not undertaking this task" (1998, p. 87).

Wittenberg (1999) states that when students are not in analysis, the role of the seminar group is additionally important, having to be "aware and receptive to anxieties and phantasies" and to take on a psychoanalytic stance, not answering questions but discussing them and, while not analysing anxieties, making the expression of them more permissible.

It is difficult to separate out the importance of the seminar leader from the seminar group. The group, and the trust developed within it, is vital in creating an atmosphere in which the observer feels safe to learn. Additionally the group provides multiple perspectives. Nissim (personal communication: research workshop at Third Tavistock Infant Observation Conference, March 2002) described research carried out in Italy into students' use of the seminar. The research found that the group operated as a "mirror" for the observer, picking up the observer's feelings, seeing ways in which the observer was unconsciously identifying with various family members, and picking up emotional states hidden to the observer. At times seminar group members may each separately unconsciously take up different identifications with different family members, and these different identifications enable enriching multiple perspectives to be seen within the group (see Harris, 1980, p. 326). Additionally, the students each learn about each other's babies and so have opportunities to learn about culture, class, and other differences. It might come as a surprise to those who think that there is a monolithic "Tavistock view" that brooks no disagreements to hear that when, in 2001, the teaching of infant observation was discussed within the senior staff group of child psychotherapists, Trudy Klauber spoke of the need for diversity and richness, and Likierman stated that the learning process should raise conflicts. Ideally, these conflicts take place within what is an essentially safe environment, although two of the staff group members remembered the persecuting nature of their own infant observation seminars, and King (personal communication, 1996) indicated that some of the reorganization of the infant observation curriculum at the Institute of Psychoanalysis had been caused by concerns about certain seminar leaders' style of teaching. Brafman (1988) also warns that students can be over-influenced by the seminar leader's own interests.

As we have seen, the task of the seminar leader is complex. Root Fortini (1997) states that while the seminar leader is apparently "just listening", he is in fact active and attentive, allowing anxieties to be expressed but not acted out. Wittenberg (1993) writes of the importance of encouraging the group to identify with the baby's experience, including contorting the body and making noises. The seminar leader often feels herself to be in a pastoral role in relation to the student. This may be defined by the training institution, or it may occur because of the small group experience and the strength of feelings occurring within it. Ruth Robinson (personal communication, 2001) feels that she often takes this position and is aware of her AFC MSc students frequently being young and from abroad. She also spoke about the need to adapt what she does to the particular group members, variations in members' familiarity with analysis and with children can make a cohesive approach difficult. She describes how she often uses role-play at the beginning as a way of finding and containing anxieties. Interestingly, Wittenberg, from a different theoretical orientation, does the same, and also advises "staggering" the starting time of each observer, so that initial anxieties can be properly attended to. Most seminar leaders seem to feel the need to avoid theory at least to begin with, lest the observer tries to take refuge in intellectualization, and all are aware of the need to rely on consecutive observations for confirmation of speculations.

Eric Rhode (1997) raises a very interesting issue when he points out that while the observer knows the baby first-hand, the seminar group can only know about him by hearsay; indeed, the importance of the observer who has had the experience being able to talk about it becomes most apparent on the rare occasions when this is not the case. Reports read without the live describing presence of the observer are poor substitutes, and much less can be understood by the reader, as shown by Canham, McFadyen, and Youell (1997). Burhouse comments: "The seminar group, the seminar leader and the training organisation ideally make up a reflective 3-D space in which to contain the observer. With this help the observer can usually contain their feelings sufficiently in order to maintain his or her quietly attentive observational stance" (2001, p. 63). In such circumstances the observer can introject the way the seminar group thinks and so in time can have an "inner voice" to help her to think on her feet.

The experience of "realization"

Although, as shown above, the observer gains capacities that are important for future clinical work, infant observation also gives the observer other learning experiences. Through the act of observing the infant in his family, the observer learns more about the complex interplay between the internal and external world, understanding more about infants and children and about infantile and non-verbal communications, together with learning about relationships. For brevity and convenience, at other points in this volume these new realizations are grouped under the heading "knowledge", but it is important to emphasize that after the experience of observing, the observer "knows" about these things in a deep and inner way, having had the opportunity to truly realize them—that is, to see and appreciate the extent of their reality.

Internal and external

Whatever the theoretical bias of infant observation teaching, all practitioners become cognizant of how much interplay there is between the internal and external. As cited above, psychoanalysis has become more interested in this area, perhaps as a result of the rich and complex awareness that observers have brought to psychoanalytic thinking. In describing the endless interaction between internal and external, Bowlby (1988) outlines the concept of "internal working models", largely derived from experience; but, of course, experience is altered by the infant's internal constitution, which influences how everything is perceived. When looking at an infant within his family, we see the interaction between constitutional and temperamental factors in the baby and the particular strengths and weaknesses of the holding environment (M. E. Rustin, 1988).

Although some writers state that having done infant observation has made them more aware of the importance of the environment, what seems most important is the awareness of "the uniqueness of each couple, how each baby develops at its own pace and relates to it mother in its own way" (Bick, 1964, p. 254). The recognition of this uniqueness, of immense value in itself, is also important in helping the prospective clinician to avoid rigid thinking. A real understanding of the uniqueness of each person should prevent a blanket application of theory.

Understanding children and very early stages of their development

It is likely that among the observed infants within a seminar group there will be babies of a similar age, so that weaning is likely to be occurring in a number of babies at the same time. In a discussion among senior child psychotherapists at the Tavistock Clinic in 2001, Miller highlighted the advantage of being able to see the "infinite variety" as well as some common features; in the same discussion, Likierman added that infant observation shows "that children are not identikit; certain experiences are universal, but every pair of mother–child in a family negotiate it in its own individual way". The student, by having the opportunity to compare the infants within the seminar, can see how very different each child's experience is. Even when the external circumstances might *appear* to be very similar, each individual and family's way of responding to them will depend on their inner resources. Moreover, seminar groups might encompass quite a wide range of cultural experiences, and so the seminar group has an opportunity to think about this too. Lacking knowledge of other cultures' ways of child-rearing can pose problems, however, and Ellis (1997) and Maiello (2000) advise that an observer's first observation should not be a transcultural one, so that the observer is not confused or diverted from the central emotional experience. Brafman comments: "Deciding what is pathological, what is cultural and what is idiosyncratic to that individual or family is the bread-and-butter of these seminars" (1988, p. 49), although some might argue that those of us with little knowledge of other cultures might sometimes make unwarrantedly Eurocentric assumptions. Trowell (1999) writes of respondents viewing themselves as using fewer stereotypes and being less judgemental as a result of infant observation seminars, feeling that they now have a deeper understanding of differences and similarities.

Many writers see infant observation as giving the observer a better knowledge of child development (Bard, 1997; Bick, 1964; Brafman, 1988; Canham, McFadyen, & Youell, 1997; Crick, 1997; McFadyen,

1991), with special emphasis on "infantile experiences". Coll (2000) writes that having observed the development of the baby's capacities, he has now has a "direct and vivid picture of the first year of a child's development" and now understands infantile experiences in a way that makes more meaningful his understanding of child and adolescent mental health. Parr (2000), describing a briefer observational experience, states that at the end the participants reported a greater awareness of both the infant's and the parents' emotional needs. Indeed, it is in terms of an infant's emotional life that the learning psychoanalytic practitioners are most interested in takes place. King (1978) states that understanding the infant's early affective development is enhanced by infant observation. In a volume of the *International Journal of Infant Observation* (2000), Asha Phillips and I offer a series of observational vignettes to the reader. While the primary purpose of this is sheer enjoyment, the collection does highlight the fact that even what might be thought to be the same activity ("a bath", "a feed") is experienced very differently by each infant—and in fact by the same infant at different times. This noticing of difference should help the observer not to "normalize" and so cease to look at what is there.

Fonagy (2001) brings together post-Kleinian and attachment theory ideas in his suggestion that the infant needs the closeness of an adult mind to internalize the experience of being thought about, leading to his own capacity for mentalization. This new approach is very much based on capacities observed within infant observation. We can observe the way in which trust, love, and the capacity to form object relations grow in the child through recurrent experiences of being understood (Harris, 1977). Moreover, all being well, observers are likely to have an experience in which they witness first-hand the baby's capacity for development and resilience. This was noted in a discussion among Tavistock child psychotherapy senior staff in 2001, with both Jonathan Bradley and Sue Reid expressing concern that observations that only last for one academic year often do not include enough of this experience, with Sue Reid describing it as follows: "Some mothers and babies, and their extended families, can get off to rather a bad start in the first year for a number of complex reasons. However, some babies when they become mobile feel better about the world. The acquisition of speech and mobility in their babies can offer real reassurance to parents that in spite of difficulties their babies are

developing ok. You can therefore sometimes get a dramatic improvement in the second year of life. For the observer carrying this observation inside one as a solid experience can be extremely helpful. I don't
mean by this to deny real pain and deprivation, but I think it can help
one as a clinician to see how some things, that can start out looking
pretty dreadful, might actually shift."

Awareness of non-verbal and infantile communication

Bick (1964) had originally stated that the experience of infant observation would increase the clinician's understanding of children's non-
verbal behaviour and play. This aspect of work relates not just to very
young children, but also to our understanding of the infantile parts of
adult patients. Wittenberg (1999) says that infant observation helps to
create an awareness of the non-verbal manifestations of unconscious
phantasies. Emotions at the most primitive level are embodied in
bodily states, and a clinician needs the experience of infant observation to integrate this knowledge in day-to-day work with adult patients. A similar emphasis on the somatic is made by McDougall in
writing about psychosomatically ill infants: "these observations play
an important role in confirming theories of early psychic functioning
and the transactional world of the infant and its mother, much as the
experiments in hypnosis in Freud's time confirmed his theories about
the unconscious and its timeless qualities" (1992, p. 8). In both these
instances the writers seem to be stating that having observed will
make the theoretical ideas more deeply convincing to the clinician.

Margaret Rustin (1988) suggests that by carefully observing infants and seeing their body language, the prospective clinician will
"struggle towards a language for describing pre-linguistic experiences" (1988, p. 20)—features that are particularly helpful in work not
just with very young children and psychosomatic patients, but also
with silent patients, patients who have little or no verbal capacities,
children on the autistic spectrum, or the kind of adolescents who are
very silent, where tiny physical shifts may be a major source of
evidence as to what is going on. In such circumstances, if the clinician
can get into an "observational state of mind", the detailed observation
and careful attention to the countertransference can enable the therapist to get into contact with the patient.

Learning about relationships

Tuters (1988) delineated that what her groups learnt from infant observation was that they discovered that not all mothers and infants were Madonna and child—each mother and infant form a unique dyad—and they learned about sibling rivalry, sexuality from birth, and the impact on a family of the birth of a baby. Certainly understanding how the baby forms relationships with others and the formation of object relations is a common and valuable learning experience. The observer can learn about relationships not just within the family, but also the relationship of the observer in the family and that between the seminar group and seminar leader, and this enables the student to "experience and learn about the effect of these relationships on relationships" (Trowell & Rustin, 1991). They suggest that "learning how and why relationships in the family arouse such strong responses in those around them and the effect of those relationships on the observer is *the* training element" (1991, p. 236).

While this largely refers to the area already covered of the observer learning to take note of her own feelings and question where they are coming from, it is also relevant to the formation of all relationships. Infant observation gives the opportunity to see particularly the relationship between the infant and mother, although we should also keep in mind the importance of the relationship with the father. McFarland Solomon (2002) writes movingly that the manifestations of transference and countertransference that are encountered in the consulting-room contain direct links to the "preverbal exchanges that happen between the first couple in love"—the mother and baby—and that it is these that form the basis of all later exchanges. According to Wittenberg (1999), through studying "the to-and-fro, the flux of interaction" between baby and mother, we can see some of the ways maladjustment and inhibition come about, as well as resilience and the capacity to preserve good experience, and to recover from misfortune. Crick (1997) says that what she has studied is called "mother–infant observation" to acknowledge the impossibility of separating the infant from the mother. While other trainings that use the terminology "infant observation" for convenience also appreciate this, this different emphasis, especially at the Institute of Psychoanalysis, is revealed in chapter 8, which describes how the research participants spoke of their experiences. Of course, for all observers it is impossible in many ways to think about the baby without thinking of the mother–baby relationship. The container–contained model, although at times used by Tavistock students rather glibly and in a shorthand way, really is a most helpful way of thinking both about mothers and infants and about therapists and patients. Knowledge of the two-way nature of relationships—accepting, of course, that each partner is bringing very different things to the relationship—is an essential feature for being aware of the importance of intersubjectivity in psychoanalytic work.

Awareness of multiple perspectives

A quality that is perhaps more important for a child psychotherapist than an adult one, the awareness of multiple perspectives, was described by Margaret Rustin in a discussion among Tavistock child psychotherapy senior staff in 2001 as follows: "I think something very central I would want to highlight is the multiple perspectives that people have to cope with in infant observation. Sometimes it is very very difficult for the observer to learn to manage it, but absolutely minimally there's going to be mother's and baby's perspective and very likely also other members of the family, quite often an older child, maybe many more, father, grandmother, nanny, etc. I think it's an incredibly valuable experience for anybody who is going to become a child psychotherapist in particular, because I think that the tension between being able to be mindful of both parent and child perspectives is something that is good practice for clinical work." Rustin then went on to refer to the second year of infant observation or young child observation as also giving the experience of "a relationship with the child and a relationship with the mother, where it's not all through the mother or not all in the mother's presence. [This] is another exceptionally useful experience of how you can be keeping loyalties to everybody in the situation and make some differentiation between what might be said to you privately by one, whether it's the small child or the mother, and being able to differentiate what is private from what is secret and reflect on all the issues about betrayal and loyalty and so on. I think a lot is explored in that experience which is relevant to child psychotherapy practice in particular."

Other child psychotherapists have commented on how the experience of infant observation has helped them to be less blaming of mothers when seeing poor mother–child relationships. The observer may learn to comprehend the impact of intense infantile anxieties aroused in the mother of a young child from allowing herself to feel her own countertransference (Harris, 1977; Merrill, personal communication, 1999). Ruth Robinson, near the beginning of her training as an adult psychoanalyst, wrote of her experience: "Over the course of the observation I became interested in the issue of the observer's identifications with the members of the mother–baby couple. I became aware of the necessity of keeping both parties in mind and of being able to move from identifying with one to the other" (1992).

I found it interesting that Jackson and Shavit, both qualified as both child psychotherapists and adult psychoanalysts, write that "the observer is often unconsciously perceived by mother as making room for the infant's emotional perspective and existence" (2000, p. 3). Perhaps "making room" links to the idea propounded in Anne Alvarez and Piera Furgiuele's 1997 paper about the development of two-tracked thinking: the authors suggest that the baby comes to expect this ability in the mother from the way she facilitates such behaviour and consequently becomes identified with an object who is capable of two-tracked thinking. Perhaps we could say that infant observation develops the capacity for having in mind two tracks, background and foreground, family/mother and infant, which is then needed in clinical work, when theory needs to be available but in the background.

Usefulness for clinical work

This topic has been addressed throughout this chapter; at this point I briefly draw attention to the ways in which the infant observation experience can be consciously felt to be useful for clinical work. Both Pozzi (2003) and Briggs (2004) give detailed case examples to show how capacities and skills developed in infant observation were of central importance in the clinical work they describe. Margaret Rustin says that the family's response to a change in the time of a meeting provides "future therapists with usually unforgettable evidence of the powerful unconscious reverberations of apparently ordinary and reasonable matters" (1988, p. 13). Bodin, an experienced Danish psychoanalyst, writes that from seeing the observed mother's withdrawal from her following the summer break, she became better at formulating interpretations to patients about weekends and holiday breaks (1997, p. 219). The observation experience teaches the vital significance of beginnings, endings, and times of transition and also shows the importance of looking beyond words and surface behaviour. All aspects of the experience of setting up the observation, arranging visits, and managing the relationship provide a helpful background for a new clinician to keep in mind when approaching her first clinical case. Ann Scott (personal communication, 2004) has also suggested that from the experience of having become very familiar with the observed family's home, the clinician may later be helped to imagine her patient's—childhood or current—home setting and, visualizing the patient at home, to attend silently to this visualization and allow it to contribute to her thinking about the patient.

"Living in the question", without premature application of theory, is very much valued. Harris (1977) says that the observation experience will add dimensions to the quality of later clinical work, anticipating that it helps to avoid premature anxiety-ridden interpretations and interventions and relaxes undue therapeutic zeal because of the deep inner knowledge that things cannot be hurried.

For practitioners within or influenced by the Kleinian school, infant observation is valued as an opportunity for getting in touch with primitive anxieties. Harris notes that the evacuation of pain is not necessarily a negative act. In the first weeks the infant needs to do this to relieve himself from intolerable discomfort (the fear of dying), and the mother needs to receive this. This model in mind can help to make experiences in the consulting-room more tolerable and more useful. She suggests that infant observation also gives the future therapist an insight into conditions that favour or impede introjection, and these are applicable to the study of analytic processes (1976, p. 231).

The way the therapist will then behave in the consulting-room will be influenced by many factors, including her own analytic experience. The mother–infant relationship should make the therapist aware of the intersubjective relatedness of the analyst–analysand relationship. Youell (1999), citing Hinshelwood's (1997) comment that the first skill a psychotherapist needs is to be able to be with the patient, suggests that such "being with" is achieved in part at least through training in observation, in which the observer/therapist has learned to be emotionally and intellectually engaged. The observational attitude of being neutral, attentive, and non-judgemental offers important attributes for clinical work (Bard & Crick, 1997). Awareness of the value of attentiveness also arises from infant observation, and Lignos describes how "our trained analytic skill, which can be sharpened through infant observation practice, permits us to see inside and outside at the same time and develop a 'binocular vision'" (1997, p. 7).

The idea of infant observation as a "practice run" is often talked about by those involved in its teaching. Miriam Steele (personal communication, 2001) said that the observation experience should engender an observational stance in the trainee, who is not expected to take on responsibilities in the way a therapist is. Of the three observation experiences students at the Anna Freud Centre are expected to have, she sees infant observation as being the one closest to the clinical situation and so the most valuable. W. Ernest Freud encouraged those he taught to think about in what ways and for what reasons their role resembles or differs from that of the analyst (1975, p. 79). He views being alone with one other—seeing the mother and baby couple as one—as good preparation for the intimacy of the analytic situation. He also suggests that both observer and analyst are sparing with information and opaque to the other.

Some types of therapeutic work are very clear about their close link with infant observation. Parent–infant and infant mental health work often acknowledges the debt to infant observation, frequently citing Winnicott (Barrows, 1999; Salo et al., 1999). Parent–infant psychotherapists use direct observation of infants in their work and also encourage parents to take a similar stance to their own children, beginning the experience of really seeing *them*—as opposed to the imagined child—and thinking about their experience. Elizabeth Bradley (personal communication, 2001) spoke of how the Tavistock Under-5s Service grew out of the observation course and described how practitioners use observation and countertransference to make a link to the family. Margaret Rustin also highlights another, perhaps less expected, arena in which the infant observation experience is useful:

> The long training in observing babies and young children within everyday family contexts is a real resource when it comes to finding ways to be thoughtful and to create space for reflexive dialogue in a room full of worried people. The infantile anxieties with which infant observation acquaints us are potent features of group life and an observational stance is a very good starting point. [2000, p. 12]

The influence of infant observation on theory and clinical practice

This large subject can only be touched on here. Some of the influences are the result of both infant observation and infant research. Trevarthen (1998) suggests that infant observation has led analysts to a better and more effective awareness of the infant's prowess and needs. We are more aware of the infant's positive capacities and this has in some cases necessitated an alteration in psychoanalytic emphasis. Before the 1950s, psychoanalytic theories of infants' emotional life were retrospective. Now, as a result of "imaginative research on paediatric experience and baby observation with psychoanalytic insights", we have a more rounded picture of infantile development (Lanyado, 1998). There have been extensive changes in analytic thinking and practice, the accent having moved from a more exclusively intrapsychic approach to viewing the interactional and interpersonal aspects as essential structuring forces for the development of mental models. This view has focused attention on the developmental factors in analytic work. The increased acknowledgement of the constant interchange between the internal and external world through the ongoing process of introjection and projection surely owes something to the experience of infant observation in which the unfolding of the primary relationship is so central.

Wittenberg (1999) also suggests that finding out about the baby's positive capacities could be important for psychoanalytic theory, adding that having seen resilience in infants can bring about a hopefulness about recovery, which leads to extending the boundaries of those to whom treatment is offered. Reid (1997) makes an associated point: that from capacities and skills learned within infant observation, as well as theoretical awareness, therapists can work more effectively with patients who are hard to reach. Alvarez's (1992, 1997) work on infants' need for liveliness also affects our clinical practice and links with work from infant research that suggests that traditional analytic practice—i.e. the use of the couch—may "down-regulate" patients who would benefit from being enlivened.

Shuttleworth (1989) writes of the way that modern infant research has increasingly borne out the Kleinian hypothesis that infants are object-related from birth. She sees infant observation as contributing specifically to an interest in how infants manage the transition be-tween states, in contrast to researchers' preferred attention to babies in states of alert inactivity. From longitudinal infant observation we are aware that a mother's mental qualities make an impact on the baby's, both indirectly through the effect her physical care has on his psychosomatic state, and directly through the infant's capacity to apprehend emotional states in others.

Wittenberg (1999) warns that although infant observation may contribute to psychoanalytic knowledge and practice in many ways, it is important to also be aware of the differences between them. Bodin comments that "different to the analyst, the observer does not formu-late interpretations in the observing situation, but will wait and share her or his reflections with a seminar leader and group" (1993, pp. 207–208). Wittenberg suggests that in clinical work interpretation plays a central role in testing the correctness of the analyst's understanding, whereas in infant observation one has to wait and see. While this is essentially true, many modern practitioners would pay less attention to the apparent immediate response to an interpretation, recognizing the situation as a very complex one.

There are few obvious examples—with perhaps the notable excep-tion of Bick's famous paper on second skin defences (1968) and Cornwell's (1983) extension of this—of the way infant observation has directly extended psychoanalytic concepts: however, I would argue that the shift in the general direction of psychoanalytic work to include more awareness of the "analytic third" (Ogden, 1997), the space created by the activity between therapist and patient, may, for practitioners trained in a culture where infant observation is taught, owe much to the unremembered unconscious influence of the latter.

Infant observation as a prognostic indicator
of clinical capacities

Those who teach infant observation often refer to it as a useful basis for making judgements about students' potential clinical capacities. In a discussion with her colleagues in 2001, Margaret Rustin said: "We do see infant observation as a very good guide of whether somebody can really learn from infant observation or not in relation to potentiality as a clinician. So in other ways one is using it to make judgements . . . it catches the question of the fundamental relationship to the observer's internal objects all unawares . . . people do reveal a good deal about themselves in doing the observation. Then one is on a very good wicket. And if they're rather stuck and they're not really provoked into questioning and shifting, really there's less optimism."

What many writers have noted is the importance of the student's capacity to change. Wittenberg states that "those who remain detached and unaffected or overwhelmed by infant observation will be found not to be suitable, or at least not yet ready, if they apply to undertake a clinical training in psychoanalytic work with patients" (1999, p. 10). Tuters describes it as follows:

> Personal struggles in terms of transference and countertransference issues were many and varied for each student because each student came into the infant observation sessions with different life experiences and at different learning points. As it was with all the infants observed, that they developed according to their genetic "givens", temperament, environmental factors and relationship availabilities, so it was with the individual students. They found out, sometimes painfully, where they were in their intrapsychic development and interpersonal development. [1988, p. 103]

Trowell (2002; Trowell & Rustin, 1991) writes of wanting to see the observer develop the "capacity to learn from experience and their ability to tolerate and share confusion and uncertainty" (1991, p. 235).

Naturally, not all who carry out infant observation want to become psychoanalytic psychotherapists. Some may imagine they want to do so prior to the infant observation experience but may be able to use the experience to know that clinical work is not for them. Reid (1997) sees infant observation as helping both selection and self-selection as students can see "if the pain/pleasure balance is right for them". Harris thinks about those for whom the experience leads to a wish for further growth: "Such detailed observation has inevitably an emotional impact on the observer which is likely to disturb complacency and to lead to the kind of self questioning that evokes an interest in personal analysis in those whose desire to get at the truth of themselves is likely to be stronger than their wish to preserve the status quo" (1976, p. 226).

The interest in spending one's working life in close contact with excruciatingly painful experiences is vital but not sufficient. As well as what Margaret Rustin (1988) describes as an "appetite" for clinical work, we also have the question of potential aptitude. The way the observer can manage the pitfalls of early observation in terms of finding a way to conduct themselves in the presence of the family is, as Dilys Daws (personal communication, 2002) has stated, a very good predictor of therapeutic capacities. As Wittenberg (1999) says, the ability to be in touch with the emotional experience of mothers and babies will give an indication of the capacity to be receptive to and able to think at depth about interactions with children.

Miriam Steele (personal communication, 2001) stated that the AFC also used infant observation as a "trial ground" for choosing clinicians and said that they were looking for observers who were interested in what was going on at an unconscious level in the mother's mind, which she described as "psychological-mindedness". Observers have to be able to connect what is seen to an inner world experience and be interested in teasing apart these issues. She described this as a "reflective function". This links with Trowell and Rustin's (1991) statement:

> We, like Fonagy (1991), are highlighting the importance of the internal "reflective self". We see trainee professionals who vary between having little or no reflective-self function to a generalised or inaccurate reflective-self function to an almost complete reflective-self function. It has been suggested for mothers and their babies that the reflective-self function is superior in predicting infant security and may be a key determinant of infant security. We may find, as we clinically suspect, a similar method for developing and predicting the capacity of the caring professional to provide an emotionally enhancing relationship for clients. [1991, p. 239]

Ruth Robinson (personal communication, 2001) raised concerns about how we view students as being suitable for clinical training. She was concerned that the system of seminar leaders doing the assessing could produce an atmosphere in which the students were anxious about making "mistakes" in the seminars or allowing such "mistakes" to be seen. She felt that trainees need to be free to learn from mistakes. She was also concerned that narcissism in seminar leaders would lead to a preference for those who resemble the current teachers, with ultimately stultifying results. However, if these issues could be appropriately managed, infant observation seminars can give valuable insight into the students. As stated previously, Davids and colleagues (1999) cite Spillius as saying that performance in infant observation correlates with later success in clinical training.

Values placed on infant observation

Traditionally, perhaps because it was first introduced into the child psychotherapists' curriculum, infant observation was thought to be of particular value to the child therapist. As long as the emphasis was on understanding child patients better, this would be a logical conclusion; however, adult psychotherapists are well aware of the "child in the adult". The emphasis on understanding infantile forms of communication, the interest in noticing detail, and attention to the non-verbal are a central part of an adult clinician's psychotherapeutic repertoire of skills. It could be argued that an interest in the primitive aspects of a patient is a particularly Kleinian approach.

Kleinian theory, with its privileging of projection as a form of communication, would pay special attention to an infant's early months. While all psychoanalytic theory rests on the assumption that later psychopathology is rooted in earlier experiences, Kleinians have been more interested in the very early months of life than have classical Freudians. Klein's view that the Oedipus complex could first be seen in the first year of life rather than in the fourth or fifth year is just one example. It is therefore not surprising that Kleinians should welcome the opportunity of close study of these early months. We can perhaps see an example of this when Borensztejn and colleagues, in summarizing what they had learned from infant observation, said (*inter alia*): "The experience of baby observation has given us an evocative linking model to conjecture and describe the more primitive aspects of our patients" (1998, p. 82). Since in their paper the theory they quote is heavy with post-Kleinian references, particularly Bion and Meltzer, one might see this as an example of circular thinking: we all find most useful that which confirms our earlier views.

However, although perhaps in the past it was predominantly the Kleinians who had a particular interest in infancy studies, this is not necessarily still the case. The work of developmentalists and infant research has also very much attracted the Independents, who have been interested in thinking about the interchange between internal and external worlds. Hamilton (1996) has shown that of the different theoretical groups it is the Independents and the British Object Relations theorists who most acknowledge their interest in and debt to infancy studies. Indeed, a very different model is privileged, as emphasized earlier, in the current climate in psychoanalysis with its interest in the influence of the patient's internal working models—or whatever each "school" names them—on his perception of his "real" life experiences. This, together with attention to the to-and-fro between patient and analyst, with awareness that the unconscious of the analyst is in the consulting-room as much as that of the patient, calls for a different approach. This model is one that, I have suggested, is heavily influenced by infancy studies in general, although many of those who use it may not view it as in any way connected with infant observation.

Brafman (1988), writing of his experience of teaching infant observation to candidates at the Institute of Psychoanalysis, says that whereas one might expect that the experience might make them wish to train as child analysts, this was in fact not the case, and they kept to their interest in working with adults. "Some will transpose findings on to the notion of 'the child in the adult' and it can then be seen that, in fact, they are usually doing the exact opposite: they try to understand the baby in front of them by resorting to what they have learnt about reconstructions and hypotheses on adult psychopathology" (1988, p. 54).

This outlines dangers that can arise within the situation. But infant observation *is* valuable for adult work. Certainly many trained adult therapists (Bard, 1997; Crick, 1997; Harris, 1977; McGinley, 2000; L. R. Miller, 2001; M. Robinson, 1997) make parallels between the mother and the therapist and see themselves as learning how to be with the patient from seeing how a mother enables her baby to take in and

Table 5.1. The interrelationship of capacities, skills, and infant observation

Capacity	Technique	Cited in observation literature
analytic attitude: absence of narcissism	creating a setting; neutral, objective, suspension of judgement	observer stance, find a position in the family; non-judgemental
bearing humbling experience	keeping oneself back	awareness of peripheral role in family
respect for patient	respect for patient	awareness of struggle & of uniqueness
open oneself to the experience of shock	find something new	open oneself to being shocked, disturbed
tolerate anxiety & uncertainty	manage strong feelings	manage strong feelings, tolerate anxiety
wait for meaning to emerge	wait for meaning to emerge	wait for pattern to emerge
empathy	attitude to patient, hold patient inside self; receive all aspects of patient, reverie	LIMITED: awareness uniqueness should influence attitude to patient; should have increased capacity to bear strong feelings
	thoughts about how patient uses therapist, avoid acting-out responses	NOT DIRECT, but increased through awareness of countertransference
		awareness of projection increased
realistic hopefulness		see something shift over time, see infants' resilience, child development knowledge
retain apparently contradictory experiences simultaneously	shift between role participant & observer, identify & not with patient, hold different things in mind & oscillate between	shift identification, two-tracked thinking
close attention	close attention, non-verbal, sensitivity to infantile modes of communication	looking without preconceptions, awareness of non-verbal, tiny body movements, uniqueness each family teaches not to normalize

cognitive abilities	using cognitive skills to organize into patterns	NOT STRONGLY, but some aspects of writing up & presenting
	think, evaluate, remember & anticipate	some from recalling, much from thinking about
	think about what experiencing	think about what experiencing
	hold onto uncomfortable ideas & feelings, don't grab at understanding	hold onto feelings, hypothesize, realize it takes time for pattern to emerge
	create space to think about feelings	create space to think about feelings especially through the seminars
	awareness of transference & countertransference	notice own experiences, study self in response to what seeing, disentangle self & other; struggle with language helps with work re infantile transference; from exposure relationships will understand transference & countertransference relationships in clinical work better
knowledge of theory	theory informs practice	PARTIAL from infant observation but in very alive & unforgettable way
	feelings recognized by a reflective part of the mind	feelings recognized by a reflective part of the mind
	timing	PARTIAL: learn to hold onto, pain of abstinence; avoid premature interpretations not see whole pattern at once, not grab at understanding
listening & skill in communication	verbal communication: how to talk to the patient, silence, questions, clarifications	LIMITED: language to describe non-verbal, pre-linguistic experiences; think about the penumbra round language
	interpretation	NOT DIRECT: thinking that would go into an interpretation could be influenced by infant observation experience, also through monitoring of countertransference

grow. Lynda R. Miller (2001) also makes reference to her better understanding of language development, which helped her as a therapist to be more aware of her patients' "linguistic styles, distortions and peculiarities of speech". We can also see that therapists feel that they can better understand the early life experiences of their now adult patients from having seen mothers and infants. Adult therapists' papers about their infant observation experiences often concentrate predominantly on the mother's contribution. [For many examples of this, see the *International Journal of Infant Observation, 4* (2000, No. 1).]

There are certain aspects that may be of more immediate and apparent interest to the child psychotherapist than the adult psychotherapist, but if we follow the argument I have been propounding— namely, that the *experience* of infant observation gives the practitioner an opportunity for the *experience* of intense emotional feelings that have to be processed and thought about—then we can see that this is equally valuable for all psychoanalytic practitioners. (See Table 5.1.)

PART III

EMPIRICAL RESEARCH

CHAPTER SIX

Data organization

In Part II I want now to turn to my empirical research, in which I interviewed participants who were engaged in carrying out infant observation in major London psychoanalytic or psychoanalytic psychotherapy training institutions. Having in chapter 2 outlined the methodology, showing how the research was conducted and giving some attention to the theoretical principles that underlay the approach that I took to analysing the data, here I provide an exposition of how I approached the data, showing that it was possible to generate the categories using the grounded theory method. It is important to be clear that this was done only once I had conducted all the pre- and post-observation interviews. I moved from the finding of elementary statements to the generation of concepts and then of categories, following the pattern laid out by Strauss and Corbin (1998). Table 6.1 shows how and whether the groups interviewed had referred to these categories. The categories were regrouped to reduce them to seven, but each category was subsequently developed to enable a more precise picture of the subtleties indicated within each to be seen. It should be noted that I also approached the subject in a more integrated way.

Table 6.1. Second-order concepts created from texts and similarities and differences of these across groups

AFC	BAP	Institute	Tavistock
awareness of feelings	awareness of own feelings	awareness of own feelings, including intensity of feelings & anxieties at the beginning	own feelings, including primitive emotions
thoughts about what made me to feel	reflection on feelings	thinking about own feelings	thoughts about feelings
issues about being an observer, how to behave & the observer's place in the observed family	difficulties in maintaining the observer stance	difficulties in finding an observer stance	—
interest in family dynamics	thoughts about families	family dynamics & the personality of the mother	families and family dynamics
child development and the internal world of the baby	interest in the baby & the impact of the environment on the baby	—	greater emphasis on the baby
seminar	seminar	seminar	seminar
the use the family make of the observer & the effect of mother on the observer	the relationship of the observer & the family	why the family want an observer	the use of the observer & what the family get from it
identification with different family members	identification with different family members	—	identification with different family members & oscillation
painfulness of observer position	painfulness of the situation	painful	painfulness of watching something that felt wrong
length of observation		comparison of first & second observations	
struggle remembering		way what they were seeing links with theory	theoretical links
new way of thinking about things			cultural issues
learning from experience/ mistakes			experience of not knowing

Chapters 7 and 8 give the narratives of the interviews and chapter 9 draws out the significance of the data seen. I then look at the mind of the clinician at work and discuss whether, through looking closely at excerpts from the interviews, we can see similar capacities operating in the mind of the observer. The extract given in the section below gives a flavour of what complex thinking and feeling is going on within the observer. As the separation out into discrete statements may fail to recognize the complexity and interwoven nature of the data, this is later addressed in an alternative way.

Step 1: finding the statements

The following excerpt was the first statement made by the first member of the first group, interviewed at the end of his observation experience.

> *"The mother and child I've been observing—there has always been the father at home and an older sibling, so really the whole thing has been around, it's always been at least five of us in the room, so trying to observe the mother–infant dyadic has been very difficult, so when it came to writing up the early observations, anyway, I thought I was giving a good account as near as to what I can remember, and then I was completely unaware of why my attention was focusing where it was in the room, it was completely unconscious, and it was only actually being confronted in the seminar in the way that I didn't actually get to begin with, it provoked quite a lot of anxiety over time, sort of, and wrestling with it and then returning to these early observations, so I became aware of the movement of my own awareness in the room and realizing we had, why and when I was identifying with the baby or the older sibling. And also the effect that the mother was having on me and my capacity to observe and also my denial of the anxiety she provoked in me that then was discussed in the seminar. So I went through a massive learning space through that."*

Examining this piece of text, I noted the following individual statements and the issues that they might be implying or stating:

a. Mother and child: this is viewed as mother–infant observation, not infant observation. The idea that mother and infant need to be looked at together is implied.

b. Presence of father and older sibling emphasized—thinking of the infant in the context of his family.

c. Difficulties in observing the mother–infant dyad.

d. Mention of writing up as part of the task.

e. "Early observations anyway": this suggests the speaker has an idea of change over time and implies that his view would be different later.

f. "I thought I was giving a good account": thoughts about the act of remembering and writing and the possible flaws in this.

g. "Completely unaware of why my attention, etc": thoughts about the fact that attention can be focused in different ways and about what underlies where attention is focused, including unconscious reasons.

h. Confronted in the seminar: the experience of the seminar, the participant's sense of being confronted, how the seminar is used.

i. "Didn't get to begin with": idea of an understanding of seminar/ seminar leader's purpose, which only emerged over time.

j. "It provoked . . . anxiety": anxiety; awareness of feelings that engendered.

k. "Over time": sense of feelings building up.

l. "Wrestling": idea of struggling, actively engaging with feelings engendered. Awareness of resisting: again paying attention to own feelings and responses.

m. Awareness of "movement of awareness in room": as before about focus. Implication here that this idea/capacity developed over time.

n. Thoughts about identifying: who with, different family members.

o. Thoughts about mother's effect on the observer in general.

p. Thoughts about mother's effect on his capacity to observe specifically.

q. Respondent's denial of anxiety: this implies he is now aware that he *was* anxious, although he had denied it at the time, so awareness of feelings and his defences about those uncomfortable feelings. Suggests change over time.

r. Seminar used for discussing those feelings.

s. Sense of massive learning experience, which arose as a result of the observation.

This example shows how, by subjecting a piece of text to microanalysis, it is possible to generate initial categories, each with their own properties and dimensions. Some of the statements (as, in the example, h, i, and r about the seminar, and j, l, and q about an awareness of feelings) show that the same theme is repeated, although with subtle differences; others introduce significantly new elements. I noted and numbered each "new" statement. For all of the post-observation interviews this generated well over 50 separate categories.

Step 2: gathering the statements into concepts

Treating each specific interview as a separate entity at this point, I then looked at all these different statements, now thought of as initial concepts, and thought how they could be clustered together. This creation of over-arching groups then meant that a number of statements that might have been viewed as fairly disparate could then be conceptually related in a preliminary way. For example, for the BAP group the cluster that became the category that was eventually labelled "thoughts about the observer and the observer's relationship to the family" included (1) a sense of anxiety; (2) awareness of the impact of oneself on the family, thoughts about the use mother makes of the observer; (3) the idea that things would be different if they were not there; (4) the difference when the observation takes place outside the home; (5) questions about why the family allowed them in; (6) thoughts about what a missed week meant to the baby; (7) how the observer is viewed by the family; (8) the way the family behave in the presence of the observer; and (9) anxieties about the premature termination of the observation. Some of these statements could also be assigned to other categories that emerged—for example, "thoughts about families" or "reflection on feelings".

Step 3: concepts become categories

According to Strauss and Corbin, certain concepts can be grouped under a more abstract higher-order concept that is based on its ability to explain what is taking place. The basic statements form concepts, and as concepts accumulate, they can be grouped or categorized. The name or label given to each category depends on the phenomena contained within it. They comment that "other researchers might use other labels, depending on their foci, training or interpretations" (1998, p. 106). Strauss and Corbin also consider the label that the researcher assigns to the concepts, discussing the advantages and disadvantages to terms that arise from the literature or from the data (*in vivo* codes). It is important for the researcher and the reader to be able to see what is new in the categories, while at the same time the familiar can usefully extend the development of already used concepts. The names I gave my categories arose out of the data, but very simple terms were chosen in order to keep the concepts contained within them accessible to the reader.

Once between nine and twelve categories had been created for each group, I returned to the texts and went through them again in order to see in what ways the individual statements fitted appropriately within that framework and altering the boundaries of the categories where necessary to re-formulate what each might include. Considering how to place the data within the newly created categories led to new ways of looking at the data and often meant that headings had to be re-defined. There were inevitably some statements that did not fall within the categories; the headings of these were then compared across groups. As one would expect, many were similar, but, as shown in Table 6.1, there are differences in certain arenas of interest.

Step 4: re-ordering the categories

However, bearing in mind Strauss and Corbin's statement that "Concepts that reach the status of a category are abstractions; they represent not one individual's or group's story but rather the stories of many persons or groups reduced into, or represented by, several highly conceptual terms" (1998, p. 145), the categories now had to be re-ordered under more generalized headings that could be used for analysing the data from all the groups, both separately and across the groups. The concepts to be considered fell into the following categories:

a. awareness of own feelings, including emphasis on the painful nature of the experience;

b. reflection on those feelings;

c. thoughts about the observer stance;

d. issues about the observed family and the observer's relationship to them;

e. thoughts about families;

f. interest in a baby's development;

g. the influence of the seminar group and the seminar leader.

It is, of course, inevitable that the generation of categories was influenced by my own clinical and theoretical experiences. Indeed, as Glaser and Strauss wrote, "The root sources of all significant theorising is the sensitive insights of the observer himself. . . . the researcher can get—and cultivate—crucial insights not only during his research (and from his research) but from his own personal experiences prior to and outside it" (1968, pp. 251–252).

The conceptual mapping in which I had previously been engaged, particularly with reference to chapter 4, is also likely to have unconsciously influenced my decisions, because it had become incorporated within the scope of my "theoretical sensitivity". The emphasis that had emerged from my study of skills and capacities on the importance of attending to and reflecting on feelings undoubtedly made me aware of moments when issues relating to these emerged from the data. Chapter 8 gives a narrative of how these areas were addressed by each group, showing both the depth and richness of responses and enabling comparisons to be made across the groups.

Step 5: developing the categories into sub-categories

The seven categories developed and used for comparing the interviews across the groups turned out to be too broad for the purpose of representing in a substantial way the strands of the experiences that go to form the experience of infant observation. In order to consider aspects more closely and in a more complex manner than the seven basic categories permitted, it was necessary to develop sub-categories that reflected the variety of concepts included within the category as well as the influence of the conceptual mapping, as I was sensitized to the presence of capacities and activities that related to those shown to be useful for clinical work:

"Awareness of feelings"

a.   Registering feelings: the initial stage in which the speaker shows awareness of feeling or having felt something, which would be likely to include the experience of picked-up projections.

b.   Tolerating uncomfortable feelings: the tolerating of anxiety and uncertainty, the experience of something intense and painful, and the need to stay with these uncomfortable feelings is often mentioned in relation to the usefulness of infant observation.

c.   The processing of feelings within oneself: this includes the very important area of being able to begin to think about what within the felt feelings comes from oneself and what comes from the other. This important differentiating can be thought of in clinical work as the ability to differentiate the personal countertransference from the clinical countertransference.

"Reflection on those feelings":

a.   Finding that what had been experienced needed to be thought about and reflected on.

b.   A willingness *not* to understand prematurely, which I then also linked with the recognition of the importance of waiting for patterns to establish themselves, waiting for meaning to emerge.

c.   Calling upon theoretical models to help create understanding of the experience.

d.   Being aware of the usefulness of one's own feelings as a source of information.

e.   Having an awareness—most probably emerging from the act of writing up and from the seminar—of how much the observer had failed to notice or give sufficient weight to.

"Thoughts about the observer stance" and "issues about the observed family and the observer's relationship to them":

a.   Awareness of oneself in relation to others, including thinking about the impact that their way of being has on others.

b.   The importance of maintaining certain boundaries and thoughts about how to stay in role.

c.   Thoughts about holding back on reactions, which goes beyond just thinking about the importance of boundaries and includes considering what can evolve in the space left from doing so.

d.   Awareness of how much there is to notice within the observational hour.

The following two aspects were not explicitly drawn out within the post-observation interviews, but consideration of the list of qualities writers and practitioners claim the experience of infant observation to provide matching these with the skills and capacities needed to be a psychoanalytic psychotherapist also pointed up the importance of:

a.   An interest in seeing detail, and an awareness of the importance of close attention, together with thoughts about how to remember and marshal such thoughts.

b.   The achievement of multiple perspectives: through shifting identifications with mother and baby, and with other family members to have an awareness of other points of view.

As well as these dimensions of "capacities", infant observation should give the student a "live experience" of aspects of important realizations to do with infant and child development, the development of relationships within families, and other understanding to do with what influences a child's development, and how introjection comes about (see chapter 5). In chapter 9 there is a section on these, grouped for convenience under the term "knowledge".

CHAPTER SEVEN

Anticipations: initial interviews

S tudents were interviewed in groups, on the expectation that ideas would then be taken up and expanded by the members of the small group. Although direct questioning was likely to elicit only answers largely on a conscious level and there was a likelihood that these would be heavily influenced by what the training institutions' explicit expectations were, it was thought that in a fairly unstructured free-ranging discussion it would be possible to notice underlying assumptions and, through the use of grounded theory (Atkinson & Coffey, 1996; Strauss & Corbin, 1998; Taylor & Bogdan, 1998), to extrapolate themes that would go beyond the supposedly "correct answers". Each group was asked two questions: (1) "What do you expect to learn from undertaking an infant observation that might be relevant to you as future clinicians in training?" (2) "Was the fact that the course that you're on has an observation component something that attracted you to the course, or not?"

Each meeting lasted approximately one hour and was taped and the tapes transcribed. Each statement in turn was then examined in light of grounded theory, and the many complex issues I thought it contained extracted from it. These issues were grouped in clusters (as described in chapter 6). Some aspects did not fit within that frame-work, and these were noted.

What follows is a description of how each group in turn gave attention, or not, to these issues. The category used for the post-observation interviews of "Thoughts about the observed family and the observer's relationship to them" was not shown by any of the groups in these initial interviews. Similarities and differences be-tween the groups are addressed at the end.

An overall view from these interviews

What is striking is how "unrooted" much of what is said in these interviews is. With a few memorable exceptions, most of what the respondents say has the quality of being a regurgitation of what is known to be expected, perhaps already said to them in a different context by their teachers and seminar leaders. There may be a feeling that "right answers" have to be given, and I am told what I am presumed to want to hear. However, this "synthetic" quality may also have arisen from these interviews having taken place *before* the major-ity of participants had begun observing. The respondents could not speak of how the experience felt, as they had not yet begun it. The few who had begun could and did offer a different level of response. Without the direct experience of going into someone's home and being aware of the feelings stirred up (as we shall see vividly de-scribed in the example of being outside the cocoon), all the respond-ents could talk about was what they had been told and what they were anticipating, and this then came across as somewhat without feeling. To a great extent it seemed that emotional responses were absent and were replaced instead with comments that seemed rather pre-fabricated and glib. It is not surprising that the kind of develop-ment that I had been anticipating discovering as arising through the experience of infant observation could only be found through learn-ing from experience, and the majority of the respondents did not have that experience, or had not had it recently enough for it to suffuse their statements emotionally. Perhaps because the question was "What do you expect to learn from undertaking an infant observation that might be relevant to you as future clinicians in training?" rather than asking what they *did* learn, those participants who had previous experience of it responded in a way that failed to show the richness of their experience.

The AFC group

The AFC group had three students. The AFC MSc involves a nursery observation and a toddler observation as well, making their experiences of observing different from the that of the others. At times they were thinking about the experience of observation in general, at other times about the specifics of infant observation. None of the group felt that infant observation had been a specific attraction for them in choosing the course, and one stated: *"It feels more important now than it did at the beginning of the training, before we started, now it feels like . . . I'm really excited to get started."*

- *Awareness of feelings*

This group were very aware of how they expected the observation experience to stir up feelings. They referred to primitive feelings but, interestingly, there was also considerable emphasis on their expectation of seeing things that would be painful: *"Because you're just an observer you have to be there observing something you know is wrong and you know that it will have a bad effect on the child. I think this must be painful to be in a situation like this."* We can note the feeling of lack of power as well as the anticipation of pathology. They spoke of looking for pathology, and this seemed to have become a source of anxiety. They expected to have emotional reactions to the ordinary, albeit highly charged feelings in a family with a new baby.

- *Reflection on feelings*

One group member referred to expecting to *"get to some things about myself as well, as I think this will be unavoidable"*. They thought that the experience of observing would help to increase their empathy, and one referred to experiencing the situation from *"inside out"*. One participant spoke of protective feelings, although it was not clear whom she was anticipating protecting. When thinking of the emotional impact of it, they also mentioned the need to hold back on their reactions. The observation as perspective was mentioned, and it was also acknowledged that the observer could have a particular bias: *"When you observe something, you're not sure if it's your perspective or your angles. There's no security there."* One member suggested that as a mother herself, she thought she would identify more with the mother than with the baby.

- *Thoughts about the observer stance*

A participant who had begun an observation with a young child in the observed family mentioned concerns about how much to interact. The group also spoke of holding back on reactions, and one referred to *"going into someone's universe"*—a sense of a world in which they had little importance.

- *Thoughts about families*

This group mentioned that in every parent's interactions things go wrong and that they felt they were looking for pathology. When discussing what they hoped to get from the experience, one said: *"I hope I get to see a healthy mother."*

- *Interest in a baby's development*

Ideas about child development and especially seeing "real" children were mentioned, but there was not much emphasis on this. One group member, while acknowledging theoretical ideas about the importance of early life, questioned how much goes back to *"fundamentals"*. They anticipated seeing mother–baby interaction and later development. One group member was especially interested in the clinical situation as a recreation of the mother–infant relationship. This was linked with the importance of the non-verbal: *"I don't believe that psychoanalysis or psychotherapy is just a talking cure. It's a relationship cure somehow."*

- *The influence of seminar group and seminar leader*

This group also brought up the importance of the seminar group. This was seen as an opportunity to think: *"I get so much from it because I find other people in the group see things I didn't see. The way we go over our observations, minute by minute, is really helpful, because then that same process can happen when other people come up with the things that I didn't see."*

- *Additional issues*

They are aware of the importance of detail (*"minute by minute"*), which, the speaker suggests, is easier to notice in infant observation than with older children. The group also drew attention to the difficulties of writing up, referring to *"when you come to write it up, what you choose to remember, and also lots of events that go on in a situation that take time to process"*. This idea of remembering and also time to process was not further added to at this point, although one member spoke of observation as an opportunity to see how one's own mind operates. It would be interesting to consider how this view of observation as an opportunity to think about oneself fits in with the closing remark made by one group member: *"As an observer, you have to accept the fact that you are not the centre of attention."* (This group did not make a connection, but I think that if one is mindful of some of the earlier findings about the capacities and skills needed by the psychoanalytic psychotherapist, then it becomes apparent that while in clinical work the patient is the centre of attention, what is happening in the mind of the therapist is central to the work. The psychotherapist must use herself while keeping her patient firmly in focus.)

The BAP group

The BAP MSc group was composed of five students who had recently embarked on a two-year MSc and who had just begun or were about to begin infant observation. In considering the attraction—or not—of infant observation as part of the course, one likened it to a placement, while another said she had not really been fully aware of what the course involved.

- *Awareness of feelings*

Anxiety was the feeling of which they were most aware, with it being expressed in relation to finding a baby to observe and how to conduct the observation; the students expressly articulated anxiety about not interacting, especially once the baby was aware of this: *"What I find interesting is when it starts to be aware of other people around, how it's going to react to this person sitting in the corner, just sitting there."*

The fear of being damaging in some way is clearly underlying this and is referred to again when stating that mothers have fantasies about what the observer is going to do.

- *Reflection on feelings*

There was no evidence of this group reflecting on feelings at this point; however, they had the idea that it was something that they would do in time. They anticipated that they would learn to observe, listen, and watch, and the idea that seeing and reflecting could be valuable for a therapist was raised: *"The fact that you're seeing something but you're actually reflecting upon it when it's over—maybe that's something that could apply."* At this stage it seems to be a process in two very separate parts, with little expectation that one could see and reflect within a much closer time frame. They commented on expecting that the experience could help the observer see things from another perspective, with one saying *"I think not having children, I didn't feel that I would understand until I did have, and maybe this enables me to see it from someone else's point of view."* The implication that something will change quite radically within the observer is present here, together with the possibility of an increased capacity to be empathic.

- *Thoughts about the observer stance*

As seen above in relation to feelings, this group were preoccupied with how to conduct themselves as observers, with concerns about their level of interaction. Ideas about distance and objectivity were also thought to be something a therapist might need.

- *Thoughts about families*

They wondered how different a child might be according to his place in the family and other variables. This made some of the group feel that the experience of observing one child would be inadequate: they would need to observe more to understand the ways in which the mother–baby they were observing was in fact idiosyncratic. However, they realized that they would get to know others well through discussions in the seminar group.

• *Interest in a baby's development*

This group paid much attention to the fact that they expected that they would be learning about baby- and child development. They were surprised by the level of emphasis on infancy so far in their theoretical seminars. They acknowledged that psychoanalytic theory has a view that early life is important, *"building patterns about what you learned in the beginning"*. However, they also expressed curiosity about the influence of later experiences: *"Is it really what happens to the baby in the first two years in its life that really governs what's going to happen to the person? One of the things that occurred to me embarking on the baby observation, it would be interesting to see twenty years down the line what the baby that we observed for two years turns out like."*

The group felt that knowing more about babies and how relationships develop was valuable for thinking about adults, although this was thought about in terms of how the adult had evolved, rather than an idea of a continuing infant within the adult. They spoke of the importance of the mother–baby relationship, with one saying that *"I found that the reading that we've been doing so far, it's made me think about my relationship with my mother, and I've spoken to her—'did I do this?' or 'did you feel this?'."* Others agreed, and it is apparent that the course was having an impact on them even at this early stage.

• *The influence of seminar group and seminar leader*

This was not mentioned, apart from the opportunity of getting to know about other babies through the seminar group.

• *Additional issues*

Perhaps mindful of my question about its usefulness for clinical work, this group also pointed to what they saw as differences between observation and clinical work: *"If you are in a clinical situation, you have a client or patient or somebody who comes to you with a certain expectation, whereas a baby has no expectations"*. However, there was also acknowledgement that they felt that they did not know enough at this stage about what clinical life would be like, and the main feeling about clinical training was that it was hard to be accepted onto it.

The way infant observation could be linked to theory but was not just theoretical was an area that was given much attention and seemed important to the group. They spoke of expecting the observation experience to make the reading more "real" and more meaningful. Learning through experiencing also seemed important: *"A baby was just a baby before, . . . it could be down in a book in a million colours, but it won't speak to you the way it does when you are actually practising doing it yourself."*

The speaker's statement that a baby was just a baby before was echoed by others in the group, who made it clear that they had previously taken very little interest in babies; there was a sense that they were beginning to see that there had been a *"variety of things that are going on that you are actually oblivious to"*.

Institute of Psychoanalysis group

There were three students in the group from the Institute of Psychoanalysis. It was clear that the subsidiary question about knowing that infant observation was part of the course was an irrelevance. All had done infant observation before as part of their previous professional development, and so one of the aspects they considered— which was not of relevance to the other groups—was the possible differences between this time and the previous experience. For one of the candidates, the previous experience had not been good, and he wanted to have a better one. All were aware of changes in themselves since they had engaged in their first observation, and they wondered how that would change the experience.

- *Awareness of feelings*

This group, drawing on their past experience, spoke of the anxiety stirred up by observing, which was noted by all the groups in different ways. They spoke of how anxiety-provoking it can be, for example, to be left alone with the baby: *"I was thinking what an impact it does have, you get left in awkward positions like that."* These observers were aware of how the feelings of the mother could be projected onto or into the observer, and they also spoke of the *"sheer intensity of the experience"*. One described the experience of hearing the baby cry: *"I remember recently when one of the infants started crying . . . the piercingness of its cry really cuts into your mind and gets everywhere, and you can't think."* This inability to think brought to mind for this observer his experience of seeing floridly psychotic patients on a ward *"where you have the same phenomenon of feeling dirty, feeling really gripped by the intensity and hugeness of their experience"*.

This group mentioned the primitive states of mind in the baby and how the experience of infant observation could put the observer in touch with those. One even used the word *"survive"* in the context of struggling to understand and to think.

- *Reflection on feelings*

The impact of the experience on themselves at this point was seen as a *"downside"*. They spoke of how important it was to have analysis within which to process feelings. Being in touch with feelings and thinking about those feelings emerged as a strong theme. The feelings stirred up by hearing a baby crying, which then led the observer to think about psychotic patients, has already been cited. Another in the group referred to the way the experience of observing made him think about himself both as a baby and as a parent. They spoke of the importance of staying with the experience, the need to feel without acting as a *"struggle"*. One stated: *"You're actually told a lot if you hang on, the experience of being with an infant can make you feel a lot of powerful feelings."* There was no overt link to infant observation as a helpful way of developing attention to countertransference feelings.

- *Thoughts about the observer stance*

These clinicians, experienced in other clinical roles, were delighted by the lack of clinical responsibility in infant observation: *"You can just be there and not feel a clinical responsibility to who you're with."* They took tremendous pleasure in the way that they could *"just allow an experi- ence to be had"*. Although they were expressing this pleasure at not having to *"solve"* anything, they also spoke of how it can be difficult not to have a *"structure"*, a *"context"*, in which *"you have authority to do something"*. Non-intervention and non-interaction were both noted as something potentially difficult, but this position allowed the experi- ence to develop and meant that feelings had to be contained within the self.

They spoke of having to process feelings, not act on them: *"Still, I think there's something about sitting with things, not being in a position where you can jump in to intervene is a very good discipline. It allows you to step back and be in touch with what you are feeling or thinking or what's happening without rushing in to try to solve it. I think that would be an important skill to learn for being a clinician."*

- *Thoughts about families*

One participant was aware that his second experience led to a new perspective on the first observation and that in fact the mother–infant pair seen will alter the observer's experience. Thinking of this led the group to consider the differences one would see according to the child's position in the family. From a second observation they felt they would get a sense of common threads in child development and also a sense of each baby's uniqueness.

- *Interest in a baby's development*

There was little expressed interest in this. The emotional life of a baby and the interaction between mother and baby were mentioned, but they privileged the parallel with clinical work: *"I expect to learn more about the emotional life of the baby and interaction between baby and mother; that's exactly what you are constantly struggling to understand in our patients."*

- *The influence of seminar group and seminar leader*

One who had not been in analysis when conducting his first observation spoke of the seminar group as very important, but this led others to comment on ways in which the seminar group may not be helpful—could be an *"unsupporting environment"*—with the seminar leader having particular views that cause too much bias. However, they also saw the whole seminar group as a container and as something that enabled them to keep going during a time-consuming and difficult task.

- *Additional issues*

In thinking of ways in which infant observation could link to skills needed by a clinician, they spoke of not rushing to solve things, bearing anxiety, and not knowing the answers: *"Being able to be comfortable in not knowing, not being an expert, not having the answers, you don't necessarily know . . . over time it becomes a pattern and you know."*

This idea of a pattern that emerges over time, which is not overtly referred to by the candidate as being important for clinical experience—she is concentrating on the experience of not knowing—is, as we have seen in earlier chapters, cited by many writers as valuable in clinical work.

Another group member took the point about the mother–baby couple and spoke of having to relate to mother and infant simultaneously. He saw this as something he did in his clinical work, needing to be aware of both the adult and the infant within the same patient. They described the task of writing up the observation as difficult; the time it takes to do so and the inadequacy of language were both acknowledged.

The Tavistock group

The Tavistock group of seven students was made up of one on M16 (MA in Psychoanalytic Studies, a course with no direct clinical links, although sometimes taken by experienced clinicians) and six on M7 (MA in Observational Studies, which acts as a prerequisite for training to qualify as a child psychotherapist at the Tavistock Clinic). Most made it clear that they were wanting to go on to clinical training. They were interviewed in the first term of their infant observation experience, at a time when some had just begun infant observation and others had not yet done so.

- *Awareness of feelings*

Again anxiety was a major theme: for many of them this was or had been focused on the question of finding a baby to observe and concerns about it being the *"right"* sort of baby. One spoke very movingly of her awareness of the emotional aspects of what she was observing: *"I think it can be quite staggering how much emotion you can see when you are observing. At night, in the freezing cold, the family you are observing live on the fourth floor of a tower block. I was really struck when I went in how warm and inviting—a cocoon—it was: it just felt so high up, and outside it was cold. I also felt that the mother and baby were very cocoon-like couple— I was on the outside. How much feeling that evoked."*

- *Reflection on feelings*

Another said: *"When I'm actually doing an observation, I always feel myself struggling, noticing what's going on inside me, whether it means anything, whether it's legitimate. In a way you're a bit like the baby, in a very confused world, lots of things going on, not knowing sometimes, not knowing when to ask questions until other people in the seminar actually bring it out."*

As they had hardly begun the task of observing, members of this group gave little attention to countertransference feelings, but, as the example cited above about being excluded shows, some of the group were already aware of feelings stirred up in them by the experience.

• *Thoughts about the observer stance*

This group also spoke about *"doing it right"*, which was especially focused around the issues of the observer stance and the relationship with the mother. Students were concerned that they should not be persecutory to the mother. One spoke of learning *"how to remain detached and to observe, but also in a way that will not make the mother feel like she's so conscious"*. They also spoke of how they might be called on to meet mother's perceived needs, and how difficult this would be.

There was a lot of awareness of potentially being identified with the mother. One of the group had in fact been observed as a mother in her country of origin and spoke of feeling dropped by the observer. This experience had made her reluctant to engage in infant observation, but she was pleased now she had started it: *"I was worried at the beginning about being an observer because I could identify with the mother, and I don't know if I can remain a detached observer. I think it's going to be very hard for me."*

Another group member later questioned the concept of the detached observer, saying: *"You can't be, you're always in it, and the struggle is to be in and out all the time, and there's tension there, and I think that can be quite useful."* He linked this to the idea that *"if you are practising as a psychotherapist that you have the ability to be in and be attached and be in a relationship and to be out and thinking. I think that might be a useful experience."*

• *Thoughts about families*

The participants also anticipated and looked forward to learning about the impact of the child on the family: *"I think it might be really important, because it is understanding and more about the dynamics of the family as a whole, so it's not just observing how a baby develops but also the huge impact on the feelings of the family, the mother, the sibling, and the father in the family. If I do train as a child psychotherapist, I'll get more of an in-depth understanding of the impact of the child within the family."*

One expressed a particular interest in siblings.

• *Interest in a baby's development*

They also saw the observation as being helpful in understanding children and infants. They referred to instances in their current working lives in which understanding children, or infantile reactions, could be useful to them. They expected to learn about infant development. and some spoke from their experience as mothers about their expectations of development.

• *The influence of seminar group and seminar leader*

The use of the seminar in enabling the students to think about what they have seen and felt was acknowledged. One valued the way things that could not be thought about at the time could be later through the process of writing and through the seminar group: *"I find that during the observation itself there's so much going on, there's very little time to think what it means. Taking in all the detail and trying to remember. I find it extremely difficult to follow, but writing it down, the discussion in the group is invaluable, because things have meaning beyond what they seem to at that moment."*

From this one can see both the pressure of the situation that prevents thinking and the role of the seminar group in helping to see implications that were not obvious.

• *Additional issues*

Many of the participants referred to a sense of knowing little at this point. Perhaps because of this, there was quite a lot of emphasis on the link between infant observation and theory. Infant observation was described as having an integrative function, *"pulling everything together from the course-work"*, and was contrasted with other parts of the course, which were seen as removed from *"real people"*. One member of the group spoke of the importance in psychoanalytic theory—especially Kleinian theory—of the influence of the early months and years. Students referred to the importance of the mother–baby relationship within psychoanalytic theory and how knowledge of it could be used to understand and enrich the therapist–patient relationship. One linked this with her current work and said that children she worked with *"behave in ways that I hope the observation of a baby will help me understand in terms of sound, play games and interaction"*. This emphasis on the non-verbal was picked up by another member: *"What I think I'm hoping for is to get in touch with pre-verbal feelings and see what they look like. Psychotherapy is very wordy."*

Other group members spoke of the importance of trying to remember in sequence, which they thought would be a useful discipline. Many of the members mentioned interest in detail, which was one of the ways, the group suggested, that an observer experience could be useful for a therapist. They also saw the in–out quality, the awareness of oneself, and the parallels between the mother–baby and therapist–patient relationships as potentially valuable.

Issues about the task of observing were also raised. There was a shared feeling that there were so many aspects to attend to: *"It is using so many different parts of the brain at the same time: the language part, the part that picks up atmosphere and feelings, the part that's trying to notice every little gesture the baby makes. All these things are happening at once."*

They wondered about what was important to observe and note. There was some discussion about the micro- and macro-context, with one member suggesting that the Tavistock focus on the micro can be too narrow. The expectation of having different feelings in the future and also of seeing patterns emerging was apparent.

The question of whether the infant observation component of the course had been an attraction was answered negatively by one who said he had not been able to imagine what it would be like, but positively by others, with an emphasis on bringing theory and practice together.

Given the emphasis that teaching staff often give to infant observation as a useful beginning, a place where an observer can have *some* experience useful for clinical work when not yet ready to engage in clinical work, it is interesting that only one student spoke of this aspect of it, saying: *"I realized I was years away from any clinical work where it* [theory learned] *could be applied in a sensible way. Infant observation seemed like the one place where I could meddle and still not necessarily ruin anything."*

While teachers of infant observation would be concerned about the word "meddle", the idea of it as a "non-harming" experience has certainly been raised by many staff.

Comparing the groups

Not surprisingly, the group from the Institute, who had all observed before, had different preoccupations from the other groups. They made much of the lack of clinical responsibility in the task of infant observation—something that was not mentioned by the others. In some ways, as might be expected, they were operating at a far more sophisticated level than the other groups, although at times their responses seemed as unrooted in experience as those of the others. They were the only set that did not make a link between theory and infant observation. Interestingly, the BAP MSc group were the most interested in and concerned about this—perhaps because at this stage they were trying to make sense of why it was included in their academic course. All the groups referred to infant observation as an opportunity to learn more about babies, although the reason for wanting to do so—"*the emotional life of the child*", "*how people evolve*"— had different emphases, with the AFC and Tavistock groups express-ing a particular interest in the non-verbal. Similarly, all the groups referred to the importance of the mother–baby relationship and an-ticipated learning about the interaction between mother and infant. Perhaps because they were asked to think about ways in which doing an infant observation could be of use for future clinical activity, there was an emphasis on the mother–baby relationship as in some ways paralleling the therapist–patient relationship. Other ways in which this question was addressed included ideas about seeing and reflect-ing, which were expressed by the BAP group and were framed by the Tavistock group in terms of thinking afterwards about what had been seen, and also thoughts about the in–out quality necessary for both roles. The Institute group concentrated on the importance of bearing anxiety and not rushing to know the answers, while the Tavistock, BAP, and AFC groups all thought that attention to detail would be important.

Anxiety about observing was mentioned by all, although the groups focused on different causes for anxiety. Not surprisingly, anxieties about practical issues—getting it right, doing it right— dominated for group members who had not yet begun. Concerns about finding a suitable baby were predominant in the BAP and Tavistock groups, with the AFC students being very concerned about the quality of the mother. This was overtly about pathology with the

AFC group, but was also an issue with the Institute group, who thought about how the personality of the mother alters the observation experience. The BAP and Tavistock groups were also concerned about the observer's relationship with the mother but saw it more in terms of not being either over-identified with her or persecuting to her. How to comport oneself as an observer was an issue for all the groups. All had the idea that they "should" not interact with mother or baby, and they were concerned about how to manage this. Again the language used varied: the BAP and Tavistock groups had an awareness that detachment or non-reaction were needed, while the AFC group spoke of holding back on reactions. The Institute group, who had all observed before, spoke of not acting on feelings instead staying with them.

The BAP group had not really thought about feelings that the experience would stir up in them, but this aspect was mentioned by the other groups, although for some it had the flavour of repeating something they might have been told by others. The AFC students spoke about primitive feelings, as did the Institute group, who also spoke about receiving projections from mother and baby. The Tavistock and AFC groups thought they would learn about themselves from noticing their own feelings, while the Institute group spoke of the impact on the self and thought analysis while observing would be important for processing the intense feelings. This was not mentioned by the other groups. All, with the exception of the BAP group, mentioned the seminar group as an important part of the experience, with an emphasis from the AFC and Tavistock groups on it as helping the observer to become aware of things previously missed and the Institute group seeing the group as a container for the feelings emerging as part of the experience. Again the Tavistock, AFC, and Institute groups spoke of the task of writing up the observations, with concern about the strain of remembering.

Both the Tavistock and Institute groups referred to the experience of waiting and thinking that a pattern would emerge. The sense of the complexity of people and how they vary was mentioned specifically by the BAP group and implied by the Institute group when thinking about how the experience of the second observation would give a new perspective to the first. Building on this sense of difference, the BAP group hoped the experience would help them to see the other's point of view, which was also stated by the AFC group in terms of increasing empathy. The idea that the observer would be somehow changed by the experience was at its most explicit with the Institute group but implied by all respondents.

We will see, when looking closely at the way these same themes emerged from the post-observation interviews, that some issues were no longer of much concern, while others claimed prominence. Later chapters address whether such changes can be simply attributed to the fact that by that point participants have live experiences on which to draw, or whether we can see that the experience of carrying out infant observation impacts in significant ways on those who engage in it.

CHAPTER EIGHT

Delivery:
the narrative of the end interviews

The participants were interviewed again after an academic year of studying infant observation, and this time they were able to refer frequently to experiences in which they had recently been involved. The interviewees spoke freely about what they felt the experience had shown them and, as was outlined in chapters 2 and 6, their statements were analysed using grounded theory method. The statements were gathered into the seven categories described in chapter 6, and each group's responses were treated as a distinct entity. As one would expect, there was a difference in emphasis within the groups in the ways they addressed each category, and in the amount of attention each was given.

Awareness of feelings

All groups spoke of this, both explicitly and in relation to other issues, though it is not always clear whether what is being talked of should be categorized as reflection on feelings, as obviously these interviewees were all talking after the event.

- *The AFC group*

This group were very open about how they had been stirred up by the experience of observing and spoke at times of leaving the observations with a feeling of depression. They made passing references to anxiety as well as referring to it more directly. The rapidity of changing emotions without understanding how or why was also mentioned. The sense of exclusion from the mother–infant couple and then feeling that the mother was deliberately keeping the child away were painful experiences for the observer. The agony of watching an underfed baby not being fed was conveyed in the discussion, as were the painful feelings stirred up by being aware of the vulnerability of infants. All are compounded by the "intensity of emotion" that surrounds infants. This group also spoke about how painful it was to realize in the seminar the partial nature of what they had seen.

They were interested in distinguishing which of their responses belonged to them and which were probably the result of projections, referring to the *"anxiety she provoked in me"* or times of knowing the mother to be depressed and also feeling themselves as depressed. They clearly realized the usefulness of monitoring and noting their own feelings as a valuable source of information about the family: *"Really, our only way of understanding the internal world is seeing how we're provoked."* However, the group were also very thoughtful about what in their reactions belonged to themselves.

A group member spoke movingly about the *"odd repercussions"* that had arisen in his personal life as a result of observing: *"The infant I'm observing has an older sibling: he's two years older, and they're both male. It exactly matches my situation with an older brother, and this was quite quickly picked up on by our seminar leader, and over the next few weeks I began to really, I think, slightly unconsciously, observe what it was like for the older sib to suddenly have this annoying intrusion in their life and vice-versa. And I actually found—could be because of other reasons—that my relationship with my brother improved massively, just in terms of seeing him in a completely different light."*

They spoke specifically about experiences within the observation about which they had felt strongly. One observer felt that the mother did not want the baby to come to her, which she conceptualized as having to do with what she called the mother's transference to her. This observer was in therapy, and she used both her own therapy and the seminar group to help her think about the feelings she was experiencing. Another group member spoke of her pleasure in a situation that was going well, but being concerned that perhaps she was unconsciously idealizing the situation.

It is difficult to separate the feelings this group talked about that arose from the observations and those that arose from the seminar group. Certainly, as we shall see when looking at that section, this group found that experience very challenging and immensely helpful. The strength of feelings expressed certainly owes something, however, to the intensity of feelings that contact with primitive experiences stirs up: *"Sometimes I left the group so angry and so troubled, and so I had to go home and think about things over and over again."*

- *The BAP group*

While acknowledging a mixture of emotions—one participant described her experience of observing as a *"bitter-sweet experience"*—this group talked mainly of anxiety. The group discussion started as follows: *"Before I started the observation, I think I was the last actually to start, I was very, very worried about it and had all sorts of fears and anxieties, and even up to the last minute, going up to the door and it not immediately being answered, ... I was quite surprised by how emotional I felt when I saw the baby I was observing first."*

Others echoed this surprise, and also the anxiety, especially anxiety about *"doing it right"* ... *"what am I allowed to do, what am I not allowed to do"*, but most felt that this diminished over time, although—as becomes evident in the section on the observer stance—many were concerned that the growing baby made more efforts to make a relationship with them, which led to anxieties about how to manage that. Many of them expressed concern for the baby, talking of anxious anticipation about what each observation would hold, caused by worries about how this was going to affect the baby.

They were aware that their feelings might be caused by picking up projections. One respondent described feeling anxious about *"the times when she's [the baby] not feeling soothed, that I feel grandmother is being too intrusive, that's when I feel the impact. I don't sort of notice being anxious a lot when I'm writing up."* The reference to not being anxious at the time of writing up refers to a view others had been expressing about the process of remembering and writing up (see the section on the seminars). Many spoke about finding the remembering of it painful. The act of writing it up felt very *"demanding"* to one and the anxieties about *"doing it right"* also seemed to be engendered by writing up. They did not mention this in terms of then presenting in the seminar, but one might assume this to be so.

Observers mentioned the impact of the mood of the mother or the family on them, with one putting it very clearly: *"When I go and do the observation and the baby is smiley and happy, that's great, and I can't help but think that's fantastic, but when I go into the observation and he is maybe less playful and the mother feels she has to bombard me with everything that's going on in her life and how depressed she is, I come away feeling quite depressed myself."*

One group member spoke of an experience she had had of seeing the baby being propped up and left with a bottle. This was a baby that was often left alone with the observer: *"I felt very, quite cross with her once two weeks ago, because she was feeding the baby from the bottle, and when I first visited, she said she couldn't cope with breast-feeding, and she wasn't happy about this, but then a few weeks ago she propped up this bottle so he was more or less feeding himself. He was just propped up in this arrangement of blankets and car-seat, and she had a friend there, and she kept popping up and trying to see how he was getting on, and I felt really quite cross, and I thought, poor baby, and had she been breast-feeding she wouldn't have taken off her breast and propped it up, and I felt rather incensed, and then I thought, well, why am I feeling like this, because she has got a lot on and it's nice for her to have a friend there. . . . I felt critical and then I felt guilty because I felt critical."*

The observer describes her feelings (*"rather incensed"*) and was aware that she felt critical of the mother. However, she then felt guilt about feeling critical (see the section on reflecting on feelings). The group as a whole clearly wanted to feel positive about the situations they were observing. One was concerned that she was avoiding seeing difficulties in order to see the *"perfect"* baby.

The observer's relationship with the family could be a source of painful feelings, with participants mentioning anxiety over observing a depressed mother and concerns about the parents' capacities to look after the children.

- *The Institute group*

Although the Institute group spoke overtly about being assessed on their capacity to be in touch with their own unconscious feelings, they did not evidence this much as a concern. The first feeling that they talked about—and this was discussed at some length—was that of anxiety primarily focused on finding a baby. Although one had found one before the term started, she spoke of being aware of others in her group who had found this process difficult, while the other two participants spoke more of how anxious they had been about it. One had put a lot of effort into it—*"wore my desperation on my sleeve"*—and had lost the first observation opportunity through a process that he saw as having to do with his anxieties. The other man in the group had had considerable difficulties in finding a baby; he had had a number of failed contacts, and talk about this and its repercussions was in fact a major issue in this group discussion. There was discussion about the pain of being rejected by people he had made contact with, and concern about what other people thought of him, with the additional difficulty of being a male observer. Having struggled to find a baby, this same observer was filled with *"fury"* when the mother then decided to make an extended trip that disrupted the observation. He felt *"she ruined it for me"*, but then *"in a moment regained myself"* and worked on trying to hide those feelings, about which he subsequently felt guilty. His difficulty in finding a baby to observe had led to him receiving what he then felt was an unfair, overly harsh report from his seminar leader. For him, this had been a *"nightmare experience"* and one that he wished he had not had to undergo. Clearly the pain here is located in the experience of being judged as *"a man without bones"* by this seminar leader in a way that felt unfair and also potentially threatened his progress within the training.

The experience in general was felt to be difficult. One referred to the *"hard work of observation"* and talked about the value in *"having to stick it out"*. He felt that the requirement to observe for a chronological year, not an academic year, had been made in order to make it a lengthier experience, but not, I noticed, mentioning any ideas about child development that would make the longer time more useful. Another spoke of painful things to which she had been witness. Her observed mother had had to undergo an emergency caesarean and had later had a breast abscess. She spoke of the pain of *"being exposed to it but not able to work with it"*. Others in the group also expressed the inadequacy they felt, feeling *"the lack of interpretive tools"*. One said *"just bear it"* in response to others' thoughts about the struggle of the experience; there was a sense that these were unbearable things. However, when speaking of the baby he had observed having been born five weeks prematurely, the participant made no mention of feelings that this might have stirred up in him, referring instead to his gratitude that this had made the mother eager for the observation experience.

A group member spoke of his observed family, where the mother had a teenage daughter from a previous relationship. He saw himself as being the recipient of the murderous feelings of this girl towards the baby which were exhibited to him. She refused to acknowledge him and at times walked in to where he was as if he weren't there. The observer described how *"wiped out"* he felt and elaborated on how painful it was: *"I had feelings of inadequacy"*, which he understood as not only projection, realizing that something in him identified with them, saying *"at least they found a good home in me"*.

Another group member expressed feelings of gratitude to the mother. She had previously been invited by the mother to hold the baby and had felt that the mother was hurt by her refusal of this. The mother later gave her the baby to hold after the observation hour. Later, when the baby was crawling and put out a hand to the observer and the observer did not respond, the mother was very facilitating in *"bridging the gap"* between the observer and baby: *"Mother brought the baby back between us"*. The observer felt relieved about this. She saw mother's act as very generous and was aware that the mother could have reacted in a very persecuted way: *"She might not have bothered to help."* She saw this mother as having helped the baby get over a strange experience and appreciated that she had done so *"without intruding or pulling me out of role"*. In telling of this, the interviewee mainly emphasized her gratitude to the mother, but another group member picked up on how she could have been *"made to feel uncomfortable"* or, as the participant said, *"really bad"*. Her *"uneasy"* feelings about not responding to the baby were acknowledged but were not privileged in this discussion.

- *The Tavistock group*

One group member declared that her experience was of being *"literally catapulted into a really intense situation"*, and other interviewees referred to the intensity of feelings stirred up. Although some within this group referred to painful experiences, they also spoke of pleasure. They talked of how painful it was to watch something that felt wrong. One observer had the experience of *"a very rough kind of period, with the baby crying an awful lot and the mother trying to see what was the matter but not always managing to comfort the baby and . . . sometimes quite a mismatch between what the mother was doing and what the baby actually, maybe, needed."* She went on to say that within her seminar group she had felt *"uncomfortable about being the only one who has got a baby who is not smiley".*

Anxieties about the mother wanting to end the observation also stirred up feelings of inadequacy and rejection. A member who had recently arrived from abroad indicated that she was having to manage her own homesickness and adjust to a new culture. Ruth Robinson, who teaches infant observation for the AFC, said in an informal conversation that she is often aware how vulnerable the students can be, especially if they are newly arrived in the country, and how the observation then becomes overlaid with these feelings.

This group also spoke of the pleasures of the experience, using words like *"delight"* and *"joyous"*. One attempted to describe her feelings when the baby looked at her: *"that kind of feeling, you don't need any language actually at that moment"*, and she spoke of herself as feeling contained by the baby, saying of the observation: *"The most delightful time for me every week, I love to go."*

One participant spoke very movingly about her identification with the baby: *"I still remember one time during the observation the baby was crying because no one was in the living room, and she was crying. I felt like crying too, but maybe because I'm also in the process of adoption, to fit myself in this culture, and its quite difficult, and sometimes the family I observe provided me a kind of home . . . so when I saw the baby crying, it's quite unbearable, maybe because of my own emotional state."*

In this we can see the observer feeling intensely and then trying to disentangle why she is feeling as she is, acknowledging both her own part and having a sense of receiving projections from the baby. This and the following examples will also be looked at again in the section on reflecting on feelings.

Another group member spoke of feeling depressed after an observation visit and trying to work out why when overtly the mother was far from depressed—she was, in fact, quite manic.

The force and impact of receiving projected, often disavowed, feelings is vividly conveyed in another description by that group member: *"I had quite an amazing experience: the mother, between the second and third month, was not there at the times that we had arranged.*

About three times I was happy to rearrange, and I literally felt kind of primitive feelings, absolute nothingness and oblivion that got projected into me . . . and then I suddenly realized, I got this hunch, that perhaps the baby had been weaned. And the next time I visited, it had been weaned, and it was such an incredible experience to think that all must, may be, all connected, this complete blocking out was part of, perhaps, what the baby was experiencing."

Again we see how the observer is having the experience of feeling something and learning to think about those feelings, and then using them as possible evidence for what the baby is feeling, giving the observer the opportunity of experiencing for herself the usefulness of being receptive to one's countertransference feelings.

Reflection on feelings

- *The AFC group*

The AFC group were explicit about how important the act of reflecting on their feelings was and how much help they had had within the seminar group about this. They were interested in their own reactions to things and believed that, after consideration, their reactions could be a useful source of evidence. They were also aware of how much they had missed of what there was to be seen, and they were interested in why this might be so. Clearly, in the seminars it had become apparent to them that they had failed to notice important things as they happened, or failed to remember them for making their presentations: *"What it is that you remember, why do you remember, why suddenly this is particularly absorbing and not something else? . . . just how partial your capacity for listening to it is, even if you feel that it's been quite total."*

They spoke of the struggle of remembering and how painful it was to recognize defences that they had used. They acknowledged their own feelings in their narratives of the observation visit, stating that they had been resistant to giving this sufficient weight: *"It has happened to me that I left the observation very depressed because . . . I don't know . . . there was something I was feeling a little depressed about, the relationship with the mother, the mother was a little bit depressed. Then in writing my observation I would not put it in, or would put it in but not really make anything of it, undervalue it, and the group allowed me to be able to get more in touch with this kind of thing."*

It was important to think about why they had reacted as they did, and analysing this in the group helped this process. The act of thinking was seen as helpful. Following the statement, already quoted, about leaving the group angry and troubled and going home to think about things over and over again, the respondent went on: *"and then I would go back and really I felt that really this could really help me, thinking about things".*

This seminar group were perhaps enabled to reflect on what they had avoided feeling or seeing because there was an emphasis on the useful learning experience of "mistakes". It was explicitly stated that making a mistake could be a helpful: *"an error you're really going to expand with or grow in".* One observer spoke of her unconscious acting out: *"When the mother cancelled an appointment, the next time I arrived half an hour late, it was like I needed to punish her."* The depth of her understanding of her reaction was shown when later in the interview she spoke of her feelings about the end of the observation. She had only four more weeks to visit and was feeling a sense of loss about that. She expressed her concern that she might act out, slip up under pressure; however, it seemed that her awareness of this would protect her from enactment.

The sense of having gained something solid from these reflections on feelings was expressed by one of the group. Having been talking about the intensity of emotion and vulnerability, he went on: *"Quite often you don't recognize how much you've learned until you are with other people who are discussing these things. You suddenly realize that's where you were before, suddenly realize that you have actually grown up a bit."*

- *The BAP group*

The BAP group were less overtly aware than the AFC group about the process of reflecting on their feelings. However, there was some evidence of it in the way they described things. They referred to writing a paper about the experience and through doing so feeling that the learning of the experience takes place after the observations themselves. One said: *"The actual learning of the observation only happens with me when I start thinking about it, and I didn't start thinking about it until, I suppose, I had to write the paper."*

As mentioned in the section about awareness of feelings, one observer spoke of wondering what she was avoiding: *"I felt sometimes guilt, almost feeling, how in the beginning we said in the seminars, 'Oh, this looks like the perfect idea of a happy family.' And when it goes too well, I always wonder whether it is because I'm having a good day, I don't want to hear anything that's not going right, so I don't pick it up."*

The member who spoke of her *"incensed"* feelings with the mother who gave the baby the propped-up bottle went on: *"Then I thought, well, why am I feeling like this, because she has got a lot on."* While it is important to view all things observed in context and with a respectful attitude, this observer does not seem to have considered that she might have been feeling something on behalf of the baby. Instead, she seemed to need to rationalize and feel that what the mother had done and was doing was all right, overriding her original feelings that the "poor baby" was suffering. She felt "guilty" about her critical feelings about the mother, but the other group members stated that they had felt critical in hearing about it. Although the observer was reflecting on her feelings, using time and space away from the heat and pain of the experience to consider them, it seems to me from the way it was described that in fact the observer was retreating from knowing something rather than using the reflective space to disentangle projections, countertransference feelings, and her own contributing feelings.

- *The Institute group*

As we can see from the examples given when looking at their awareness of feelings, members of this group were thinking about what they felt and why. The group member who felt *"wiped out"* was quick to say that not all of what he felt could be attributed to projection from the child. The description of the experience with the mother of the baby who approached the observer shows the observer thinking about the experience and noticing to some extent the various feelings she had about it. All spoke about the seminars as the place where they felt such reflection happened, with one talking of the seminar discussion as *"detoxifying"*, and, as we shall see, their section on the seminar is a substantial one.

They believed that reflection about their feelings would be an aspect that their training institution would expect them to display. They expected that the Institute wanted them to be in touch with their unconscious and to put their thoughts and feelings into their reports on the sessions. In discussing the assessment function of the infant observation seminars, they anticipated being evaluated on *"how you deal with emotions in yourself, emotions in the mother and baby, the whole situation"*. They also thought that the way they *"metabolized"* their experiences would be seen as significant.

- *The Tavistock group*

As we have seen in the section on awareness of feelings, the Tavistock group showed considerable evidence of doing this without necessarily naming what they were doing. The example I cited above of the Chinese observer trying to work out what of her wish to cry belonged to her in her loneliness in a foreign land and what belonged to the baby left alone shows this, as does the episode of the observer using her reaction to the changed and cancelled meetings to help her make the leap to thinking that her experience of *"nothingness"* might reflect the baby's experience of weaning. The observer who wondered where his feelings of depression came from shows something of the process of this: *"I came out of the observation and I felt really depressed and I couldn't account for it. . . . And this is in the early period, and then I was thinking back, remembering this episode, I did think, well, is it the mother? But the mother didn't appear depressed, but then I thought . . . she was quite manic."*

This example shows us someone who at the time of the observation is aware of the feeling, but is not then, early on, inclined to think of it as having significance, having been engendered by the observation experience. It is later on, when he is more familiar with the experience of monitoring his countertransference and has become more aware of how he is at the receiving end of projections, that he then begins to wonder about the *"muddle"* and to recognize the depression that was masked by the manic behaviour.

Although reflection and not enactment are thought to be what the observer is aiming for, there was also the realization that enactment, if subsequently thought about, could be a very useful experience. One observer spoke at length about how difficult she found a depressed mother's non-responsiveness to her boisterous toddler. She described how on one occasion she had strongly felt the wish, the need, to change this situation, and how she had grabbed and tickled the child, which he loved (see section on observer stance). She said *"I probably shouldn't have done that, but I think that told me something."* Although what it taught her was not expanded on within the group interview, we have a sense of the observer being able to reflect on what had driven her out of her observer stance. As with the AFC group, it is important that valuable learning can arise from "mistakes".

The observer stance

This was an issue that received varying degrees of emphasis, with the Tavistock group speaking very little about it *per se* and the others reflecting on it more explicitly.

• *The AFC group*

This group's discussion began with a participant talking about how difficult he found it to observe the mother–infant dyad in a family of five, and how the mother impacted on his capacity to observe. He went on to talk about identifying with family members and how at times *"I would laugh, where I was identifying with somebody else, and then defensively. Now, I think, was it defensive for the infant, or was I actually defensive for myself?"*

The group expressed various concerns about how to conduct themselves as observers—*"being an observer is a very particular position"*. One said that she had found it very hard and felt confused *"in terms of how much I would reveal about myself or not reveal about myself or how much was natural in the situation to talk about or how much was unnatural to hide."* She felt she had indicated to the mother that she knew nothing, which led to the mother *"teaching"* her, but then she felt that she was *"not really being myself in the situation"*. She had been shown this in the seminar group and had learned to be more natural and acknowledged that she did have some experience. Two group members expressed concerns about being intrusive, feeing that they should *"be present and minimize the impact"*.

Only one member said explicitly how difficult it was to do nothing, when describing her feelings about sitting and watching a mother postpone feeding an underweight baby. Another said: *"I haven't done anything, I'm not a therapist, I'm not a clinician or anything like that, but they managed to use me"*. One contrasted the situation with therapy, saying *"you don't get feedback"*, but then suggested that the feedback was in fact evidenced in the countertransference.

All compared this observation experience with others (nursery and toddler) undertaken as part of their AFC MSc and viewed themselves as more *"invested in this situation"*. They saw this observation, not carried out in an institution, as lacking the *"protection"* of other settings, saying that the situation makes demands that they *"self-manage"*, leaving them simultaneously wishing for rules, but also knowing that they wanted the rules to *"hide behind"* and that they had learned more from the *"struggle"* and the *"mistakes"* made.

- *The BAP group*

This entire group talked about the struggle they had experienced in attempting to maintain an observer stance. One felt that because of her sense of anxiety, it had been harder to begin with, but that she had now found her place and was comfortable with it, even though the baby was reaching out to her more. Others felt that it had become harder as the baby had got older, with one suggesting it was because the family were more familiar with her: *"I feel that I'm only recently discovering the difficulty of maintaining that observer stance and not engaging with baby, parents, mother/father too much, which in the beginning seemed like the most natural thing."*

They questioned how to behave to both family and growing baby. One participant said: *"I feel big anxiety about the baby looking at me and I feel I'm not responding. I feel the baby wants to almost rocket towards me, interact, expects me to, and I don't."* She also expressed anxiety that the mother thought she was too distant, although she was quick to say the mother did not seem to, so we might hypothesize that she is attributing this view, which she holds to some extent, to the mother. This group expressed anxiety about keeping boundaries, with one saying that it *"feels like constant negotiation between whatever is going on, whether it's the baby coming towards you or the father making conversation or engaging or not engaging, all of that"*. However, one suggested that perhaps she had been too careful to keep a distance and on recently reading *Closely Observed Infants* (Miller, Rustin, Rustin, & Shuttleworth, 1989) to prepare for her paper, she had been surprised to find that many observers there described interacting more than she had previously believed appropriate.

One observer had been left alone with the baby much of the time, which had posed different problems about the observer stance. Once she had wondered, should she go and tell the mother, who was in another room, that the baby had been sick. She had managed this by doing so as she was saying goodbye at the point of leaving soon after. On another occasion she had been concerned about a bit of plastic on the playroom floor: *"There was a bit of plastic, a torn-off bit, I felt that . . . perhaps I ought to take it out of harm's way so I just took it through to the kitchen thinking I feel a bit intrusive doing this, but on the other hand I don't think it's good for it to be around."*

Another participant expressed considerable anger about being left alone with the baby by a father: *"I'm not being left alone with the baby, unless he is asleep and I feel quite comfy about that. . . . Times like last week, the nappy had to be changed, father didn't, and he just put the baby on the floor with a toy and then he went off to the living room, put on his shoes because he was planning to go out, and I was there in the room by myself with the baby looking straight at me, waiting for me to do something, and I felt so cheated, I felt like, who are you to put this baby in front of me to interact with me, I am here to observe you and that baby. I really felt ambushed."*

The group raised the question of what it was they were looking at, was it *infant* observation or *mother–infant* observation? They stated that they often wondered where to focus their attention when there was so much going on. One participant expressed a sense of achievement for staying with it, which was echoed by the others.

- *The Institute group*

The Institute group described being aware of there always being a *"line or boundary about what you say or don't say"*. They spoke of having been allowed into a *"very intimate space"* and thought it was then difficult not to say much. Perhaps because of their usual position as clinicians, they seemed to find this loss of their verbal skills particularly hard, saying *"we don't have interpretive tools, we're very exposed"*. They described being exposed to the situation but not able to work with it. One said that they *"couldn't offer the family anything"* and then corrected himself, adding *"or anyway we're not able to talk about it"*.

As we have seen in previous sections, one member of the group had the very common experience of having the mother offer that she—the observer—should hold the baby. She felt the mother was hurt by her refusal to do so. The mother later offered her the baby to hold after the "official" observation time, making it clear that she understood the observer's previous refusal as caused by the need to maintain the observer stance *during* the observation. In relating this, the observer felt that her taking and holding the baby was important to mother and described mother as more *"settled"* after that, noting that mother no longer spoke of the baby wanting to play with the observer. In telling of this, the observer did not emphasize how hard *she* found it to refuse the offer or whether she had any wish within herself to hold the baby, but she emphasized the importance of having both maintained the boundary and having found a flexible way of negotiating the problem.

With their concentration on what they imagined their training institution was looking for, this group expected their seminar leaders to be looking to see how they managed these difficulties. They thought they would be evaluated on *"how able you are to stay in your role of observer even when it's difficult . . . how you negotiate that role, because I guess a lot of what you do as an observer is a bit of what you do as an analyst"*.

In making this parallel, the interviewee explained that, like an analyst, an observer is frustrating and does not tell a lot about himself, and said that one needed to feel comfortable about that. They also suggested that the seminar leader would be noting and reporting on *"how easily you are pushed out of role, and how can you think about it when you are"*.

• *The Tavistock group*

This group said little explicitly about this. They had thoughts about the observer's relationship to the family, which is addressed in that section, but they were less explicit about the observer stance *per se.* They spoke of a need to hold the boundary and thought this was more difficult if the family have needs of the observer. One mused about what the family needed the observer for and what was being enacted in front of her: *"There was quite an interesting dynamic going on, and it made me realize how much gets enacted in front of the observer on all sorts of different levels."* The family's needs of the observer and ways of relating to the observer were also mentioned by the Chinese observer when she spoke briefly of the problems caused for her by being treated as an honoured guest and having food prepared for her visits. Other group members referred to the way parents chat, feeling they were being told *"everything"*.

As mentioned above, one participant spoke of a time when she had been pulled out of observer role. She spoke about a mother of a *"needy and energetic toddler"* who *"was never able to match his mood. No matter how excited he was, she was really calm, though she patently felt some anger that she was holding in, and the calmer she was, the more the little boy was angry and energetic. And I just desperately wanted her to pick him up and tickle him or match his level somehow, and it was very hard to sit through so many observations where I could see that and not say anything. Finally, during one last observation, the baby was on the floor, and I was sitting against the wall, and this little boy was right between me and the baby, doing everything he could to get attention, and I had been aware how hard he has to work to get attention, and I just grabbed him and I tickled him and he absolutely loved it. And after months and months of sitting and watching, I just decided, it was just an impulse that I had. But I wanted so much for the mother to be able to do that, and I probably shouldn't have done that, but I think that told me something really."*

Although in this meeting the observer did not explicitly specify what she felt she had learned, she went on to talk in a sympathetic way about *"how hard it is for this mother to have two children in mind at the same time"*, so it seemed as if her stepping out of observer role had helped her to fully realize the internal struggles someone might be experiencing.

The observer's relationship to the family

All the groups had an interest in this, and all expressed thoughts about how they might affect family dynamics and why the family might have welcomed an observer.

- *The AFC group*

This group were rapidly approaching the end of their observations and were reluctant to end their relationships with the families. One thought that she would want to make occasional visits as *"People have really let us into their lives and we are a piece of their family constellations."* In addition to having felt involved with the families, this group had a sense of having been able to give something of value to them. The opportunity for the family and observer together to focus on the baby was indicated by a respondent who spoke about her experience of watching the baby dreaming. She emphasized that the mother had joined her in looking at the baby: *"I think I'm helping her look at the internal world of her baby, of this child, but there's a certain resistance to doing it. Somehow in a normal world we would like to pretend it doesn't exist somehow."* They mentioned giving the space for the parents to think about their child so that *"it provides some strange sort of structure for them to build their own awareness of themselves as parents".*

Naturally not all of the group felt as positive all the time. The same observer had previously spoken of the effect of the mother on his capacity to observe, and his denial of *"the anxiety she provoked in me".* As discussed above, one observer felt that the mother was keeping the baby away from her, and she felt at that point that the mother was hostile to her. There were some thoughts, related to another family, about what it might be in mother's internal world that made her as she is. They referred to identifying with different family members at different times and were aware that by their presence they were affecting the dynamics of what was going on in the observations and wanted to avoid this: *"That was the hardest thing, to be present and to minimize your impact on what was going on."*

- *The BAP group*

This group thought a great deal about how each of them related to their observed families and had very different experiences. One observer, who was left alone with the baby a lot, felt very isolated, while another said: *"It seems we do the observation together."* One participant spoke of the mother using the observer as a *"confidante",* while the observer of the depressed mother thought that when she visited, *"maybe it gives her time to play with the baby when she wouldn't, with someone there she thinks she has to".* They were very interested in the question of why the family had agreed to the observation, with a suggestion to one member from another that the observed mother had hoped to use her as a sort of babysitter. There were concerns about how the observer was seen by the family. One spoke of the family's—presumably expressed—expectation that the observer was there to *"watch what they do and report anything wrong",* while another spoke of a time when mother referred to *"a posh lady"* coming to the house and the need to tidy the house. While this ostensibly referred to someone else, the observer had some sense of it referring to her.

The group did not express much sense of being valuable to the families. There were anxieties about whether the observations could continue into the second year, with one in particular being very concerned that the observation would come to a premature end, saying, *"we practice a lot in saying goodbye"*, referring to the baby's waving at the end of each visit. Another had seen significance in mother not answering her calls and taking longer on a break than the observer had expected. However, another had some sense of the baby having a wish and a need for her to come: *"Is it my imagination that when I missed a week, as happened two weeks ago, he's not been quite so pleased to see me the following week? I think it's probably my imagination."* Although she resists taking on board that the absence had an impact on the baby, she does allow herself to think of it.

Many expressed the idea that the family would behave differently if they were not there. One spoke of the mother making *"a big effort"* to play with the baby. They also talked of the observations often taking place within one room and feeling cramped, and of how different the observations had felt when they had gone outside.

- *The Institute group*

This group also wondered why families invited in observers and what they got from the experience. One participant, in describing his observed mother's traumatic birth experience, spoke of her as *"gushing with the experience"* and *"desperate for the observation"*. He felt he had been very lucky to have a mother who *"needed"* the observation and whose *"reasons for need were benign"*. Perhaps because of the group member who had so much difficulty in finding a family willing to be observed, there was discussion about what aspects of him—being male, having a "thick accent"—might have put them off. Others felt the commitment of one year was off-putting at the time of setting up the observation, although as time went on it did not seem that long. The question of why the family should *"trust"* the observer was raised, with them feeling that trust could only be *"passed on down the line"* through personal relationships.

One group member said that he thought the family wanted him to come because they were from abroad and needed a *"paternal figure to see the baby"*. It was also mentioned that a family had asked to see the observer's notes and final paper at the beginning, but that it was hoped that this would subsequently be forgotten. They spoke about the family allowing them in to *"a very intimate space"* and there was some sense of gratitude for this. Despite having thoughts about the families' need of them, they did not seem to feel they were giving much to the family, with one saying he was *"not offering anything—well, offering something, but not able to talk about it"*.

- *The Tavistock group*

One participant said the observer was *"drawn into almost right into the heart of the family"*, and they had a sense of having become valuable to the families. Although one spoke of her expectation that the observed mother would call a halt to the observation, in fact her visits were valued. The importance of the relationship became clear to one of the group members who had not visited at half-term, presuming this as agreed and understood. She had felt badly then finding a message on her answering-machine from the observed mother, asking *"Where are you?"* She said she had not realized how important her visits were for this *"lonely, isolated mother"*. Another participant also thought of her mother, from another country, being lonely, and partially understood this as a reason why her visits to them had become a *"big social event"*. This group had a strong underlying feeling of gratitude to the mothers.

One interviewee speculated about the way a family could use the observation time. Having wondered what it meant to the non-religious father that the mother visited the priest at the time of the observation, she felt, *"it just made me realize how much gets enacted in front of the observer on all sorts of different levels"*.

Thoughts about families

This topic received a markedly different degrees of attention from the various groups: the Institute group showed very little interest in it, and the AFC group, although more overtly interested, did not have much to say about it; the BAP group spoke at length about it; and the Tavistock group's interest could be inferred but was not that explicit.

- *The AFC group*

This group, who had been together as a single seminar group, felt that by chance they had had very different families to observe: *"Three very different families. Three very different situations. Just really different, like we represented families in a way."* One said that he felt he now knew more about families, not having been a parent himself. They were aware of how difficult it was to observe the mother–infant dyad in a large family and also spoke about the observation experience being different when either mother or father was there, noticing that the baby behaved differently. They mentioned being able to see the development of relationships within families. One participant spoke of her observation experience with a mother who, she felt, attempted to be *"perfect"*, and yet there were still deficits. This led to the question of what was a *"good-enough"* experience for the baby, what constituted a *"good-enough mother"*. It seemed that the realization of how complex a task parenting is was leading them to be less harshly judgemental in their attitudes.

- *The BAP group*

The BAP group had quite a lot of interest in the families. They felt that seeing the different families highlighted the *"uniqueness of each situation"*. The group thought that the baby's position in the family—regarding birth order—made a difference, and one spoke of the mother of a first baby being *"really lost"* in the experience, contrasting it with the experience of a third. One observer spoke of a sibling as *"murderous"* saying *"she asked me on my first or second visit if I want to kill the baby"*.

The relationship between parents and babies came up frequently. One participant felt she understood the baby and understood his father's ambitions for him better on hearing something of father's history. She explained that mother had told her that father had been adopted and that in her—the mother's—view there is an element in father that makes him very self-sufficient. The observer had seen the father as detached, noting how frequently the father commented on the baby's ability to be self-sufficient, and she now felt she understood why. The fact that it took time to find out these things and appreciate their relevance was emphasized. They spoke of having an *"evolving awareness"* of family dynamics, which was then linked to the question of why some families welcomed observers. Awareness of the impact of the parental past and parental personality on the infant's development was implicit in this. They were conscious of the effect on the baby—and on the observer!—of different sorts of mothers and the *"luck"* of what one gets. One participant who observed a depressed mother spoke of how courageous she felt it was to let someone in under the circumstances. More than one group member spoke of how different the observation experience is according to which adults are there, mentioning tension with intrusive grandparents, resentment of nanny, and especially the difference in parental styles between mother and father. One participant said that her experience of observing is very different when father is there—the father says *"Let's show what we can do now, and he's so much trying to show me the things that happened last week."* She contrasted that with mother's approach, although there was also an agreed view that families tended to make an effort for the visits and so what was seen was not necessarily typical of the rest of the week.

- *The Institute group*

This group made no explicit statements about having been brought into contact with different sorts of families, but by talking about the *"luck"* related to what sort of mother the observer got to observe and the importance of the mother's personality, they were implicitly acknowledging that there are different sorts of families.

One participant spoke about the interesting family dynamics he encountered. The family he was observing were *"strongly Christian, but divorced, not married when the baby was born"*. The mother had a teenage daughter from her previous marriage, who seemed to find both the new baby and the observer difficult to bear. The observer noticed that once the parental couple got married, the daughter then acknowledged his presence. Mother commented on how difficult it had been for her to change her name. The observer was interested in the family dynamic and in the idea of an *"emergent family"*. Close personal experience of the painfulness of this situation will surely have given the observer and the other members of his seminar group a deep internal knowledge of how complex families can be.

- *The Tavistock group*

The Tavistock group were interested in families, saying that the observation experience had given them an opportunity to see different sorts of families, especially those with or without siblings and also the wider family network.

One described somehow not having realized this beforehand: *"I've observed the mother and father and the baby, which is something that I hadn't thought it would be, [pause] that I'd learn from the observation is learning about the broader family dynamics, there is also quite a lot about the grand-*

parents of the baby as well, and I think that is quite an important aspect to doing an observation, in terms of then going on to possibly train as a therapist, learning about that side of the effect that the baby has on the whole family."

The idea that mother and baby act as a system with one influencing the other was also raised. One participant said: *"Mother is now managing to relate to her* [the baby] *better, so they're both managing better, and I think probably because the baby has come through that difficult stage, that has helped the mother."*

This inter-relatedness is also addressed when looking at their thoughts about infants. There was considerable sympathy and respect within the group for mothers. The particular loneliness of mothers who are away from their native land and families was picked up on as a theme.

Interest in babies and how they develop

In line with predictions that one might have made about people engaged on courses where they are, or might be, training to be adult therapists having less interest in babies than those offered as pre-clinical experiences for a training in child psychotherapy, the Institute and BAP groups had very little to say about babies, with the Tavistock group being clearly very enthusiastic on this topic. The BAP group's emphasis on the external world impinging on the baby rather than thinking about the baby's internal world may also show a difference in emphasis influenced by the seminar leader. Certainly the BAP Child Training views itself as being heavily influenced by Winnicott, with his ideas about impingement—ideas that both the AFC and Tavistock child psychotherapy trainings would be interested in, but would not privilege over internal world ideas, however they were expressed.

- *The AFC group*

The AFC group were observing only for an academic year and were due to be stopping soon after the interview, with their observed babies aged approximately seven months. They expressed their regret at stopping, mourning the loss of the opportunity to see continuing development. Watching development was described as *"exciting"*, *"you see the differences and changes and now he's starting to be like a little person"*. One felt that the baby's relationship with the mother was changing all the time, *"in a month's time it'll all be a totally different experience"*, and they referred to having ideas about how the baby was going to grow up, with many hypotheses about the future.

One described in detail an experience she had had of watching the baby sleep and cry in her sleep. She understood this as watching the baby dreaming. Apart from this there was little reference to ideas about the internal world of infants.

- *The BAP group*

This group spoke mainly about babies in terms of the impact on the baby of those around them. One commented that the observation had been *"more about baby and mother, baby and father, than just baby"*. Development was referred to, but the emphasis was on the baby being impacted on by the adults. As discussed before, the story of the adopted father and how his emphasis on self-sufficiency led him to seeing and valuing this quality in the baby raises the issue of the influence of parental personality on infant development. They also saw the baby behave differently with different parents and other carers, but they did not speak at all about what the babies brought to these relationships.

- *The Institute group*

The Institute group had very little to say about this. As can be seen in the section on the seminar, they were very aware of the way that their seminars focused on mother–infant interaction, or possibly on mothers, and not on the infants as much as their previous observations had done. One group member was very dissatisfied about this, but the other two were satisfied with it as a useful experience in a different way—and, they thought, one more directly relevant to analytic work with adults. In talking about the seminars, one member said that there was an emphasis on *"developmental pathways"* and not on pathologizing mothers, but this remark was not elaborated on.

- *The Tavistock group*

The Tavistock group was the group most interested in babies and their development. They gave a substantial amount of the interview time to thinking about this. As other groups did, they spoke about the impact on babies of carers and others in the babies' external worlds, but they also thought in terms of the baby's experience and internal qualities. In fact one said that she felt that she had learned that *"babies are born with personalities and that they are all different"*. Infants' resilience was referred to, as well as the idea of a baby *"helping" "teaching both her parents almost what she wants and what she needs"*. One participant spoke of feeling that the baby *"contained"* her parents, and there was a lovely brief description of a baby who could be easily comforted and seemed to *"forgive . . . quickly"*.

The group also thought about the impact on the baby of life experiences. In one observation experience *"immediately after that newborn was born his older brother, who was eighteen months, had a seizure and had to spend several days in the hospital. And during this first observation the mother was depressed and very preoccupied with the older boy and didn't seem to be aware at all of this little baby, she didn't really connect with him, and the next week the newborn was very ill and had to be hospitalized for several days."*

The impact on the new baby of a depressed and shocked mother seems probably to have resulted in his own propensity to illness. The observer went on to say that subsequently *"the mother was very depressed during the first few months of the observation, and it was really interesting to see the effect this had on the baby and also his older brother. And the baby ended up being very placid and quiet, and I never heard him cry for the first few months, never, and I was very concerned, and I wondered if maybe he was so identified with the mother who was very quiet and withdrawn."*

One participant said that he had become very aware *"that how babies are treated largely depends on adults who take care of them, of who happens to be around . . . and I suppose what the observation has taught me is looking at the individual child and their agenda, needs and interests and what happens when these are overridden, how they manage those feelings."*

Here we see both the impact on the infant and what is done with the feelings. One observer commented on how different the baby is when he is with various others: *"This brother has had a big effect on this infant's life. Whenever the brother is in the room, the infant is quiet and withdrawn, and when the brother leaves the room, the infant expresses his personality. And it's just been fascinating to see the two sides of this personality."*

She went on to say *"how different the infant is when the father is there and when the childminder is there, so I guess I'm just amazed at all these different parts of this infant's personality"*. This observer wondered what kind of relationships the baby would have in the future. Future development was referred to when she said, *"I'm looking forward to seeing how this little baby develops into a toddler"*.

The use of the seminar

It should be noted here that the AFC and BAP groups had both been together as a group in their seminars throughout the year, whereas the Institute and Tavistock participants had been in different infant observation seminars and had come together for the purpose of the research. Both the AFC and Institute groups spent much time thinking about the importance of the seminar, while the other two addressed it, but far from centrally. It may be that this was a result of the individual members' experiences—as one Institute group member had found his seminar leader very harshly judgemental—but it may also be of significance that at the time of conducting the research I had no connections with either the AFC or the Institute, while I was involved with both the BAP and the Tavistock, and this might have inhibited those respondents from commenting more on their experiences of the seminar.

I have included comments about the experience of writing up notes of the observation visits, and, where relevant, of writing a paper on the experience, within this section on the seminar, as they can all be thought about under the broader heading of thinking about the experience and processing it in a disciplined way.

- *The AFC group*

The seminar was very important to this group in a number of ways. They spoke of both trying to remember things point by point and the discussion of it in the seminar as helping them to recognize what they had left out and so recognize certain defences in themselves. They mentioned the group confronting them with what they were not seeing—*"every time I do a presentation, it confronts me with what really went on"*—as well as helping them analyse why they had reacted as they did. One spoke of the seminar helping her to see that she was not being natural with her observed mother, acting as if she were more ignorant of babies than she was.

The seminar leader was obviously very important, but the group itself was also seen as having a value. One said that they *"slightly defended each other"* within the seminar group, and they spoke about unconsciously taking up different roles in identification with family members. However, the group member who had been first to find a baby also spoke of how hard this had been at the beginning: *"I was the first to go, and at the start, before the group had really formed, I found it provoked so much anxiety in me because there were issues that I didn't feel that I wanted to talk about in front of the group. . . . It might be different to go to an analyst on your own with that."*

The other group members recognized this, also acknowledging that they had not appreciated the strains of observing until doing it themselves: *"At the beginning . . . I felt so clever because I had all these answers about the mother and the infant . . . it's a totally different thing when you do it yourself."*

This observer also emphasized how valuable she had found the experience of making "mistakes", such as being half an hour late, and learning to think about why. They admired their seminar leader, feeling that the group had been *"well managed"*. They suggested that they had been a difficult group at first, turning up late and missing times, but that over time they had learned what in the observation situation had led them to behave in this way. The seminar leader's emphasis on *"conjectures"*, *"not saying that something is necessarily what is happening"* had also taken some adjusting to for one member.

- *The BAP group*

This group never mentioned their seminar leader, but they did think about the group as being a place where they compared their observed babies and observed families with others. They described feeling protective about their babies in this arena, and one said that they were like a group of mothers concerned with their children's progress, but she added that they also compared the *"mothers' progress"*. One said that she had felt concerned that others had seen things she had not, such as breast-feeding or bathing, but in comparing her observed mother's behaviour with that described by others, she felt proud of her.

The writing-up of the notes was commented on by this group. There was a feeling that negative things are given more attention: *"The things you do remember and write down are the not positive things, the positive things you don't really write them down. You take them as a matter of course."* Others agreed with this, referring to the *"prodigal son"*.

- *The Institute group*

This group had a lot to say about the seminar group experience. Although one member had had a very difficult time—a *"nightmare experience"*—because of his seminar leader's reaction to his failure to find a baby, other group members had seen it as a helpful experience. The seminar leader had helped one learn how to be *"natural"* with the family. One described the seminar discussion about his *"wiped-out"* feelings as *"very good"* and *"detoxifying"*. He also saw the seminars as a place when *"you can grasp something, or where things seem to fit together"*.

Perhaps because they had all had previous experience of infant observation seminars, this group were very aware of the influence of the seminar leader: *"The quality of the seminar leader decides the quality of the experience."* They saw the seminar leader as *"directing the themes"*, influencing what they *"look at, and focus on, what they notice"*. There was agreement that the Institute seminar leaders picked up different things than they had previously experienced, with less emphasis on the baby. One described this as the baby being *"completely neglected. There's emphasis on the mother, the mother–observer, but the baby is put aside."* Others put it less strongly, stating that there was *"more looking at the mother, thinking about it in the context of seeing patients, what patients mean when they say this or that."*

This group were acutely aware of how the seminars were being used to evaluate them. The infant observation seminars are held before candidates begin with training patients, and so *"it's the Institute's only way of seeing how you might be with somebody in a way the other seminars don't"*.

Another group member agreed with this, saying: *"I feel we're being encouraged to speak with our unconscious, be deep with our unconscious. . . . I think they are wanting to see what you're going to make of the first patient."*

In contrasting earlier and current observation seminar experiences, it was agreed that they valued the seminars being smaller.

They had previously been in seminars with six members and currently had only three; as a result they felt that presentations could be more detailed, which was much appreciated.

- *The Tavistock group*

With one notable exception, the Tavistock group gave very little attention to the seminars as separate from other aspects of the experience. It was implied when they spoke about seeing different types of families and babies, and with the *"non-smiley"* baby, where the observer had felt uncomfortable about having a different experience from others in her seminar group.

The Chinese observer felt that her seminar group had helped her to see how important she was to the observed mother, because the mother's family were far away, and that it had also made her think about cultural issues: *"When I was in Taiwan, I never thought about cultural differences that clearly, and since I was here, because I have to . . . sometimes I take it for granted . . . but my colleagues will point it out."*

Differences between the groups

It may be useful to remember that there were five participants in both the BAP and Tavistock groups (one participant, the one from M16, in the original Tavistock interview, had not been able to attend the second interview) and only three each in the AFC and Institute groups. As acknowledged in chapter 2, obviously group dynamics play a part in any group interview, and when one member responds in a certain way, the others "run with" the theme introduced, whether agreeing and expanding on it or disagreeing. The individual composition of the groups certainly led to the emphasis in the Institute group on the assessment nature of the seminar, although as experienced professionals, possibly themselves teaching on other trainings, they would have had more awareness of this than the members of the other groups.

Themes not common to all groups

Differences in external circumstances led to some issues being high-lighted, with the Institute group comparing previous observation experiences and the AFC group contrasting some aspects of infant observation with their nursery and toddler observations. The AFC group was dominated by the fact that their observations were soon coming to an end. The length of time of the observation was men-tioned by the other groups, but in a far less significant way.

The Tavistock group was the only one to think about cultural issues. Although this may be because there was one Chinese member in the group who brought this up and so led the others into thinking about how they had also seen aspects of this in their observations—the Tavistock group commented on religion, distance from family, different expectations about, for instance, when to give an injection—all the other interviewed groups had members who clearly had come from other countries, presumably with other cultures, and yet this was not brought up as an issue.

The Tavistock and Institute groups both commented on the links between infant observation and psychoanalytic theory. The Institute group expressed satisfaction felt when seeing theories *"in action"*: *"actually you can grasp something . . . and that's very gratifying"*. The Tavistock group felt that the observations brought alive theory they had been studying and expected that studying different theory would lead to seeing other aspects of the infants, wondering *"what shifts our perspectives on what we've seen in relation to what we are learning at the time"*. Neither the AFC or BAP groups made any reference at all to theory.

The Tavistock group also spoke of how doing infant observation led them to look for and see the infantile in their current client population, whether it was autistic children or acting-out adolescents. They also spoke of how they had become more attuned to the visual, the non-verbal. One said: *"As a teacher, I now pay attention to the way a student walks across the room, which I had never thought about in fifteen years."* This was not mentioned by any of the others, although both the AFC and the Institute groups linked the experience with that of working with patients.

With the exception of the Institute group, all spoke of the expe-rience of identifying with different family members, although it was not really substantially taken up by any of them other than the AFC.

Evaluation of the significance of differences

As stated before, had each group had different individual members within it—although still members of that same training institution—inevitably the topics discussed and the issues raised would have been different. Nevertheless, it seems to me that certain differences could be thought of as being validly between the various trainings and not just a matter of the participants who made up the separate groups.

The point made by the Institute group about there being less emphasis in the seminars on the baby and more on mother–baby interaction seems validated by the transcripts, which show them as having very little to say about infants, in marked contrast to the Tavistock group, who were very involved with that topic. It also seems to confirm something that was commented on in a discussion in 2001 by the senior staff child psychotherapists at the Tavistock Clinic, when they described noticing this different emphasis in papers written by adult analysts in the *International Journal of Infant Observation*. This might seem to confirm a hypothesis I raised on setting out on this research: namely, that those involved in psychotherapeutic work with adults might value less one of the outcomes of infant observation experience—that is, greater familiarity with infant and young child development—than do those who are involved in work with children. People on the Tavistock Observation Course, with a psychotherapy training in mind, would be very likely to intend to train as child psychotherapists and would probably be currently involved in some sort of work with children. This, together with the fact that their seminar leaders were likely to be overwhelmingly—although not exclusively—child psychotherapists might account for this group's enthusiasm for thinking about the child.

All groups showed an awareness of feelings, although some participants gave examples that evidenced this more vividly than others. In many ways the Institute group did this the least. This may be a result of the discussion being skewed elsewhere, although perhaps it is also accounted for by this being their second observation experience and possibly therefore lacking some of the raw impact of the first. Certainly the AFC group had most to say about reflecting on those feelings. I wonder if the Tavistock experience of teaching a large number of students, many of whom are not in analysis and many of whom do not intend to go on to clinical training, inhibits the seminar leaders from confronting the students in the way the AFC seminar leader was described as doing. Obviously the personality and capacities of the seminar leader will be very influential here.

Summary

In chapter 4 we saw those involved in thinking and writing about infant observation claim a vast number of positive benefits. The transcripts of these interviews show that some of those skills and capacities are overtly evidenced, while others are implied and can be inferred from close examination of the texts. The following chapters detail how the ideas looked at in depth in this chapter can "map" onto the capacities previously cited.

CHAPTER NINE

Comparing the results
of the initial and end interviews

Issues for consideration

There are some issues that it is important to address before looking closely at these areas. Students interviewed before they had had much experience of carrying out observations had little or no "real" experience to talk about. Apart from the Institute group, who referred to their previous observation experience—for some as long as 10 years earlier—they could only talk about what they anticipated, what they had been told in seminars or had read or imagined. The rather glib quality and lack of emotionality of the early interviews could be understood as inevitable without the lived experience in which to root ideas. However, we could also argue that the infant observation experience enables participants to be more in touch with their emotional experiences.

Once observers had begun—and as interviews were conducted towards the end of the first term of observation seminars, many had at least begun the experience—and speak of what they have experienced, there is a very different quality to their responses. The Tavistock interviewee who speaks in the initial interview about her experience of visiting a mother and baby *"cocooned"* in the warmth on a cold night and her feelings of isolation is exhibiting many of the features of awareness of feelings and processing of them, thinking and reflecting on the experience, that are on the whole absent in the initial interviews.

What this study is unable to show is how quickly a student might gain those capacities once she has begun observing. In this instance, the interviewee could not have had much observation experience. Do some students need longer than this, with only the most talented "getting it" so quickly? My experience as a teacher of infant observation would seem to confirm that, but a Norwegian study (Abrahamsen & Morkeseth, 1998) of a brief observation experience suggests that benefits emerge within the first three months. Although some of the "realizations" could only be gained from longer exposure to a growing child, can some of the central capacities be gained from a briefer observation period? It was not possible to address this in this study, but future research—perhaps meeting with students at three-monthly intervals throughout their observation experience—could try to examine the growth of such capacities.

When considering how frequently ideas emerged, we also need to be aware of the disparity between the sizes of the groups interviewed. Two of the groups—the AFC and the Institute—had three members, the others five and six, respectively. As an episode or reference counted as one each time a concept was raised, but not as more than a single episode when it was expanded upon by the same speaker within that conversational paragraph, more respondents in a group might well lead to more references being noted. Similarly, as stated when comparing the responses of each group at the post-observation interviews, such small numbers mean that a group can be strongly influenced by a single member with a particular "agenda" in mind.

Table 9.1 shows how frequently each concept was mentioned by each group in both the pre- and post-observation interviews. We see, for example, that the BAP group did not mention being aware of their feelings as being important in the initial interviews, but they mentioned it 22 times in the post-observation interview; the other groups showed similar, although less dramatic, increases. All categories to do with feelings and thinking about the usefulness of them, awareness of self in relation to others, and the importance of maintaining boundaries increased substantially, as did the idea of using theory to help understanding. However, others related to "realization" or knowledge of children and their relationships, the interplay between the internal and external, and other aspects cited in the literature about the gains infant observation brings did not evidence much increase and sometimes none at all. Surprisingly, there was little evidence of an increase in interest in the idea of not understanding prematurely, letting the pattern evolve over time, and I later speculate on why this might be so. However, certain issues are talked about much more frequently, which indicates considerable changes in the participants.

Results

1.   Awareness of feelings

The BAP group did not have much idea of this in the initial interviews. They spoke of the *"objective observer"*, and anxiety was the only feeling mentioned. Although the other groups mentioned anxiety, the awareness of emotions was shown in other ways. The AFC group spoke of feeling *"on the spot"* when presenting their observations and spoke of the conflict that the mother has to go through *"generating feelings, protective feelings"*. Here we see a hint at projection, with perhaps an awareness that the protective feelings might come from some other part of the observer's self. The Institute group, with their previous experience, spoke of being in touch with primitive states of mind. The rather removed quality of this statement is not so evident in another statement, that *"the experience of being with an infant makes you feel a lot of powerful feelings"*. They also commented that the non-interventionist approach of the observer stance allows the observer to *"step back and be in touch with what you're feeling"*. One of the Tavistock group commented on *"so many emotions, feelings involved in the process"* and in the example cited of the *"cocoon"*, we see an interviewee acutely aware of her feelings and having an idea about why it might be so.

None of the pre-observation groups mentioned this aspect more than a few times. In the post-observation interviews the registering of feelings and ideas about picking up projections were massively increased. Although the BAP group (with 22 references altogether) still spoke a great deal about anxiety, and the Institute group (8 references altogether) also emphasized anxiety in terms of finding the baby, the groups all showed much more emphasis on this category. However, it must be noted that, of course, individual responses were variable. There were times when feelings were not spoken of when I would have expected them to be—for example, when an AFC member described her experience of watching a mother avoid feeding her underweight baby as *"interesting"*, or an Institute candidate described the mother's reaction to the observer not holding the baby, but did not mention her own feelings.

2. Tolerating and staying with feelings

The Institute group mentioned this 4 times in their pre-observation interviews, talking of staying with the experience and struggling with it at two separate times. They also spoke of the anxiety stirred up by watching what is going on and spoke particularly vividly of the unbearable feelings, close to a psychotic experience, stirred up by hearing a baby crying. The AFC group also had expectations about this, twice mentioning painful feelings and that they expected it would stir up feelings in them when seeing something they felt to be wrong. The Tavistock group had one member who anticipated *"struggling, noticing what's going on inside"*, while the BAP group did not explicitly mention this.

In the post-observation interviews again the emphasis on this aspect had increased. The Institute group mentioned it only 5 times, one of which was saying that anxiety was less than it had been the first time, but all the other groups mentioned it significantly more often. One Tavistock member spoke of some difficult months and the feeling that mother, baby, *and* observer had come out the *"other side"* of something painful. However, as commented on in the section on post-observation interviews, occasionally there was avoidance of recognizing some feelings, as with the BAP student who could not allow herself to feel the pain of the baby's experience or stay with her fury— possibly a projection of the baby's rage—with the mother who fed her baby with a propped-up bottle.

Table 9.1. Frequency of the incidence of comments relating to relevant capacities and skills

	Pre-observation				Post-observation			
	AFC	BAP	Inst	Tav	AFC	BAP	Inst	Tav
register feelings, pick up projections	2	—	2	2	13	22	8	10
tolerate feelings, hold onto painful feelings	3	—	4	1	7	8	5	4
recognize usefulness of own feelings as information	—	—	—	—	4	—	—	2
process, think about what is happening inside oneself	3	—	2	2	12	13	4	6
think, reflect	—	2	—	3	9	8	6	10
willingness not to understand prematurely, capacity to wait, let pattern evolve over time	—	—	2	1	1	2	1	2
use of theory to help understanding	—	—	—	—	7	2	6	2
awareness of what not noticed	2	—	1	2	5	1	—	—
awareness of self in relation to others	2	2	2	2	6	15	7	8
awareness importance of maintaining boundaries	2	2	3	1	4	11	6	1
hold back on reactions, avoid acting-out responses	2	1	3	1	1	—	1	1

awareness of so much to notice	2	1	2	2	3	—	—
close attention, including the importance of remembering	—	—	—	1	2	—	—
the achievement of multiple perspectives	3	—	3	4	1	1	—
"knowledge":							
a. better knowledge of child development	2	—	—	1	1	—	1
b. understanding children & early development, awareness of non-verbal & infantile communication	—	—	—	1	3	—	2
c. seeing relationships grow	7	-	8	1	6	2	5
d. uniqueness of mother baby couple	4	3	3	2	1	2	2
e. awareness of other cultures	3	—	—	—	1	—	—
f. noticing of difference to avoid "normalizing"	2	—	1	1	—	—	—
g. better awareness of children's (& adults') emotional needs	2	—	—	1	—	1	—
h. seeing development & resilience	2	—	2	—	—	—	—
i. interplay between internal & external	1	—	2	—	—	1	2

3.   Processing of feelings

Apart from the BAP group, who did not anticipate this, the other groups all spoke of it in the initial interviews. One member of the Tavistock group spoke of it as a good way of understanding oneself but did not say how; another member spoke of *"noticing what's going on inside and questioning whether it means anything, whether it's legitimate"*. The AFC group thought that they would see how their own minds operated and expected to *"get some things about myself"*. The Institute group spoke of the experience of hearing the baby cry, again a "real" current experience, and the way this led the observer to think of his experience on acute psychiatric wards. They also mentioned the importance of being in analysis and the help of the seminar group in processing feelings. Although the word "process" was mentioned, no examples that give evidence of doing such things were provided.

In the post-observation interviews there was both more mention of processing and examples that showed such an experience taking place. This was less evident in the Institute group, perhaps because of their previous experience. They only made 4 references to it, while the AFC and BAP mentioned it 12 and 13 times, respectively. The BAP group is particularly remarkable, as at the beginning they had given no evidence of being interested in thinking about where feelings came from. The Tavistock group only made 6 references to it, but the examples were very rich, including, for example, the Chinese observer trying to sort out why she felt like crying in the presence of the crying baby. This increase in the observers' interest in and capacity for trying to process their feelings is a remarkable change.

4.   Reflecting on and thinking about experience

Neither the Institute nor the AFC group mentioned this in the pre-observation interviews. The BAP group thought that they would be seeing something and reflecting on it once it was over. One also said that she had been thinking about her experiences when a baby and asking her own mother about this. The Tavistock group spoke of discussion in the group, together with writing down, helping them to see things that had not been seen before.

Mention of this was much increased in the post-observation interviews. The AFC and Institute groups spoke of it 9 and 6 times, respectively, with the Institute group thinking about how different seminar leaders drew out aspects according to their interests and experiences. Although both the BAP and Tavistock groups had mentioned this in their pre-observation interviews, the frequency (BAP 8, Tavistock 10 times) was significantly increased. Some group members seemed able to process their feelings almost simultaneously with having them, while the examples given by others showed that there was often quite a time lapse between the experience and the ability to begin to sort it out.

5. Waiting for meaning to emerge and tolerating not understanding

In the initial interviews neither the AFC group nor the BAP group mentioned this. One member of the Tavistock group suggested that *"looking back in six months' time, and thinking 'this is how I felt then', it's clearer to see this, this, and this in the baby and to have that experience of looking back and seeing what's particularly meaningful and what's not."* The Institute group, perhaps because of their previous experience or greater level of sophistication, mentioned it twice, once in terms of allowing room for the picture to develop, and the other in terms of the need to be comfortable with *"not knowing, not being an expert"*.

Although there was an increase of interest in this aspect, there was in fact less than I would have anticipated, given the way that writers and practitioners have emphasized it as a feature of infant observation. As we have seen, it directly maps on to the capacity to wait for meaning to emerge within a session and within the course of psychoanalytic psychotherapy. The Institute group mentioned it once in the post-observation interviews, saying *"you can't capture the meaning in an acute moment"*, and the AFC group spoke of looking back and seeing what was significant, saying that the experience of not knowing was *"difficult but important"*. The Tavistock group spoke of it twice, commenting that *"it takes time to pull it together"*. The BAP group said that the development of an observation takes time and gave an example of how the observer's understanding of ways of relating within a family had emerged over time.

I wonder why this aspect of waiting for meaning to emerge was not privileged as a feature of the discussion. It seems to me possible that the observers, through their seminars, had learnt to do this in such a way that they were not consciously aware of doing so. However, the transcripts of the interviews do not actually give evidence of that in the way that more detailed discussion of observation material, especially consecutively over a number of weeks, would.

6.   Use of theory to aid understanding

None of the groups talked of this in advance, while all evidenced it, without putting it in those terms, in the post-observation interviews. The BAP and Tavistock groups only referred to it twice each, while the AFC and Institute groups showed it 7 and 6 times, respectively. The Institute group referred, *inter alia*, to a paper on the experience of male observers, which some of them had found helpful, while the AFC group used psychoanalytic understanding in describing why a parent had behaved as she did. They also clearly used theory to help them understand themselves.

7.   Awareness of the usefulness of feelings

Significantly, none of the group mentioned this in the pre-observation interviews, and yet it featured importantly for both the Tavistock and AFC groups afterwards. The AFC group were explicit about how they saw this, while the Tavistock group were not explicit but gave vivid examples, which have been cited above, as to how the observer's feelings of depression led him to retrospectively question whether depression had been projected into him from a mother who appeared lively, perhaps manic, or from her baby. The example of the observer who intuited that the baby had been weaned from her own feelings of *"being wiped out, made nothing"* with a series of cancelled appointments also clearly evidences the participant finding her own feelings a useful source of information.

I wonder why this was not shown in either the BAP or the Institute groups. It seems unlikely that they did not have this experience, but perhaps it was not something that was drawn out for them by their seminar leaders. The BAP participant who could not allow herself to recognize her feelings on seeing the baby with the propped-up bottle could not then recognize those feelings as a useful source of information. Other BAP members *did* recognize their feelings—e.g. being depressed after being with a depressed mother, anxious when grandparents were there—but did not overtly make the next step—to wonder what this might have taught them. The Institute group clearly understood this concept theoretically, but they seemed to be concentrating more on the feelings of the observed than looking at their own feelings in the experience.

8.   Awareness of failure to notice

Only the BAP group did not have this in mind in the initial interviews. The AFC group twice mentioned that through their write-ups they became aware of what they had not noticed. The Tavistock group spoke of the seminar showing them what they had not noticed, while they also commented on how their selves were inevitably in what they were seeing. One member of the Institute group spoke of the *"inadequacy of professional notes compared with what we're seeing"*, which rather privileges the problems of *describing* what is seen over the problems around seeing.

Neither the Institute group nor the Tavistock group mentioned this afterwards. The BAP group mentioned it once, but the AFC group were preoccupied with it, mentioning it 5 times. While this group were very aware of this as an issue and openly discussed how difficult it had been at times to realize how much they had missed, this was a group that emphasized the usefulness of learning from mistakes. Perhaps they were better able to be aware of what they had missed in a climate that overtly valued "failure" as an opportunity for learning. It is possible that the emphasis it received in the initial interviews arose from the participants' feelings of being overwhelmed by so much at the beginning of the experience and that they had in fact acclimatized and become much more comfortable with the task over time.

9.   *Awareness of the impact of the observer on the family*

Not surprisingly, all the groups had thought about this to some extent in the initial interviews. The AFC group had mentioned it in terms of the observer "position" and needing to accept that one was not at the centre. The BAP group thought that the mothers would have fantasies of what they would be like or do as observers. They also thought that it would be *"safe"* to be *"non-reactive"* to a baby, but that this would not be right later. The Institute group had mixed feelings, welcoming the lack of clinical responsibility in the task but also regretting that there was *"no structure, no authority"* in the observer position. One member spoke of his supervisor encouraging him to be more *"human"* and *"generous"* in his responses, learning to be himself more. One Tavistock participant wondered if the mother who let a stranger in might feel herself judged. One saw it as an opportunity to *"meddle and not ruin anything"*. Another spoke very sensitively about the process of remaining detached and observing, *"but also in a way that will not make the mother feel like she's so conscious. I'm trying very hard to find a family between—really watching and noticing everything but also being natural and melting into the environment in a way that the mother is comfortable and she's herself and I see a relatively realistic picture of what the relationship and home-life is like."*

The issue of how to be an observer and how to relate within the family assumed increased importance in the post-observation interviews: it was mentioned 15 times by the BAP group, and 8, 7, and 6 times by each of the others. Their real and current experiences that are very much in mind at the time of the second interviews could account for this. We also have the likelihood that the experience of carrying out the observation has made the participants very mindful of this aspect. One BAP participant expressed the idea that her preconceptions of what an observation would be like and the way she behaved with the first mother influenced that mother's way of behaving with the infant and to her. When the observer shifted her expectations, a second mother behaved differently.

10. *The importance of boundaries*

All the groups had anticipated or had early experience of the way the keeping of boundaries would be an issue in the observation experience. They all expressed thoughts about not expecting to interact, with the BAP group being particularly concerned about that. The Tavistock group expressed concerns that it might be hard not to get involved because of the mother's needs, while the AFC group spoke of *"going into someone's universe"*. The Institute group described themselves as *"not there to do anything"*.

In the post-observation interviews the Tavistock group were least concerned with this, mentioning it only once, with the AFC, BAP, and Institute groups referring to it 4, 11, and 6 times, respectively. The BAP group was clearly very much concerned about how they interacted with the mothers and the infants as they got older. The AFC and Institute groups also gave examples of babies approaching them or the issue of feeing that the mother did—or, in one case, did not—want them to hold the baby. The Institute group also paralleled the withholding of information as an observer with the opaque manner of the analyst. We might view this increase in discussion of the issue as arising from their direct experience.

11. Holding back and avoiding showing reactions

All the groups had anticipated this as an issue. The BAP group imagined that as observers they would be able to think and apply concepts because they were not directly involved. The Institute group saw the value in not intervening in a number of ways: they described it as allowing the experience to develop to its fullest extent. They also felt that *"not jumping to intervene"* was good discipline for them, and they spoke of the *"struggle to first contain feelings within oneself"*. The AFC group suggested that they would have to learn to hold back whatever reactions they were having, and one member of the Tavistock group said that he felt there was always a struggle and a tension in the experience of being in the relationship and "out" of it and thinking.

Interestingly this particular aspect of holding oneself back, as separate from other aspects of the observer stance, was not referred to by the BAP group in the post-observation interview and was only mentioned in passing by one member of the Institute group when he spoke of his fury on finding that his much-waited-for observed family were now planning an extended holiday. He spoke of his rage: *"She ruined something for me, . . . I really was struggling to keep it inside, not to do this in the moment, regain myself, but in the first moment that was kind of difficult."*

The Institute group were aware of not being able to offer anything interpretive, but it is interesting that they could not see themselves as offering anything else useful. Bearing in mind the increased emphasis on the interactional nature of psychoanalytic psychotherapy and the valuing of much that is helpful in the experience apart from interpretations, this seems a somewhat narrow view. The AFC group also referred to it in terms of finding that they had acted out, while one member of the Tavistock group spoke at some length of how hard she had found it to watch the mother mismatch a toddler's approaches and how in the end she had tickled him. One member of the AFC group also thought that despite doing nothing, they had offered something useful to the family and this idea was also expressed by one of the Tavistock group.

Again we see that few of the participants seem to be that consciously aware of this issue after the observations, although it had seemed problematic to them before.

12. Awareness of much to notice

Only the Tavistock group commented on this in the initial interviews, and that remark came from someone who had done her first observation visit and spoke of *"information overload"*. All the groups referred to it, although each with only one or two references, in the post-observation interviews.

13. Attention to detail

Interestingly, this did not seem to be an important issue for these groups, either in the initial or in the post-observation interviews. The Tavistock group mentioned it in the pre-observation interview, talking of *"looking in incredible detail at tiny, minute responses"*, and at another point mentioning the attempts to remember everything. None of the other groups addressed it at that point, and only the AFC group mentioned it afterwards.

It is interesting to speculate about this, given that infant observation is often said to teach the importance of attention to detail and the capacity to evidence it. Moreover, it is one of the capacities that is also needed for clinical work. There is no reference to it or evidence that it has been achieved within the interviews as conducted. However, I would expect written presentations of the observation hours that the students take to their seminars to give evidence of this attention to detail. Certainly, when marking infant observation portfolios and essays for both the Tavistock and the BAP, I would look for, and generally find, evidence of such attention to detail.

14. Awareness of multiple perspectives

All except the BAP group spoke of this beforehand, with the Institute group saying that they would have to relate to the mother and the infant simultaneously, and one member of the AFC group stating that she expected she would identify more with the mother than the baby. Members of the Tavistock group said something similar. Another AFC group member spoke of *"experiencing someone's universe from inside out"*. The idea of perhaps being able to better understand and empathize with others as a result of the observation experience was stated.

In the post-observation interviews only the Institute group did not refer again to this idea, and in fact the Institute group spoke very explicitly about how they felt they had been encouraged to privilege looking at the mother and her relationship with the observer over looking at the baby alone. This idea, examined more closely in the section on the end interviews, did not encourage shifts of perspective. The shifting of identification with mother or baby, or with other family members, was discussed twice by the AFC group; they also felt that in the seminar group they had taken up identifications with different family members. The Tavistock group mentioned their shifting identifications; the BAP group also spoke of this, wondering whether the task should be called infant observation or mother–infant observation. They also spoke of siblings and how the observer could identify with both the sibling and the baby—something we also saw in the Tavistock group. One member of the Tavistock group expressed an awareness of how the baby can be different when he is with different family members, and the same idea was noted by members of the BAP group.

15. "Knowledge"

Writings about infant observation emphasize aspects expected to be gained that could be grouped together under the heading of "realizations". (As described in chapter 5, I am calling this "knowledge".) This includes understanding children and early stages of development, seeing the way relationships grow, together with knowing something about the uniqueness of the mother–baby couple and seeing the interplay between internal and external. One aspect cited, that of achieving multiple perspectives, has been addressed above. Interestingly, some of the more overtly didactic aspects were more in evidence in the initial interviews than in the post-observation ones. Perhaps at that early stage, with little experience behind them, the participants could only think of the less personal gains that the experience might bring them. For three of the four groups infant observation was taking place in the context of an academically validated course, and so they might have expected at that stage that the didactic aspects would be privileged. Once the participants have engaged in the experience, these aspects fade into the background, and an emphasis on feeling and paying attention to feelings emerges.

a. Child development

All the groups except the Institute group stated that they thought that they would have a better knowledge of child development and understand more about children and early stages of development, with the Tavistock group mentioning this 3 times and the BAP group twice. However, the AFC were the only group to refer to it overtly in the post-observation interviews. It is likely that the discussions in the regular seminars would have shown evidence of this in a way that the post-observation interviews did not.

b. The non-verbal and infantile communication

Similarly, the Tavistock group spoke twice in the initial interviews about awareness of the non-verbal and of infantile communication. None mentioned it overtly in the post-observation interviews, but when two Tavistock participants spoke of the influence of infant observation, they cited noticing more how people move.

c. Relationships

From the literature and in discussion with the community of practitioners, seeing the way relationships grow had been privileged. This encompassed the child's relationships with both parents, with siblings, and with the extended family, as well as the observer's relationship to the family. All the groups had some thoughts about this in the pre-observation interviews, with the Tavistock and BAP groups mentioning it most often. It was spoken of especially by the BAP group in their post-observation interview and was of interest to the Tavistock group especially in terms of siblings. The others did not overtly address it, except in references to the baby's approach to the observer, but different implications were drawn out of those examples.

d. Uniqueness of the mother–baby dyad

It was suggested that infant observation would make the observer more aware of the uniqueness of the mother–baby dyad, especially through the opportunity to hear about different babies within the seminars. The Institute group implied this in their pre-observation interview, with the emphasis on the *"luck"* of finding a helpful, non-pathological mother. We must remember that this was the second observation experience for all of them, and they were able to compare their current experiences with previous ones. None of the other groups showed awareness of this in the pre-observation interviews, but it was again a feature of the post-observation interview for the Institute group, and also for the AFC and BAP groups. These groups had both been together for their infant observation seminars throughout the year, and they spoke of how different the babies within the seminar group had been. Only one member of the Tavistock group overtly compared her experience with that of others in her group—noting that hers had been the only non-smiley baby—but the Tavistock group had an interest in cultural aspects that was absent in the other groups.

e. Awareness of other cultures

It had been suggested in chapter 5 that infant observation would give practitioners an awareness of other cultures, but this was not mentioned by any of the groups except the Tavistock, who had thought vaguely about it in the pre-observation interview—talking about a micro- or macro approach—and who concentrated on it substantially in the post-observation interview.

f.   Avoidance of normalizing

It was also suggested that by noting the difference between their observed baby and others discussed in the seminar group, the participants would learn not to "normalize". This idea was not in evidence at all in the pre-observation interviews and was implied only at one point in the post-observation interviews within the BAP discussion, and not by any of the others. Again it may be that this would have been evidenced in close discussion of some observational material within a seminar but was not seen in the group discussions.

g.   Awareness of emotional needs

The section on expected gains cited having a greater awareness of children's—and adults'—emotional needs. The BAP and Institute groups both referred to this in their initial interviews, but only the AFC group did so in their post-observation interview, although thinking about infants' internal worlds and their emotional experiences was evident in each "live" example the participants gave when describing something to do with the infant.

h.   Awareness of development and resilience

The idea of the participants finding out about development and resilience was also cited. None of the groups indicated this in their initial interviews, but it was evident in different ways in the post-observation interviews in the AFC, BAP, and Tavistock groups. The BAP group thought about the question of "good-enough" experiences, and the AFC group were aware of how things could and would change after they stopped visiting their babies. The Tavistock group thought about the way a baby helped her "failing" parents and referred to having come through a "rough patch". One participant also spoke of a mother who had refused to continue an observation early on because of how difficult things were, who, when met later, had said that things had improved after eight weeks.

i. Interplay between internal and external

In chapter 5 I also cited the idea that practitioners would see the interplay between the internal and the external. We see some evidence for this in the initial interviews, with one member of the Institute group comparing her first observation with her second and seeing the *"magical"* precious position of a first child in a family as different from the *"part of the family"* experience of the second. The BAP group were similarly interested in the way the child's position in the family could affect the way they grew up, with speculation about why children in the same family turn out differently. In the post-observation interviews the way of thinking about this was more sophisticated. The BAP group thought about the way a father was with his child and the influence of family culture on the child, although they did not specifically link this with whatever innate characteristics the infant brought to the experience, nor with much thought about what the infant did with the experience he had. The Tavistock group showed more expectation of this, describing the infant's way of *"helping"* her parents, as well as giving the example of the infant who became ill following the impact on the mother of an older sibling's illness. The AFC group wondered about a child dreaming, but did not link this with the external world.

* * *

It is noticeable that the Institute group's post-observation interview hardly figures in any of these examples. It may be a feature of the fact that this group had previous experience of observation, so that some of these aspects did not seem comment-worthy to them. However, as one of the participants said, he was aware of how little experience he had *"with children, never mind infants"*, so it seems unlikely that this was the case. It seems more probable that this was partly to do with the way the group discussion concentrated on certain issues to do with the evaluative function of the seminars, because of one participant's experiences, and partly to do with the aspect that the group themselves highlighted: that their seminars had a different focus, less on the infant and more on the mother–observer relationship. It also must be noted that in the other trainings the participants would have been attending lectures on child development during the academic year that could have had an influence on their greater awareness of these things. Infant observation alone might not be responsible for the increase in interest in and appreciation of these dimensions, but certainly seems to have contributed substantially to them.

Additional aspects

The capacities and skills claimed to be promoted by infant observation, as detailed in chapter 5, do not precisely match those developed from the pre- and post-observation interviews using grounded theory. The way that these emerging data differ from the literature is addressed in chapter 11, which discusses how this shows that I was, as any researcher should be, open to finding the unexpected.

Here, in order to see the nuances, it seemed more useful to specify the attributes and then look at ways in which they did and did not match, rather than only re-examining these capacities in their earlier groupings. Some of them, such as the capacity to wait and the ability to tolerate not knowing, becoming aware of one's own states of mind, and the capacity to think about emotions and issues to do with the observer stance were all thoroughly addressed in the analysis above. Other dimensions, such as looking without preconceptions, the awareness of the emotional content of observations, the position of detachment, and the act of being an "other" have not been previously explored. We could, of course, argue that aspects of these have been implied in previous categories, so that thoughts about being an "other" are included in ideas about the observer stance. However, I think that looking at these particular issues separately adds a further element of understanding to our task. A section in chapter 5 links these to clinical work. I shall briefly look at evidence for these in the pre- and post-observation interviews, and Table 9.2 shows the relationship evidenced in diagrammatic form.

• *Looking without preconceptions*

The initial interviews do not address preconceptions as such. The AFC group make it clear that they expect to see things that they will find painful. They also raise the issue of seeing things from their own perspective, as does one Tavistock participant, who suggests that one might miss things—have a *"blind spot"*. Apart from these, the issue did not seem to merit attention.

In the post-observation interviews it was not explicitly mentioned by the Tavistock group, but it was given attention by all the others. The AFC group spoke of their awareness of what they had failed to notice: *"I was completely unaware of why my attention was focusing where it was in the room, it was completely unconscious."* The BAP group also showed sensitivity to this issue, with one member questioning whether she avoided seeing certain things because she wanted to see her observed family as *"the perfect idea of a happy family"*, and others wondering how much their mood affected what they saw. Another participant thought that her preconceptions of how the observation would proceed had influenced the way the mother behaved. One member of the Institute group spoke of being aware of seeing things through his *"own eyes"* but also immediately added that what he saw *"fit the theory beautifully"*.

- *Observing in a particular way, awareness of emotional content*

The literature on observation writes of observing in a particular way, aware of the emotional content. This issue though not addressed directly, could be seen in descriptions of what was seen—nothing was described without an emotional penumbra, and most of the examples given showed the observers' awareness of their feelings about what they saw as well as speculating at times about what the mother or baby felt. Naturally the initial interviews showed much less of this. Although the Institute group indicated it twice, the most outstanding example comes from the Tavistock student talking about a real experience that she has recently had, of feeling excluded from the *"cocoon"* of the mother–baby relationship.

- *Detachment*

Writers on infant observation focus on the idea of detachment, a concept mentioned by Bick (1964) and expanded on by Crick (1997). While some of this is addressed in the issue of the observer stance, it seems worth while to look at it specifically here. The AFC and Institute groups both mention this in their initial interviews, anticipating it as being useful. One member of the Tavistock group questions the idea, perhaps missing the subtleties of the term and viewing it as a

Table 9.2.   Relationship between capacities, skills, and infant observation, including data from interviews

Capacity	Technique	Cited in observation literature	Pre-obs.	Post-obs.
analytic attitude: absence of narcissism	creating a setting; neutral, objective, suspension of judgement	observer stance, find a position in the family; non-judgemental	✓	✓
bearing humbling experience	keeping oneself back	awareness of peripheral role in family	✓	✓+
respect for patient	respect for patient	awareness of struggle & of uniqueness	—	✓
open oneself to the experience of shock	find something new	open oneself to being shocked, disturbed	—	✓
tolerate anxiety & uncertainty	manage strong feelings	manage strong feelings, tolerate anxiety	✓	✓+
wait for meaning to emerge	wait for meaning to emerge	wait for pattern to emerge	✓	✓+
	attitude to patient, hold patient inside self, receive all aspects of patient, reverie	LIMITED: awareness uniqueness should influence attitude to patient; should have increased capacity to bear strong feelings	—	—
empathy	thoughts about how patient uses therapist, avoid acting-out responses	NOT DIRECT, but increased through awareness of countertransference	—	✓
		awareness of projection increased	—	✓
realistic hopefulness		see something shift over time, see infants' resilience, child development knowledge	—	✓
retain apparently contradictory experiences simultaneously	shift between role participant & observer, identify & not with patient, hold different things in mind & oscillate between	shift identification, two-tracked thinking	✓	✓+
close attention	close attention, non-verbal, sensitivity to infantile modes of communication	looking without preconceptions, awareness of non-verbal, tiny body movements, uniqueness each family teaches not to normalize	✓	✓

cognitive abilities	using cognitive skills to organize into patterns	NOT STRONGLY, but some aspects of writing up & presenting	—	✓
	think, evaluate, remember & anticipate	some from recalling, much from thinking about	✓	✓+
	think about what experiencing	think about what experiencing	✓	✓+
	hold onto uncomfortable ideas & feelings, don't grab at understanding	hold onto feelings, hypothesize, realize it takes time for pattern to emerge	—	✓
	create space to think about feelings	create space to think about feelings especially through the seminars	—	✓
	awareness of transference & countertransference	notice own experiences, study self in response to what seeing, disentangle self & other; struggle with language helps with work re infantile transference; from exposure relationships will understand transference & countertransference relationships in clinical work better	✓	✓+
knowledge of theory	theory informs practice	PARTIAL from infant observation but in very alive & unforgettable way	—	✓
	feelings recognized by a reflective part of the mind	feelings recognized by a reflective part of the mind	—	✓
	timing	PARTIAL: learn to hold onto, pain of abstinence; avoid premature interpretations not see whole pattern at once, not grab at understanding	✓	✓
listening & skill in communication	verbal communication: how to talk to the patient, silence, questions, clarifications	LIMITED: language to describe non-verbal, pre-linguistic experiences; think about the penumbra round language	—	—
	interpretation	NOT DIRECT: thinking that would go into an interpretation could be influenced by infant observation experience, also through monitoring of countertransference	—	—

synonym for "uninvolved", as he argues that it is necessary to be both *"in"* and *"out"* at the same time, to be involved and thinking. The BAP group anticipate what I would judge to be too much detachment in their initial interview, talking of being objective and anticipating this detachment as helping them be more scientific. None of the post-observation interviews picked up this aspect. Although all the groups showed evidence of thinking about what they saw and, as we have seen, being able to stand back from themselves and consider what they felt and why, none used the term "detachment" or referred back to the idea of being slightly outside the process, which had been implied at the beginning.

- *Of being "an other", in the third position*

Teachers of infant observation, in speaking about the experience of observation, gave considerable attention to the idea, put most clearly by Suzanne Maiello (1997), about the value to the observer of having the experience of being "an other"—in the third position. In the group interviews this idea did not emerge at all. At the end of their initial interview the AFC group stated that in the observation they were not at the centre of things. In the post-observation interviews a number of participants made reference to their feelings of exclusion from the mother–infant union, but the particular aspects that Maiello draws out were not in evidence. For those participants who are in therapy while studying infant observation, the private therapeutic space might give an opportunity for addressing such feelings. It may also be that all the participants were too close to the experience to be able to see this aspect of it, which might evolve only slowly and in a way that was not necessarily recognizable to them themselves. One of the AFC group drew attention to feeling that he had changed in the course of the year but did not specify in what ways.

Value to clinical work

Various authors write on the ways that they overtly claim infant observation could be of value to future clinical work (see chapter 5). Some of these ways, such as getting in touch with primitive anxieties, experiencing projective identification, bearing feelings within oneself, and looking at details have all been addressed in the main section on the comparison between the two sets of interviews. However, other dimensions were also mentioned:

- *Experiencing features important within the therapeutic setting*

Clinicians suggest that the experience of infant observation, with the regularity of visits, gives the prospective therapist the opportunity of experiencing some of the features that are important within the therapeutic setting. In the initial interviews we see the participants concerned about how they are going to manage the experience and how they will conduct themselves with the families. In the post-observation interviews we see that this aspect has been significant for some of them, at least. The AFC group recognize the impact of lateness and cancellation, and in the Tavistock group one member talked of her shock at finding how much her cancellation at half-term meant to the observed mother.

- *Awareness of intersubjectivity*

There was also the suggestion that the observation experience would help future clinicians to have a greater awareness of intersubjectivity that would be valuable in clinical work. Perhaps not surprisingly, this is not addressed explicitly, but in the post-observation interviews we see numerous examples of the participants referring to ways in which the behaviour of one person has a subtle impact on the other: examples of countertransference and projective identification are cited above, aspects of the parents' ways of being with a child (expectation of independence, a withdrawn affect), which are then thought to alter the child's way of being. Although the term "intersubjectivity" is not used as such, it seems likely that the experience of witnessing and being involved in these experiences would deeply imprint the realization of the "to and fro" nature of relationships.

- *Observer's attention to the family*

It was suggested by the community of practitioners, both in writing and in discussions, that the way an observer attends to the family, offering something neutral and attentive, is somewhat similar to the way the clinician attends to the patient. I have already addressed the neutral, non-judgemental aspect of this. The idea that attention of a particular kind in and of itself could be a resource to the family and child is mentioned by some writers and is an idea that often emerges in the course of discussing individual observations. In the initial interviews there was no awareness of this. In the post-observation interviews some participants, especially one from the AFC, had a sense that they had offered something helpful to the family through the very act of paying a particular sort of attention. It was not clear from these interviews whether that would translate to it being considered as valuable within therapy.

Conclusions

From looking closely at the pre- and post-observation interviews in terms of the specific categories drawn out through the use of grounded theory it seems apparent that the participants are more in touch with their feelings and far more able to process those feelings and question where their responses come from. Their ability to think about and reflect on their experiences is much increased, although some of this could be accounted for by the fact that in the post-observation interviews they were able to draw upon recent experiences and evidence thinking there, rather than talking about it in a more hypothetical way, as at the beginning. The idea of using their own feelings as a useful source of information was a new development. Thinking about the impact of themselves as observers showed an increase in frequency. However, other dimensions that had seemed important to the participants before starting did not receive much attention afterwards, presumably because the didactic elements that had seemed safer and more familiar at the beginning no longer seemed as important as the other aspects that were privileged.

It is worth noting that the AFC group explicitly referred to having more self-knowledge through the experience of infant observation, while this idea is implicit in others. One member of the AFC group (see Chapter 10) talked of how his relationship with his brother had changed because of his observation experience, leading him to think about his brother's experience when he was a baby. The same participant also referred to his experience of at times being with people expressing certain views and realizing that *"I was there"* but that he had now moved on. While one cannot attribute all of the emotional growth that someone makes in the course of an academic year to their experience of infant observation, especially if that person is also in psychoanalytic psychotherapy at the time, nevertheless in this instance the participant is clear about the changes within himself and his view that it was the observation experience that had led to these changes.

Among teachers of infant observation there is a consensus that it can be and often is a life-changing experience. Yet this view, which is perhaps shared within the community of practitioners, is not actually stated explicitly in any of the extensive literature I reviewed, except for the abovementioned work of Suzanne Maiello (1997), in which she writes of how the experience of being in the third position can bring gains in personal growth and understanding to the practitioner. It seems important to notice changes in the participants that the literature had not signposted.

We have looked closely at changes that have taken place between these two sets of interviews. In addition to their observation experience, much else had also happened to the participants in the intervening six–nine months, so it would not be possible to claim that all the changes were due to this alone. The participants were all on courses in psychoanalytic institutions and would have attended other seminars and been exposed to various theoretical ideas; however, many were not yet practising clinicians and would not be supervised on clinical work. Some were in their own personal analysis, and, of course, we cannot know about other important life events that took place for them. Nevertheless, we have seen substantial changes, and even if we cannot prove that what we see in the post-observation interviews is uniquely the outcome of infant observation, we have evidence of qualities that are seen clearly in relation to the observational work, and it seems likely that the experience of infant observation is at least in part responsible for these.

It therefore seems that if we return to the capacities and skills that the literature and community of practitioners claimed for infant observation we could see that many of them have been met. While interviews alone did not show evidence of *all* the many capacities and skills written of, most were shown to have increased and some were shown to have appeared for the first time.

PART IV

CONCLUSIONS

CHAPTER TEN

Integrating the issues

The mind of the clinician at work

Although so far throughout this work the activities taking place within a psychoanalytic psychotherapy session have been broken down to their separate components, this approach, with its emphasis on capacities and skills and things that can be discretely identified, inevitably fails to acknowledge the importance of the work as a whole. The art of successful therapeutic work is more than the sum of its parts: it is lifted to a different level by the way that those parts are woven together, informing and drawing out each other.

Occasionally we are privileged to be able to see the mind of the clinician at work when leading practitioners in the field present case material and then take the reader through their—the therapist's—process of thinking that caused them to act in the way described. In fact, remarkably few practitioners describe their work in this way: many of us are perhaps too persecuted by the anticipated hostility of our imagined readers to display ourselves so nakedly. More often case examples concentrate on the patient and what the patient did, with the therapist's understanding of this being a necessary part, but presented more as an overview and less as the to-and-fro of the "bi-personal field" within the session.

Thomas Ogden is a writer and clinician who shares with the reader what has been going on in his mind during the session and how all that he has thought, felt, and experienced influences what he then says to the patient. In *Conversations at the Frontier of Dreaming* (2001) he includes examples of how what he calls "reverie" form an essential component of his responses to the patient.

There is insufficient space within this book to look closely at his description of what he does—nor, indeed, is it the main point of this study. It is useful, however, to be aware of the immensely complex weaving-together of elements that takes place in his work. I suggest that a similar complexity exists in most psychoanalytic psycho-therapy encounters, although few of us have Ogden's skill and self-awareness.

Considering again now the therapist's inner instruments and the way that these are deployed to make the "music" of the psycho-therapy sessions, we can see how Ogden uses them: "The psychoana-lytic frame ... and psychoanalytic technique ... are designed to enhance the capacity of each participant to achieve a state of mind in which he might gain access to the continuous unconscious conversa-tion within himself" (2001, p. 5).

Ogden sees that for the analyst his reverie experience is an indis-pensable source of experiential data concerning the leading uncon-scious transference–countertransference anxiety at any given moment in an analytic session. He describes these reveries as momentary thoughts, sensations, even snatches of music—and he emphasizes their visceral nature—that the analyst experiences which *seem* to be unconnected to the patient but are in fact deeply connected to what the patient is experiencing and trying to communicate. He is clear that although his subsequent responses to his patient come *from* his ana-lytic reverie, they are not *about* it. For example, he describes in detail a very harrowing session with a man who had been abused as a child. At one point Ogden remembers his own son, when very young, being measured against a wall, and in doing so has a sensation of the softness of his skin. This thought–sensation–experience puts him in touch with how small and vulnerable the patient had been at the time of his abuse, and he talks to the patient about how very physically small he must have been at the time and therefore how terrifying the "tree-height" abusing man was. In giving this example, Ogden is also aware of himself using a tone of voice, saying things and behaving in ways that are unusual to him—and he uses his awareness of that to think further about what was happening within the session. In chapter 4 we noted the importance of noticing and feeling, which can then be thought about and in time harnessed to create an appropriate interpretation.

This ability to think about himself and his experiences, his ways of being, seems very important: "A good deal of my work as an analyst involves the effort to transform my experience of 'I-ness' (myself as unselfconscious subject) into an experience of 'me-ness' (myself as object of analytic scrutiny)" (Ogden, 2001, p. 19).

This seems to me to resonate with the work done by Britton about "the third". Writing about the successful outcome of negotiating the oedipal situation, Britton, says that at that time the third position comes into existence, and we can both observe object relationships and think about being observed: "This provides us with a capacity for seeing ourselves in interaction with others and for entertaining another point of view whilst retaining our own, for reflecting on ourselves whilst being ourselves" (1989, p. 87).

Reflecting on ourselves is an essential tool for psychoanalytic work, as has been emphasized in chapter 4, in the section on the use of the countertransference. Combined with Ogden's ideas about the use of reverie, we can see more clearly how it is put to use within a psychotherapy session. He describes how transference and countertransference, which are largely unconscious, have to be transformed into "more usable forms": something verbal that can be "considered, reflected upon and linked (in both primary and secondary process modes) to other thoughts, feelings and sensations" (2001, p. 42). Here we see the experience and the reflecting upon it, which are so vital.

In taking the reader through the case example mentioned above, Ogden reflects on why he said "I won't let that happen" to his patient when the patient expressed his fear that he would never recover from the feeling of "going crazy" in which he was then immersed. He examines his motivation for making such a statement, feeling that it was not a reassurance but, rather, one that emerged from himself "as an analyst taking responsibility for the thinking and clinical judgements that are part and parcel of analytic work with a patient who is struggling with psychotic-level anxiety and feelings of impending disintegration" (2001, p. 170).

The reader may question Ogden's conclusion here, wondering what fuelled the motivation and need for making such a statement. Some of the authors cited in chapter 3 who considered capacities such as neutrality or the ability to hold on to uncomfortable feelings as those needed for psychotherapeutic work might doubt whether Ogden showed enough of those qualities, but others who wrote on the need for authenticity and compassion might feel that he had displayed those. We might consider this statement in the light of the literature, cited in chapter 4, on creating an analytic setting in which the patient feels safe, how to offer an interpretation that can be heard usefully by the patient, and also Stern and colleagues' (1998) work on "moments of meeting".

Ogden then delineates what he sees as the considerable demands of such responsibility, adding: "I would not have made such a statement if I did not believe that as a consequence of my training and experience, I could provide the necessary physical and emotional presence during the hour, and in the days and months to follow" (2001, p. 170).

He goes on to detail how very demanding such work can be. The capacity for resilience and realistic hopefulness are displayed. Here, I think, we also see a clinician drawing on his theoretical knowledge, which has remained in the background. Earlier in the session he describes how he had made an intervention that, in retrospect, he felt had been emphasizing his knowledge of child abuse. In his description of the session he acknowledges that this had been unhelpful. We see Ogden's ability to consider his own behaviour critically, to return to the analytic attitude in which he places the patient's needs above his own, to move from the more comfortable position of being the one who theoretically knew about child abuse rather than being more deeply in touch with, permeated by, the patient who knew it from experience. All these capacities are delineated in chapter 3. Ogden's theoretical knowledge about psychotic states and his professional knowledge about the demands of engaging with a patient in such a state are present and inform him but do not take centre stage. We have seen earlier in this chapter and in chapter 4 that theoretical knowledge needs to be available but kept in the background.

Ogden is a most sophisticated thinker and clinician. From this brief extract we can see that many of the capacities and skills addressed in earlier chapters are evidenced in his honest description of a piece of clinical work, although his intention in describing it was not to demonstrate these capacities but to give his reader a flavour of his use of "reverie". However, as stated before, I think that we see a whole that exceeds the sum of the parts: there is a psychoanalytic approach to thinking about how to be with and respond to a patient that, even allowing for a difference in emphasis because of theoretical orientation, can be seen to permeate the whole work of a session.

I now examine whether anything in the participants' responses in the interviews can be seen as having something of the depth and complexity of this, in order to consider whether we can say that the experience of infant observation shows evidence of a deepening of professional development as well as enhancing certain specific qualities.

The mind of the observer at work

If we return to some excerpts from the post-observation interviews quoted in previous chapters, we can see some of the complex issues considered when probing the working mind of the clinician. Having given some attention to Ogden's concept of reverie, we saw how in his model the therapist's capacity to experience something, to "catch the drift of it" and bring it to reflection, lies at the heart of analytic work. His response to the patient is then suffused with this experience, with theoretical knowledge and experience forming a steady background to this.

Two brief excerpts cited earlier are repeated here to show that we can see a similar process in these participants.

A member of the AFC group spoke movingly about the *"odd repercussions"* that had arisen in his personal life as a result of observing: *"The infant I'm observing has an older sibling: he's two years older, and they're both male. It exactly matches my situation with an older brother, and this was quite quickly picked up on by our seminar leader, and over the next few weeks I began to really, I think, slightly unconsciously, observe what it was like for the older sib to suddenly have this annoying intrusion in their life and vice-versa. And I actually found—could be because of other rea-sons—that my relationship with my brother improved massively, just in terms of seeing him in a completely different light."*

Here we see that the experience—one that the seminar leader helped the student to be aware of—helped the participant to, as Britton (1989) puts it, entertain "another point of view while retaining his own". He can intuitively imagine what it was like for the *"older sib"* to adjust to a new baby in the family, and from doing so his relationship with his brother *"improved massively"*. The participant could first feel what his brother's experience might have been like and then reflect on it in such a way that this influenced his interaction with his brother. The to-and-fro, moving, changing nature of this is implied.

In another example a participant from the Tavistock group who observed the depressed mother of a toddler, whom she saw as *"needy"* and boisterous because of his neediness, spoke of how difficult she found it to watch the mismatch between them and felt herself pulled out of observer role. It is worth while to repeat this here in order to study the implications. She spoke about a mother who *"was never able to match his mood. No matter how excited he was, she was really calm, though she patently felt some anger that she was holding in, and the calmer she was, the more the little boy was angry and energetic. And I just desperately wanted her to pick him up and tickle him or match his level somehow, and it was very hard to sit through so many observations where I could see that and not say anything. Finally, during one last observation, the baby was on the floor, and I was sitting against the wall, and this little boy was right between me and the baby, doing everything he could to get attention, and I had been aware how hard he has to work to get attention, and I just grabbed him and I tickled him and he absolutely loved it. And after months and months of sitting and watching, I just decided, it was just an impulse that I had. But I wanted so much for the mother to be able to do that, and I probably shouldn't have done that, but I think that told me something really."*

We see the observer experiencing very strong feelings, *"desperately"* wanting to interact with the child, *"matching his level"*. We see her evaluating her feelings and using a theoretical framework to understand them when she talks of the child feeling some of the anger that mother was holding in. The observer also implies, from the way she describes her own feeling of *"desperately"* needing to act on feelings, that she, as well as the child, were experiencing something on behalf of the mother. Here we see evidence of the observer being aware of very strong, uncomfortable feelings, tolerating them—although also feeling impelled to act on them—and reflecting on them, understanding them through further thought, and using a theoretical framework about projection. We see that in fact the observer went beyond the accepted conventions of the observer role and tickled the toddler, and we are shown how this "acting-out" enabled her to think further about what she had been feeling and why. In recounting this episode in the interview, the participant was also able to go on to talk sympathetically of the mother and the strain of attending to two children. It seemed that her experience and her reflection on it had brought her to this approach.

As the reader will be well aware, a similar process could have been noted in many other instances cited above. We see that from the observation experience the participants are at times able to engage in some of the joined-up thinking—it really should be thinking-and-feeling—that is at the heart of therapeutic work. Although, as with so many other capacities in evidence at the end of the infant observation experience, we cannot be sure that they were gained *from* the infant observation experience (or from it alone), I would contend that the depth and complexity of the experience are vital in producing a depth and complexity of response.

Moreover, if we go back to the interviews conducted when the participants had not begun observing or had only recently done so, we find far fewer examples of thinking of this depth and complexity. As has been highlighted before, we have the example of the participant who stated: *"I think it can be quite staggering how much emotion you can see when you are observing. At night in the freezing cold, the family you are observing live on the fourth floor of a tower block. I was really struck when I went in how warm and inviting—a cocoon—it was, it just felt so high up and outside it was cold. I also felt that the mother and baby were very cocoon-like—couple—I was on the outside. How much feeling that evoked."*

While this example shows a very sensitive and aware observer becoming aware of her feelings and tolerating the uncomfortable feelings of being *"on the outside"* of the *"cocoon"*, we do not at this stage see the further dimension of reflecting on those feelings. Additionally, this is one of the few examples from the initial interviews where such depth and strength of feeling are apparent at all. I would argue that close examination of the texts of both sets of interviews provides evidence that the participants are responding differently by the end interviews and that a complex professional training process is quite well established by this point, in a way that is not apparent in the initial interviews. By the time of the end interviews, most participants make statements that show that processes that the literature review and findings would suggest a fully developed clinician would have— such as the capacity to be emotionally open, to distinguish the personal and the clinical countertransference, to maintain a stance when feeling pulled out of it, to think about what to do with all this, and to take such material to a seminar or supervision in order to see new meanings in it—are well developed.

Naturally, at the outset of the observation process many of the students were sophisticated thinkers, experienced professionals, and a few of them working clinicians, so it is not surprising that we find traces of the complex interweaving of capacities that are a prerequisite for clinical work. But the evidence of such capacities is rudimentary in the initial interviews, whereas by the end interviews we see much more substantial evidence of those capacities that training as a psychoanalytic psychotherapist is intended to develop being in place.

CHAPTER ELEVEN

Implications and validity of the findings

Following on from the discussion of the reflective aspects of the mind of the clinician and the mind of the observer at work, I now want to draw out the significance of the findings from this study.

Looking at the validity of the research method

In evaluations of the validity and usefulness of research, the literature often refers to "reproducibility" (Atkinson & Coffey, 1996; Fern, 2001; Glaser & Strauss, 1967; Hersen & Bellack, 1984; Kratochwill, Mott, & Dodson, 1984; Kazdin, 1998; Sechrest, 1984). However, in qualitative research it is acknowledged that it is impossible to replicate exactly the original conditions under which the data were collected or to control all the variables that might affect the findings—indeed, as Strauss and Corbin (1998) state, in qualitative research the researcher is not trying to control the variables but, rather, to discover them. While clearly any other group of students interviewed about the subject of this research would, in semi-structured discussions, bring up certain different topics, I think it is very likely that most of the same themes would emerge. In this sense we can see the likely generalizability of these findings. Strauss and Corbin describe "substantive theory" as one developed from the study of one small area of investigation and from one specific population from which the data are drawn. Such a study, while not having the explanatory power of a larger, more general theory, still has considerable worth as "the real merit of a substantive theory lies in its ability to speak specifically for the population from which it was derived and to apply back to them" (1998, p. 267). My research derives from and applies to those studying infant observation in psychoanalytically oriented training institutions who are intending to go on to train as clinicians, although some aspects of the findings could apply to a wider group of observers.

Researchers conducting their study in an area of which they have some experience will enter the arena with certain knowledge and expectations. According to Strauss and Corbin, researchers should be "unafraid to draw on their own experiences when analysing materials because they realise that these become the foundations for making comparisons and discovering properties and dimensions" (1998, p. 5).

Experience sensitizes the researcher to significant problems and issues in the data, and while it is important not to treat such experience as statistics, the researcher can use it to select and order the data in a conceptual way. Knowledge and experience enable the researcher to "recognise incidents as conceptually similar or dissimilar and to give them conceptual names" (p. 47). It is important, of course, not to pre-judge and only see what one expects to see. Researchers have to question whether the concepts are truly emergent or whether they are seeing them because they expect to.

Andrew Cooper considers this question in a paper (2004) in which he discusses psychoanalytic research methods. He questions whether, when research subjects respond in ways that are anticipated by the researcher, one could say that these experiences had occurred for the research subjects, or whether, in some way or to some measure, this "pattern" had been *introduced* into the textual material. He concludes that the answers are not simple, but that "at a minimum one can make the following comments": that it is possible in principle and in practice to "check" the evidence for claims, finding in the texts various reports of experiences that seem to accord with the descriptive names—for example in my research registering, tolerating and processing difficult experiences—given to them. Importantly, he goes on to state:

> it is reasonable to assume that [the researcher] was sensitised to the presence of this pattern in the data by virtue of herself being an experienced clinician and trainer of clinicians. This is quite different from saying that she "introduced" the pattern into the data, or that we are faced here with an example of a researcher finding what she already assumes to be there.

While acknowledging that it is reasonable to assume that a researcher with different theoretical and practical sensibilities would see other kinds of patterns or accounts of processes in the data, he emphasizes the absurdity of claiming that *any* proposed patterning or description of this data would be valid. It would be possible to engage in a process of open and public testing of the validity of this kind of data analysis by exposing a number of "raters", all of whom are deploying the same analytic categories, to the textual material and seeing what kind of agreement or disagreement they come up with. Cooper describes particular skills that the researcher familiar with observation and psychoanalytic clinical work is likely to use when engaged in research. He points to the expectation that

> the clinician can "access" at least to some degree not just the behavioural gestures and verbal utterances [discourse] of the patient, but something of their emotional states, non-verbal communications, and silent responses to the clinician. In observational study, something similar but slightly less complex is usually happening—concentrated more on understanding states of mind and relationships in the "observed subjects" and less the relationship with the observer—but still *as these processes are registered in the experience of the observer.*

My examination of the way the findings mapped onto what is cited in the literature on infant observation shows a number of ways in which capacities cited in the literature were *not* in evidence in the sample and also the ways in which the groups differed. The fact that there were differences between the groups suggests that the data were looked at in a careful, differentiating way, not in a more global, assumptive manner. The fact that certain capacities cited in the literature were not found provides some confidence in the belief that I did not simply impose preconceptions upon the data, but, rather, that the categories developed were truly emergent and reflect use of a procedure that considered in what ways these concepts are the same as, and in what ways different from, those cited in the literature. I have given considerable detail from the raw data in the hope of showing that the categories I created were discovered rather than constructed. From the results of my research it seems that I have discovered what I already believed—but the discoveries prove to have a basis in empirical reality and to have been refined and deepened in various respects. When tested, the reality proved to be close to, but not identical with, my expectations.

It is generally accepted by those in the research community that any approach to research has inherent advantages and disadvantages. As Michael Rustin (2002) points out, when a researcher deconstructs the "world" that is being looked at in order to study it in a systematic way, some aspects of its essential connectedness are then lost. By looking at the mind of a clinician as being made up of various competencies or by delineating all the varied learning outcomes that the study of infant observation may bring about, we are at risk of ignoring the "gestalt"—the idea of the whole being greater than the sum of its parts. In this research I have attempted to keep "both ends of the telescope" in mind and to attend to both the individual parts and the whole to which they aggregate in a complex and interconnected way. Chapter 10 also attempts to acknowledge what a complicated and interwoven process both becoming familiar with and using psychoanalytic ways of thinking can be.

In this research the categories have been conceptualized in a systematic way, generating important descriptive knowledge. In order to build a theory, a researcher, having conceptualized, defined, and developed categories, then relates these through hypotheses or statements of relationship. Through a close examination of the texts and the creation of higher-order categories, I have shown what we might think of as the building blocks that together form the "experience of infant observation". The category names used are deceptively simple: "awareness of feelings" may appear to be simply a descriptive name, but when it is unpacked and explored in a more substantial way, we can see that it is a concept containing phenomena that represent properties and dimensions in a form that goes beyond the descriptive. The creation of the category has involved an analytic more than a descriptive process. While "awareness of feelings" and "reflection on feelings" may be the two most complex categories, all of them represent a form of conceptual ordering that is analytic in its essence.

I have formulated systematically what appears to be the range of central experiences that students report in interviews as forming the core of the infant observation experience after they had been involved in it. There were interconnected features of the experience that this research has shown to be present. Infant observation facilitates complex emotional and cognitive growth. The research shows some of this more complicated internal process at work and describes in an abstract form those processes—e.g. tolerating feelings, reflecting, being drawn out of observer role—that take place within an observer. In considering conditions for something to take place, it is not necessarily helpful to think in terms of causal connections in a simplistic "A leads to B" sense: "conditions and consequences usually exist in clusters and can associate or covary in many different ways" (Strauss & Corbin, 1998, p. 186). There are multiple and diverse patterns of connectivity. However, while being aware of the complex interweaving of events, we can think of specific sets of conditions creating circumstances that lead to actions—in this case the experience of infant observation carried out in a psychoanalytically informed institution, with the aid of a seminar group, leading to an increase in interest in and sensitivity to feelings and the importance of reflecting on them. This study has indicated that participants' responses in certain categories increased significantly: as can be seen in Tables 4.1, 5.1, and 9.2, concepts that match the capacities and skills discussed throughout the work are shown to have been spoken of more frequently in the interviews. To an extent this increase could be attributed to the fact that they had recently experienced infant observation and had readily accessible vivid examples to draw on, but it is my contention that its significance goes beyond this. I have uncovered evidence of complex processes happening within trainees which is very consistent with our professional and psychoanalytically informed understanding of how clinicians work inside themselves and indeed with how trainers conceive of their task with trainees. The literature also suggests concepts of the above types.

Linking the conceptual and the empirical research

It is clear from the chapters 3 and 4 that a psychoanalytic psychotherapist needs more than simply a repertoire of specific skills. A psychoanalytic psychotherapy training places very little emphasis on the teaching of skills—it operates as a time period within which the trainee develops capacities. We could also state very clearly that infant observation does not teach skills; however, it does, through learning from experience, increase capacities.

Chris White (1994) and Richard Morgan-Jones (1995) have both written about this subject, albeit rather briefly, in the context of the growing emphasis on the concept of "competencies" in professional training. White (1994) writes of an attempt within the United Kingdom Council for Psychotherapy to participate in a process that aims to define the competencies deployed in psychotherapy. However, he begins his paper by saying that, for example, understanding, sustaining the countertransference, and containing anxiety should not be viewed as "performance", and free-floating attention, empathy, and analytic neutrality are *not* skills, for "such things involve 'being' rather than 'doing'; they require emotional capacity rather than competent action. They are based on receptivity not activity" (p. 568). He continues that a "certain frame of mind" is important for engaging in psychotherapy, and this, once adopted, may lead to certain behaviour, but the frame of mind is necessary or the behaviour is a "sham" (p. 569). Morgan-Jones follows up White's article and looks at the way psychotherapeutic competency can be related to the process within the session. He describes both basic and more advanced levels of competency, moving from "the ability to recognize and empathize verbally with a range of consciously felt emotional states" (1995, p. 444), through the ability to perceive the transference of unconscious feelings by projection and projective identification into the therapist, to creating links and making mutative interpretations. He privileges interpretation as a "core competence" (p. 442). I would suggest that in the framework of this study, the ability to create an interpretation, while deploying various capacities including thoughtfulness, receptivity, and attention to the countertransference, is in fact a skill and, as such, calls upon many other aspects of the therapist's aptitudes.

At the same time as creating a very clear seven-part basic and three-part advanced-level list, Morgan-Jones questions the value of academic training in psychotherapy and cites Bion on how intellect can be used defensively:

> The task of psychotherapy training is to help trainees live with their mixture of terror and fascination with their own mental pain and history that has led them to train, sufficiently to be able to grasp hold of and claim it, and through the disciplines of personal analysis, supervision, infant observation and theory and clinical reading and writing to be emotionally available within a professional training. [1995, p. 442]

Morgan-Jones claims infant observation as one of the necessary activities that, together with others, will lead the trainee to the essential state of mind in which to carry out effective clinical work. It has not been possible within the scope of this study to look at the contribution of other parts of the training experience; I have concentrated on looking at the contribution of infant observation alone, while acknowledging that many strands will be interwoven. I am sure that it could be cogently argued that other aspects of the teaching and learning of prospective clinicians also contribute substantially to an increase in capacities. Thus it is not my intention to claim that all the credit is due to infant observation alone but, rather, to show the ways in which it is useful, especially at the beginning of a clinical training.

The capacities that fully developed clinicians would have available within themselves include, as outlined elsewhere, most centrally the capacity to be emotionally open, to manage strong feelings and to reflect on them, to pay close attention to all that is going on, to wait for meaning to emerge, to distinguish the personal and the clinical countertransference, to have the ability to maintain the appropriate stance when feeling pulled out of it, the capacity to think about what all this may signify and so how to respond to it, and the willingness to take such material to a seminar or supervision in order to see new meanings in it. Training for becoming a psychoanalytic psychotherapist would surely aim to develop these capacities. We see from Table 9.2 that many of those capacities are in place at the end of the observation experience when they were not in evidence, or at least not to such an extent, in the initial interviews. We have seen the development of an observer who will, much of the time, have an open, reflective, emotionally available stance and who will find herself affected by what she experiences and then reflect on this. She will, often not deliberately, give space to thinking about personal counter-transference issues—what in her life and experience might be making her feel this way—and about "clinical" countertransference issues—what her feelings might tell her about the mother's and baby's states of mind—and will reflect on what such feelings mean. She will reflect on the observer stance and consider the meaning of not being able to adhere to it, and she will use the seminar to make sense of the experience. In this way we see that the processes elicited within the observer are those that are clinically relevant.

I have demonstrated that infant observation initiates or at times catalyses processes of development in its participants. The external situation, the emotionally charged atmosphere of an observation, arouses something in the internal life of the observer, which opens out into a reflection on one's self and one's own relationships and history. From the categories about registering and processing feelings, we see that the process involves internal work that will take demonstrably different forms—as we see in the examples about thinking about the effect of the sibling or about the infant's experience with a preoccupied mother. This is a painful experience—which might be given the opportunity to be processed if the observer is in analysis at the time—and the toleration of this pain is part of the process of growing into being a clinician. The observer is encouraged to engage in a particular kind of reflection. We see within the data analysis references to the function of the seminar group in helping the participants make sense of this. We could describe the seminar as the apparatus for the thinking of difficult thoughts. In this description we can see how the developmental process arises and some of the stages it goes through, with its interlinked developments. Within the four research groups, clearly there were differences in the interests and attitudes of the seminar leaders. From the way the participants spoke, I gathered that some concentrated mainly on looking at the mother–infant couple, some were more interested in the infant's extended world, and others placed more emphasis on managing the task and learning from that experience. Certainly it was apparent that the particular quality and interests of the seminar leader could increase the kinds of benefit that the participants felt able to derive from it.

Infant observation teaching in the twenty-first century

This research has shown that, as we would expect, infant observation is at the centre of the process of developing the prospective therapist's capacities that she will need in future clinical work. However, I would argue that some of the conditions under which infant observation is now taught potentially work against that. The emphasis on the acquisition of skills and abilities that can be evidenced in a transparent manner suitable for evaluation by an academically accrediting body may mean that less emphasis is then given to the development of the deeper capacities. This research reveals tensions inherent in the current situation.

Interestingly, although currently infant observation usually takes place within this new context, there is still comparatively little described about the trainings in general, or the infant observation components of trainings, in terms of learning objectives. Indeed, as the reader will see, writers still emphasize the emotional dimensions, and it might be said that there is now more emphasis on these than when Bick wrote her now famous "Notes" (1964), delineated in earlier chapters, which outline what she saw as some of the benefits of carrying out infant observation. Similarly, some three decades ago W. Ernest Freud saw it primarily as a preparation for training in analysis: "The overriding objective and commitment are to initiate the student into the world of analysis . . . so that perforce we will often find ourselves discussing analysis rather than infantile development" (1975, p. 90).

This is very clearly a particular model, and I think perhaps it is not much in use now. Klauber and Trowell (1999) outline the way attitudes to infant observation have changed over the years. They highlight the original emphasis on enhancing trainees' capacity for understanding early, pre-verbal development and experience, bringing them more in touch with the infantile in their patients. They suggest that now we are also aware of the opportunities infant observation gives for allowing the observer to develop the capacity to tolerate uncertainty and take the time to reflect before coming to conclusions or offering premature interpretations. Observers can also see the rich complexity of parent–infant interactions. We have also seen more recent writers describe the aims of infant observation in wide-ranging ways, but which privilege the emotional dimensions of the experience (see chapter 5). Barbara Segal (2003) emphasizes the experiential form of learning and suggests that the learning objectives are complex and subtle.

However, interestingly, this increase in more deeply personal capacities is not much referred to in course handbooks. For example, the Tavistock M7 (M.A. in Psychoanalytic Observational Studies) course outline is couched in terms of aims and objectives.

Aims:

- to facilitate the task of observing—establishing boundaries, noting any concerns about child protection issues;
- to become a disciplined observer—able to write good notes, reflect on the experience of the task and of the personal impact of paying close attention to a baby and her experience;
- to explore possible conscious and unconscious meanings of events and behaviour and aspects of the infant's early relationships;
- to study the growth of mind and personality from a psychoanalytic perspective, behaviour and the internal world in terms of one's own reactions to observed behaviour;
- to promote awareness of a range of experiences through varied observations in the seminar group;
- to promote awareness of and sensitivity to varied ethnic/cultural/ socio-economic issues.

Objectives:

- understanding the complex role of observer and remaining in role;
- the ability to prepare and participate in the seminar;
- producing a portfolio of observations;
- writing an infant observation paper.

It is worth noting that this gives little flavour of the emotional aspects of the task—those that, in my opinion, are really crucial for developing skills as a psychoanalytic psychotherapist. However, the information sheet on which they appear does have a paragraph that precedes these aims, which talks about the necessity of containing emotional impact and "complicated emotions evoked in the self". Perhaps the aims and objectives stated represent something that can be evaluated fairly, while it might be more problematic to evaluate the development of the capacities I am concerned about. Although it would be challenging to examine them transparently in an academically validated course, teachers in the field are increasingly attempting to make explicit to the students both the academic and experiential aspects of learning that they are intended to achieve.

The issue of concurrent analysis

When actually trying to organize the interviews, I came across an important factor. At the turn of the twenty-first century it seemed that, with the exception of the Institute of Psychoanalysis, the training institutions I approached were rarely or never taking students into clinical training and beginning their training with infant observation, as had been the case some years before. Now infant observation often takes place in a pre-clinical context. Rather than being accepted for clinical training and engaging in infant observation at the start of a recognized clinical training, most people undertaking it nowadays are involved in academically validated courses, MA or MSc, which "stand alone" but which are for some institutions prerequisites for the clinical training. The Tavistock Child Psychotherapy training had had a two year pre-clinical training for many years, and more recently this was adapted into an MA course, taken by those who wanted to train as child psychotherapists alongside others who were using the course to find ways of working better in their current roles. The MA in Observational studies at the Tavistock (M7) has become virtually the only route into training as a child psychotherapist there. In the other trainings I studied, an MA or an MSc were not a prerequisite for clinical training but were nevertheless a route taken by a number of successful applicants.

As described in chapter 2, when I was interviewing research participants, the BAP Adult Training (Psychoanalytic Section) had no new intake of students in the year in question, and the MSc students were considered to be a viable alternative group to interview—had a cohort been available, their position would have been closer to the Institute participants. The BAP MSc students could have decided to apply for either child or adult psychotherapy trainings afterwards—or, of course, for neither. While many AFC MSc students and

Tavistock MA students would not necessarily wish to embark on any further clinical training, those who did were more likely to be looking to train as child than as adult psychotherapists, although they could have used their academic qualification and the experiences gained on the course to take them to an adult psychotherapy training.

This change—the separation of the infant observation experience from clinical training—actually has major implications for the relevance of the study of infant observation. People interested in attaining an academic qualification, and perhaps at the point of starting the "observation plus" course not clear in their minds about wishing to take on a clinical training, may well not be in analysis at the time of undertaking their infant observation. For some training institutions with a two-year observation, where students wished to proceed directly to clinical training, it is most likely that for at least the second year of the infant observation the student would be in analysis, as one year of analysis is a common minimum requirement before embarking on clinical training . However, even if the analysis coincides with the second year of infant observation, it would mean that the first year would not, and it is often the beginning of infant observation that is the most alarming and disturbing, with the observer being in contact with the raw feelings of the baby and the attendant emotional disequilibrium within the family. Of course, students on psychoanalytically based courses may well already be in therapy or analysis, and it is quite common for students to decide to enter therapy partly as a result of the feelings stirred up by infant observation. However, if for any reason the student did not enter a clinical training directly from the academic course, or could not, perhaps for financial reasons, begin therapy or analysis at the time, it could well be that the entire infant observation was taken without the observer being in analysis during the process.

Other chapters in this study have addressed the many ways in which studying infant observation can help a trainee achieve various capacities and skills necessary for clinical work. Many of these would not necessarily be significantly affected by whether or not the observer was in analysis at the time. However, there are certain aspects that I think are directly related to the simultaneous experience of observing and analysis, just as later in training the experience of being in analysis while struggling with one's first clinical cases seems a necessary conjunction. In the same way as close attention to the clinical material addressed in supervision makes the trainee aware of all sorts of issues that then need to be thought about in analysis but are inappropriate for discussion within supervision, so the seminar group provides an important forum for the observer to become aware of all kinds of feelings and concerns stirred up by the observation that cannot and should not be directly addressed within the seminar. We have seen at various points throughout this work the vital role the seminar group plays in enabling the observer to stay with and think about the maelstrom of feelings being experienced. Nevertheless, in my view the seminar is a semi-public forum, and there are issues that it may not be suitable or helpful to address within it. I am concerned that without the opportunity to get sufficiently in touch with the feelings stirred up by observing and a place to reflect on those feelings, the observer may inevitably erect defences that then prevent her from getting in touch with and making use of a most central part of the experience.

The way of learning

So how might these enormous contributions that I am claiming for infant observation have come about? Clearly, one of the major influences is the way in which what is learned is learned. The learning that takes place is emotional learning—that is, the type that Bion (1962) describes as learning from experience rather than learning about something. This encompasses, but in my view goes beyond, what is meant by experiential learning. Of course, all learning, however apparently formal, is met with and understood by the student in a way that uses his or her emotional, often unconscious, self. Salzberger-Wittenberg, Henry, and Osborne (1983) looked at this for those involved in education in a way that continues to be developed by staff at the Tavistock Clinic, although it is not overtly transmitted to those who teach infant observation there. Ruth Robinson (1992), in an infant observation paper written as part of her training at the Institute of Psychoanalysis, wrote that "It is possible that its main value is that some of the lessons it teaches students can only be learned from experience". Having begun with a model of learning about the development of an infant and the developing mother–infant relationship, she moved to a model of learning taking place at multiple levels.

However, she says that she wishes the process could have been more conceptualized at the outset. Muir, Lojkasek, and Cohen (1999) state that although in their teaching experience the original aim was to facilitate the understanding of the internal world and develop awareness of infantile experience, they realized that the difficulties the students experienced in observing actually added another training aspect.

As has been shown throughout this work, this other aspect—the emotional learning—is of immense value for becoming a psychoanalytic psychotherapist, although given that many of those who carry out an infant observation are *not* doing so as part of a psychotherapeutic training, we might wonder if this is so for all observers. Perhaps others might not privilege this dimension. Carlberg, Dagberg, and Nilsson (1993) describe a study that evaluated how infant observation contributes to the students' development of psychoanalytic ideas. The students reported that it made theories more alive, their knowledge of child development became more integrated, and it increased their knowledge of the relationship between mother and baby. They also responded with remarks about their increased intuition and sensitivity. This study points out that that cohort of students only carried out 24 observations over three years and suggested that the model of observing once a week gave more opportunity for primitive anxieties, while less frequent observations made less impact. Blomberg (1999) reports that subsequent observations were carried out more frequently and that the intimacy helped the students to capture what she called the "being" aspect of the task.

It is well acknowledged that experiential learning offers something that "academic" learning does not. Kernberg (2000) suggests that analytic training has three strands: the experiential, the academic, and interactive feedback. The potential therapist has to learn ways of being, and infant observation seems to offer the opportunity to experience some of these ways. Many students approaching infant observation have a background in which intellectual capacities have been privileged. Lignos points this out, saying: "they are very much in need of a different kind of knowledge: knowledge enveloped in emotionality" (1977, p. 2), and Margaret Rustin (2000) states: "I think the genius of Bick's idea lay in the fact that it offered a context for learning from experience which would greatly deepen what was otherwise too theoretical a form of learning in the early stages of training" (2000, p. 3).

It is not simply the avoidance of the potential sterility of the theoretical that is important. Green and Miller suggest that "The experience of feeling what an infant and its family feel is the way to learn in depth about these people" (2001, p. 6). Maiello puts it even more forcefully: "My experience with infant observation has taught me that the observer does not learn only *about* the relationship between a mother and her baby, but that the experience sets in train an intense emotional learning process at deep pre-verbal levels of mental functioning" (2000, p. 82). "[I]nfant observation is a learning experience that involves, often to the surprise of the observer himself, much more than a cognitive process of learning about it. It has deep emotional implications and contains an extraordinary maturational potential" (1997, p. 49).

The influence of theory on what is seen

This research began by asking whether infant observation is differently valued by different theoretical schools. It must be acknowledged that what psychotherapists think and notice about the material in front of them will be culturally determined. Chodorow (1989) surveyed 44 female psychotherapists trained between 1920 and 1944. She discovered that things that were important to her—such as the women's movement and gender theory—were not seen as significant by them. The "Ways of Seeing" conference (1987) in which leading exponents of the different theoretical schools in Britain gave their responses to the same piece of videoed infant observation material made clear that the same event can be—must be—seen through different eyes, which are inevitably influenced by a theoretical framework. Greenberg and Mitchell sum it up as follows: "The very same patient in the eyes of theorists of different persuasions is a very different creature. . . . Diagnosis does not and cannot stand prior to and independent of theoretical commitment" (1983, p. 387).

Similarly, there cannot be straightforward "out there" observation of "external reality" that would be seen and perceived in the same way by all observers. As we shall see, what proponents of different schools make of what they see can influence the way infant observation is then valued.

Theory and an interest in infancy studies

Hamilton pays considerable attention to the strong associations between an interest in infancy studies and both group affiliation and clinical practice (1996, p. 99). She describes a preconscious, logical link between beliefs in the existence of an external/public reality and the validity of observational studies and finds that the influence of infancy studies is clearly associated with positive responses to the idea of the real relationship and, to a lesser extent, the therapeutic alliance. She points out that the growing awareness of the "contribution of the developing infant to his own destiny" (p. 96) affects the way analysts think, giving them an increased interest in the effect of the external world, although, of course, with an acknowledgement that the effects may be experienced and understood in a very distorted way. After noticing from her questionnaires and interviews that child clinicians were the group most open to a diverse range of theoretical influences, she noted that among adult analysts neither the Contemporary Freudians nor the Kleinians had an interest in infancy studies, and they had a corresponding lack of interest in "external reality". This is not in accord with my expectation that Kleinians, with their interest in primitive anxieties, would value infant observation more highly. This may be due to the difference between "infancy studies", suggesting infant research, and naturalistic infant observation, which offers the observer, as we have seen, the opportunity to both observe and experience, through the countertransference, the strength of very early feelings. Hamilton notes that among Independent analysts only the British group indicated that they were strongly influenced by infancy studies, having always focused on the early mother–child relationship, both fantasied internal object relations and the way these fantasies represented actual experiences.

According to Hamilton, Contemporary Freudians objected to the way the concept of holding/containment seemed to have been taken from infant development straight to the analytic situation. Here we see a theoretical school stating that one aspect of the study of infant observation is actually unhelpful—but it is worth emphasizing that it is not actually the study of infant observation as such that is objected to but, rather, the *misuse* that is—in their view—made of it. Similarly, Jon Sklar, a British Independent analyst was concerned (personal communication, 2001) about what he saw as the doctrinal nature of the teaching of infant observation. While seeing the observation experience as an opportunity for the observer to think and feel and develop a countertransference attitude, he states that in recent years he has felt that what he calls the "Kleinian metapsychology" of what a baby is thinking, feeling, and doing has impinged "as a theoretical blanket" over the purpose of the experience. This attitude, also mentioned by Brafman (2002), may account for some suspicion and subsequent disapproval of infant observation. However, as a teacher of infant observation in the Independent tradition, I would argue that it is important for those who hold a non-Kleinian theoretical orientation to engage wholeheartedly in the teaching of infant observation so that students realize that the same material can be thought about in many different ways and that it is the teacher's curiosity and openness to wondering what is going on that can be so enhancing.

How the theoretical framework may alter what is understood

However, as we have seen, there is disquiet over the idea that observed experiences are understood and therefore described in a form heavily influenced by a certain theoretical framework. Certainly at the time of the Controversial Discussions in such a combative atmosphere they indubitably were. Glover railed against the evidence given by Kleinians:

> There are no such direct notes, views, studies and observations. There are only *interpretations* of the child's behaviour and utterances from which *hypothetical reconstructions* of psychic situations or stages of child development are arrived at. *Other child analysts with precisely the same opportunities of observing child behaviour and utterance hold that Kleinian interpretations and reconstructions are inaccurate,* and that their own observations confirm the formulations set forth by Freud as the result of his study. [King & Steiner, 1991, p. 713, italics in the original]

Reading this made me wonder to what extent early Kleinian interest in infant observation might have been increased by the wish to "find evidence" for strongly held theoretical beliefs. Of course, Klein acknowledges at the end of her paper "The Emotional Life and Ego-Development of the Infant", given as part of the Controversial Discussions—which, incidentally, contains some extremely fine and detailed observation material—that as well as observation, she is also using "some degree of inference drawn from our knowledge of the unconscious of somewhat older children" (Klein, 1944, p. 788), and that "We could not expect by observation alone to get to full proofs for the unconscious processes at work in infants" (p. 774), though perhaps there was a hope that observation would help. Significantly, infant research, and, I would say, infant observation, have shown some of Klein's ideas to be accurate. For example, in the Controversial Discussions she takes issue with Anna Freud about the idea that there are no object relations in the first six months, and more recent infant research now seems to disprove the idea of primary narcissism. Similarly, we could make a very direct connection between Klein's thoughts about an early ego, which were thought to be rather ridiculous when first stated, and infant research that shows how infants behave in alert states (Wolff, 1963). The idea that an alert baby, not driven by fear or hunger, can be interested in studying objects, would (if we use that terminology) seem to suggest the existence of an ego that can be interested in the outside world.

The problem of describing infantile states

I wondered whether there might be a theoretical bias here and whether Kleinians, with their emphasis on primitive mental states, might be more adept at using appropriate language, or whether the very act of *talking*, and therefore using language about experiences that took place in the earliest, pre-verbal, months, is inevitably imposing a structure that could be viewed as "adultomorphic".

Interestingly, this point is raised in the Controversial Discussions, where Klein's ideas and the language she used to describe them were criticized. In typically measured form, Brierley states: "A difficulty arises in the fact that we have to describe pre-verbal experience in words in order to discuss it, but we know perfectly well that the use of words and the construction of sentences imports a kind of degree and organization into our description that is not native to the primitive experience itself" (in King & Steiner, 1991, p. 470). Brierley wonders whether in trying to make infantile experience intelligible, it is subject to a degree of falsification and retrospective sophistication. Surely the act of putting any experience, especially one heavily rooted in the body and sensations, into language is a very imprecise and subjective task. Writers and poets struggle and frequently fail at it, and we rejoice in their achievement when it seems to us they have "got it right". So it seems reasonable to agree that an element of active interpretation and construction is a part of rendering such primitive, inchoate feelings into language. There is some attention paid to this in Chapter 5, with one student writing of this difficulty in her final paper. When describing the many ways in which the experience of infant observation can be valuable for future work as a psychoanalytic psychotherapist, Margaret Rustin suggests that students can learn "to struggle towards a language for describing pre-linguistic experiences which will serve them well in work with patients if the infantile transference is to be tackled" (1988, p. 20).

Although we have seen that leading proponents of the Independent group have expressed their concerns about the way infant observation teaching is often carried out, this does not mean that they valued it less than do their colleagues in other theoretical groupings. In this study involving trainees on courses in institutions with different theoretical orientations, although we saw that the emphasis and focus of interest varied according to the groups in a way that could be thought to be theoretically determined, the valuation of infant observation *per se* was no different.

Is infant observation valued differently by child or adult psychotherapists?

I started my research with the view, shaped by informal discussions with child or adult psychotherapists who were often involved in the training of future generations, that infant observation was valued more highly by child psychotherapists than by adult psychotherapists. While I still think that this may be the case, this research has demonstrated that there is little valid reason for this. Its value hinges on the question of what the infant observation experience is for, what it is intended to achieve. If we see it as an opportunity for learning about child development, then it may seem more relevant to clinicians working with children. It was interesting to note the emphasis that the candidates from the Institute of Psychoanalysis placed on the mother rather than on the infant. Teaching the seminars with such a different focus must affect what the participants gain from the experience. However, when we take on board the myriad ways in which it can be useful to the developing clinician, then its lesser value to the adult therapist is surely contentious. Appreciation of the value of infant observation could be held equally by any psychoanalytic practitioner who recognizes that it offers access to both *external* knowledge about child development and the formation of relationships and *internal* capacities to do with waiting, tolerating feelings, and creating an internal thinking space.

However, most trainings in child psychotherapy in the United Kingdom demand a two-year infant observation, while most psychoanalytic or psychoanalytic psychotherapy trainings for adults offer only a one-year experience. Much emerges in the second year of observation: patterns change, resilience may become apparent, issues of separation and individuation arise in the second year. The observer who only observes for one year misses all these experiences. Nevertheless, if we follow the main point to emerge from my findings—namely, that the experience of infant observation gives emerging clinicians an unparalleled opportunity to become aware of and reflective about their own feelings—then this gain certainly arises within the first year.

Infant observation teaches the embryonic therapist much about how people develop, and knowledge of the parent–child relationship, showing how experiences are internalized. This can influence thinking about how to make aspects of the therapeutic relationship more readily internalizable (Pine, 1985). Sandler and Dreher (1996) point to something rather less specific that infant research—and surely also infant observation—can bring to therapeutic technique in terms of the usefulness of analysts seeing impediments to normal development. These are useful things for both adult and child therapists to keep in mind. Attention to the non-verbal aspects of communication may be heightened in a child psychotherapist who is accustomed to her child patients using forms of communication other than language. However, it is surely important for every therapist to be aware of and pay attention to, for example, how a patient walks, moves, takes off his coat, stays very still or not, and how some of these observed actions are long-standing ways of operating within one's body while others vary from day to day, displaying the patient's changing state of mind.

The observational vignette at the beginning of this book shows the observer paying close attention to Elliott's body movements, which were thought about, in part, as communicating his states of mind. The idea that the creation and maintenance of boundaries creates a space within which something hitherto unformed can evolve is vital to all therapeutic work.

When I considered whether there were specific areas of a child psychotherapist's work that would make the experience of infant observation more valuable to it than to an adult psychotherapist, a few that were mentioned in the literature stood out. Knowing about the complexity of family life should help the child psychotherapist to mitigate an unhelpful climate of blame or rivalry with the parent, while acquaintance with developmental milestones gained from infant observation can help the therapist to think more about the behaviour of the child in the room. Margaret Rustin (2000) says that understanding the unconscious processes triggered off around a disturbed child is an essential component of our work. While I think it would be overstating the situation to suggest that this understanding can be gained from infant observation alone, experiencing the strength of infantile projections and being aware of their impact on those around them is a useful grounding for recognizing these phenomena in other settings.

Awareness of the complications of family life as seen in infant observation—as well as often experienced personally—can help the child psychotherapist to avoid rescue fantasies by maintaining a more balanced attitude towards parents who may themselves be very damaged and deprived. Awareness of resilience and the ordinary developmental thrust can also help stem the child psychotherapist's arrogance about the importance and efficacy of her work. Referring to the changes in socialization that usually occur as children enter latency, Winnicott says: "In the analysis of small children the analyst is considerably helped by the tremendous changes that take place in the child" (1958b, p. 172).

While I can accept that there are these additional areas for the child psychotherapist that are not of relevance to the adult practitioner, I would suggest that these are not in themselves sufficient to justify the difference in the valuation of infant observation that my discussions with colleagues and the lack of interest in certain parts of the literature have led me to believe exists. The difference in valuation, where it does exist, arises, I suspect, from historical ideas about infant observation as originally described by Bick (1964). If we become more aware of the tremendous opportunities that infant observation gives for developing the necessary capacities outlined above, related to becoming aware of, tolerating, and reflecting on feelings, then what I believe to be its rightful place at the heart of training for psychoanalytic psychotherapy will surely be acknowledged.

REFERENCES

Abrahamsen, G., & Morkeseth, E. (1998). "What Kind of Quality Do Family Daycare Homes Provide for Children under Three?" Paper presented at the 22nd World Congress, OMEP, Copenhagen, Denmark, 13–16 August.

Alexander, F., & French, T. M. (1946). *Psychoanalytic Therapy: Principles and Applications*. New York: Ronald Press.

Alvarez, A. (1992). *Live Company: Psychoanalytic Psychotherapy with Autistic, Borderline, Deprived and Abused Children*. London/New York: Tavistock/Routledge.

Alvarez, A. (1997). Projective identification as a communication: Its grammar in borderline psychotic children. *Psychoanalytic Dialogues, 7* (6): 753–768.

Alvarez, A., & Furgiuele, P. (1997). Speculations on components in the infant's sense of agency. In: S. Reid (Ed.), *Developments in Infant Observation: The Tavistock Model*. London: Routledge.

Atkinson, P., & Coffey, A. (1996). *Making Sense of Qualitative Data: Complementary Research Strategies*. London: Sage.

Aveline, M. (1990). The training and supervision of individual therapists. In: W. Dryden (Ed.), *Individual Therapy: A Handbook*. Milton Keynes: Open University Press.

Bard, E. (1997). Difficulty in "casting off": Observations on the task of separation. *Psychoanalytic Psychotherapy, 11* (3): 257–269.

241

Bard, E., & Crick, P. (1997). Mother–baby observation: Introductory remarks. *Psychoanalytic Psychotherapy, 11* (3): 243–244.

Barrows, P. (1999). Editorial. *International Journal of Infant Observation, 3* (1): 1–10.

Bellack, A. S., & Hersen, M. (Eds.) (1984). *Research Methods in Clinical Psychology.* New York: Pergamon.

Bick, E. (1961). Child analysis today. In: M. Harris Williams (Ed.), *Collected Papers of Martha Harris and Esther Bick* (pp. 104–113). Strath Tay, Perthshire: Clunie Press, 1987.

Bick, E. (1964). Notes on infant observation in psychoanalytic training. In: M. Harris Williams (Ed.), *Collected Papers of Martha Harris and Esther Bick* (pp. 240–256). Perthshire: Clunie Press, 1987.

Bick, E. (1968). The experience of the skin in early object-relations. *International Journal of Psychoanalysis, 49*: 484–486.

Bion, W. (1962). *Learning from Experience.* London: Heinemann.

Bion, W. (1970). *Attention and Interpretation.* London: Tavistock.

Bion, W. (1974). *Brazilian Lectures.* Brazil: Imago Editora. London: Karnac Books, 1990.

Bion, W. (1976). Making the best of a bad job. In: *Clinical Seminars and Four Papers.* Abingdon: Fleetwood Press, 1987.

Blomberg, B. (1999). *Baby Observation as Part of Psychotherapy Training* (in Swedish). Stockholm: Ericastiftelsen.

Bloor, M., Frankland, J., Thomas, M., & Robson, K. (2001). *Focus Groups in Social Research.* London: Sage.

Bodin, G. (1997). The value of infant observation in the psychoanalytic training. *Scandinavian Psychoanalytic Review:* 207–226.

Bollas, C. (1987). *The Shadow of the Object.* London: Free Association Books.

Bollas, C. (1989). *Forces of Destiny.* London: Free Association Books.

Borensztejn, C. L., Kohen de Abdata, N. G., Dimant, S. N., Nemas de Urman, C., & Ungar, V. (1998). Infant observation and its relation to our work as psychoanalysts. *International Journal of Infant Observation, 1* (2): 71–83.

Bowlby, J. (1988). *A Secure Base: Clinical Applications of Attachment Theory.* London: Routledge.

Brafman, A. (1988). Infant observation. *International Journal of Psychoanalysis, 15*: 45–58.

Brafman, A. (2002). Infant observation: What *do* you see? In: L. Caldwell (Ed.), *The Elusive Child.* London: Karnac.

Brazelton, T. B., & Cramer, B. (1991). *The Earliest Relationship.* London: Karnac.

Brazelton, T. B., Koslowski, B., & Main, M. (1974). The origins of reciprocity: The early mother–infant interaction. In: M. Lewis & L. Rosenblum (Eds.), *The Effect of the Infant on Its Caregiver*. New York/London: Wiley.

Bridge, G., & Miles, G. (Eds.) (1996). On the outside looking in. In: *Collected Essays on Young Child Observation in Social Work Training*. London: Central Council for Education & Training in Social Work.

Briggs, A. (2004). The importance of clinical observation for understanding a difficult-to-reach young boy. *International Journal of Infant Observation, 6* (2): 33–52.

Briggs, S. (1997). *Growth and Risk in Infancy*. London: Jessica Kingsley.

Britton, R. (1989). The missing link: Parental sexuality in the Oedipal couple. In: J. Steiner (Ed.), *The Oedipus Complex Today*. London: Karnac.

Bruner, J. S. (1977). Early social interaction and language acquisition. In: H. R. Schoffer (Ed.), *Studies in Mother–Infant Interaction*. London: Academic Press.

Buechler, S. (1997). The right stuff: The analyst's sensitivity to emotional nuance. *Contemporary Psychoanalysis, 33* (2): 295–306.

Burhouse, A. (2001). Now we are two, going on three. *International Journal of Infant Observation, 4* (2): 51–67.

Canham, H., McFadyen, A., & Youell, B. (1997). "Rating Observation: Is It Possible?" Paper presented at Second International Infant Observation Conference, Tavistock, September. *International Journal of Infant Observation, 2* (1999, No. 3): 66–80.

Cantle, Alison (1995). "Counter-transference in theory, practice and in infant observation." Unpublished Masters' dissertation.

Cantle, Anthony (2000). Maternal disavowal in the face of abuse of an infant by its sibling. *International Journal of Infant Observation, 4* (1): 7–25.

Carlberg, G., Dagberg, K., & Nilsson, W. (1993). *Emotional Learning through Observation* (in Swedish). Stockholm: Ericastiftelsen.

Carpy, D. (1989). Tolerating the countertransference: A mutative process. *International Journal of Psychoanalysis, 70*: 287–294.

Carvahlo, R. (1990). Psychodynamic therapy: The Jungian approach. In: W. Dryden (Ed.), *Individual Therapy: A Handbook*. Milton Keynes: Open University Press.

Chodorow, N. (1989). *Feminism and Psychoanalytic Theory*. New Haven, CT: Yale University Press.

Coll, X. (2000). Who needs to observe infants? Infant observation in the training of child and adolescent mental health workers. *Child Psychology & Psychiatry Review, 5* (1): 25–30.

Coltart, N. (1993). *How to Survive as a Psychotherapist*. London: Sheldon Press.

Condon, W., & Sander, L. (1974). Neonatal movement is synchronized with adult speech: Interactional participation and language acquisition. *Science, 183*: 99–101.

Cooper, A. (2004). "Clinical and observational research methods in psychoanalysis: Some philosophical considerations." Unpublished seminar paper.

Cooper, C. (1990). Psychodynamic therapy: The Kleinian approach. In: W. Dryden (Ed.), *Individual Therapy: A Handbook.* Milton Keynes: Open University Press.

Cooper, C. L., & Payne, R. (Eds.) (1980). *Current Concerns in Occupational Stress.* New York: John Wiley & Sons.

Cornwell, J. (1983). Crisis and survival in infancy. *Journal of Child Psychotherapy, 9* (1): 25–33.

Crick, P. (1997). Mother–baby observation: The position of the observer. *Psychoanalytic Psychotherapy, 11* (3): 245–255.

Davids, Z., Miles, G., Paton, A., & Trowell, J. (1999). Issues for seminar leaders in infant and young child observation. *International Journal of Infant Observation, 2* (3): 16–29.

Daws, D. (1986). Consent in child psychotherapy: The conflicts for child patients, parents and professionals. *Journal of Child Psychotherapy, 12* (1): 103–111.

Dean, J., & Moore, M.-S. (2001). Untitled. Presentation at Infant Mental Health Workshop, Tavistock Clinic.

De Casper, A. J., & Fifer, W. P. (1980). Of human bonding: Newborns prefer their mothers' voice. *Science, 208*: 1174–1176.

Dowling, S., & Rothstein, A. (Eds.) (1989). *The Significance of Infant Observation Research for Work with Children, Adolescents and Adults.* Workshop Series of The American Psychoanalytic Association, Monograph 5. Madison, CT: International Universities Press.

Dreher, A. U. (2000). *Foundations for Conceptual Research in Psychoanalysis.* London: Karnac.

Dryden, W. (Ed.) (1990). *Individual Therapy: A Handbook.* Milton Keynes: Open University Press.

Ellis, L. (1997). The meaning of difference: Race, culture and context in infant observation. In: S. Reid (Ed.), *Developments in Infant Observation: The Tavistock Model* (pp. 56–80). London: Routledge.

Emde, R. (1988). Development terminable and interminable: Innate and motivational factors from infancy. *International Journal of Psychoanalysis, 69*: 23–42.

Etchegoyen, H. (1991). *The Fundamentals of Psychoanalytic Technique.* London: Karnac.

Fantz, R. (1961). The origins of perception. *Scientific American, 204*: 66–72.

Farber, B. A. (1995). The genesis, development and implications of psychological-mindedness in psychoanalysts. *Psychopathology, 222*: 170–177.

Fern, E. F. (2001). *Advanced Focus Group Research.* London: Sage.

Ferro, A. (1999). *The Bi-Personal Field: Experiences in Child Analysis.* London: Routledge.

Fisher, J. V. (2002). Poetry and psychoanalysis: Twin "sciences" of the emotions. *Journal of the British Association of Psychotherapists, 40* (2): 101–114.

Fonagy, P. (1993). Aggression and the psychological self. *International Journal of Psychoanalysis, 74*: 471–485.

Fonagy, P. (2001). *Attachment Theory and Psychoanalysis.* New York: Other Press.

Freud, E. (1975). Infant observation: Its relevance to psychoanalytic training. *Psychoanalytic Study of the Child, 30*: 75–94.

Freud, S. (1905e [1901]). Fragment of an analysis of a case of hysteria. *S.E., 7* (pp. 7–122).

Freud, S. (1910d). Future prospects of psychoanalysis. *S.E., 11* (pp. 139–151).

Freud, S. (1912e). Recommendations to physicians practising psychoanalysis. *S.E., 12* (pp. 109–120).

Freud, S. (1913c). Further recommendations on the technique of psychoanalysis: On beginning the treatment. *S.E., 12* (pp. 121–144).

Gayle Beck, J., Andrasik, F., & Arena, J. G. (1984). Group comparison designs. In: A. S. Bellack & M. Hersen (Eds.), *Research Methods in Clinical Psychology* (pp. 100–138). New York: Pergamon.

Glaser, B., & Strauss, A. (1967). *The Discovery of Grounded Theory: Strategies for Qualitative Research.* New York: Aldine.

Goldberg, A. (1994). Farewell to the objective analyst. *International Journal of Psychoanalysis, 75* (1): 21–31.

Goldberg, A. (1999). Between empathy and judgement. *Journal of the American Psychoanalytic Association, 47* (2): 351–365.

Gordon, K. (1997). An advanced training in the supervision and teaching of psychotherapy. In: B. Martindale (Ed.), *Supervision and Its Vicissitudes.* London: Karnac, for EFPP.

Graham, R. (1999). "O" is for observation. *International Journal of Infant Observation, 2* (3): 54–65.

Greben, S. E. (1975). Some difficulties and satisfactions inherent in the practice of psychoanalysis. *International Journal of Psychoanalysis, 56* (4): 427–434.

Green, A. (1975). The analyst, symbolization and absence in the analytic setting. *International Journal of Psychoanalysis, 56*: 1–23.

Green, P., & Miller, L. (2001). Editorial. *International Journal of Infant Observation, 4* (3): 5–12.

Greenberg, J. R., & Mitchell, S. A. (1983). *Object Relations in Psychoanalytic Theory*. Cambridge, MA/London: Harvard University Press.

Greenson, R. (1974). *The Technique and Practice of Psychoanalysis, Vol. 1*. London: Hogarth Press & The Institute of Psychoanalysis.

Greenson, R. (1978). *Explorations in Psychoanalysis*. New York: International Universities Press.

Guy, J. D. (1978). *The Personal Life of the Psychotherapist*. New York: Wiley.

Hamilton, V. (1996). *The Analyst's Preconscious*. Hillsdale, NJ: Analytic Press.

Harris, M. (1976). The contribution of observation of mother–infant interaction and development to the equipment of a psychoanalyst or psychoanalytic therapist. In: M. Harris Williams (Ed.), *The Collected Papers of Martha Harris and Esther Bick* (pp. 225–239). Strath Tay, Perthshire: Clunie Press.

Harris, M. (1977). The Tavistock training and philosophy. In: M. Harris Williams (Ed.), *The Collected Papers of Martha Harris and Esther Bick* (pp. 259–282). Strath Tay, Perthshire: Clunie Press.

Harris, M. (1980). Bion's conception of a psychoanalytic attitude. In: M. Harris Williams (Ed.), *The Collected Papers of Martha Harris and Esther Bick* (pp. 322–340). Strath Tay, Perthshire: Clunie Press.

Hedges, L. (1983). *Listening Perspectives in Psychotherapy*. New York: Jason Aronson.

Heimann, P. (1950). On countertransference. *International Journal of Psychoanalysis, 31*. Also in: M. Tonnesmann (Ed.), *About Children and Children-No-Longer: Collected Papers of Paula Heimann*. London/New York: Tavistock/Routledge, 1989.

Heimann, P. (1962). Response in symposium on "The Curative Factors in Psychoanalysis". *International Journal of Psychoanalysis, 43*: 228–231.

Hersen, M., & Bellack, A. S. (1984). Research in clinical psychology. In: A. S. Bellack & M. Hersen (Ed.), *Research Methods in Clinical Psychology* (pp. 1–23). New York: Pergamon.

Hewison, P. (2004). "Conceptualising audit in couple psychoanalytic psychotherapy." Unpublished thesis.

Hinshelwood, R. (1997). *Therapy or Brainwashing? Does Psychotherapy Differ from Coercion?* London: Karnac.

Holmes, J. (1998). The changing aims of psychoanalysis. *International Journal of Psychoanalysis, 79*: 227–238.

Houzel, D. (1999). A therapeutic application of infant observation in child psychiatry. *International Journal of Infant Observation*, 2 (3): 42–53.

Hunter, V. (1994). *Psychoanalysts Talk*. New York/London: Guilford Press.

Jackson, J. (1998). The male observer: An evaluation. *International Journal of Infant Observation*, 1 (2): 84–99.

Jackson, J., & Shavit, N. (2000). Editorial. *International Journal of Infant Observation*, 4 (1): 3–6.

Joseph, B. (1982). Addiction to near death. *International Journal of Psychoanalysis*, 63: 449–456.

Joseph, B. (1985). Transference: The total situation. *International Journal of Psychoanalysis*, 66: 447–454.

Joseph, B. (1998). Thinking about a playroom. *Journal of Child Psychotherapy*, 24 (3): 359–366.

Kazdin, A. E. (Ed.) (1998). *Methodological Issues and Strategies in Clinical Research* (2nd edition). Washington, DC: American Psychological Association.

Kernberg, O. (1993). Nature and agents of structural intra-psychic change. In: M. Horowitz, O. Kernberg, & E. M. Weinshel (Eds.), *Psychic Structure and Psychic Change: Essays in Honor of Robert S. Wallerstein M.D.* Madison, CT: International Universities Press.

Kernberg, O. (2000). A concerned critique of psychoanalytic education. *International Journal of Psychoanalysis*, 81: 87–120.

Kimberly, R. P. (1970). Rhythmic patterns in human interactions. *Nature*, 228: 89–90.

Kimble, G. A. (1998). Psychology from the standpoint of a generalist. In: A. E. Kazdin (Ed.), *Methodological Issues and Strategies in Clinical Research* (2nd edition). Washington, DC: American Psychological Association.

King, P. (1978). Affective responses of the analyst to the patient's communication. *International Journal of Psychoanalysis*, 59: 329–334.

King, P., & Steiner, R. (Eds.) (1991). *The Freud–Klein Controversies*. London: Routledge.

Klauber, J. (1972). On the relationship of transference and interpretation in psychoanalytic therapy. *International Journal of Psychoanalysis*, 53: 385–391.

Klauber, J. (1986). *Difficulties in the Analytic Encounter*. London: Free Association Books.

Klauber, T., & Trowell, J. (1999). Editorial. *International Journal of Infant Observation*, 2 (3): 2–3.

Klein, M. (1944). The emotional life of the infant. In: P. King & R. Steiner

(Eds.), *The Freud/Klein Controversies* (pp. 752–788). London: Routledge.

Kohut, H. (1959). Introspection, empathy, and psychoanalysis: An examination of the relationship between mode of observation and theory. *Journal of the American Psychiatric Association, 7*: 459–483.

Kratochwill, T. R., Mott, S. E., & Dodson, C. L. (1984). Case study and single-case research in clinical and applied psychology. In: A. S. Bellack & M. Hersen (Eds.), *Research Methods in Clinical Psychology* (pp. 55–99). New York: Pergamon.

Lampl-De Groot, J. (1979). Psychoanalysis: Frame of reference for training. In: W. De Moor & H. Wijngaarden (Eds.), *Psychotherapy: Research and Training: Procedures of the Eleventh International Congress of Psychotherapy* (pp. 213–221). Amsterdam, The Netherlands, 27–31 August.

Langs, R. (1973). *The Technique of Psychoanalytic Psychotherapy, Vol. 1.* New York: Jason Aronson.

Langs, R. (1978). *The Listening Process.* New York: Jason Aronson.

Langs, R. (1982). *Psychotherapy: A Basic Text.* New York: Jason Aronson.

Lanyado, M. (1994). In the beginning . . . Observations of newborn babies and their families. *Journal of the British Association of Psychotherapists, 26*: 22–39.

Lanyado, M. (1998). Review of "Postpartum Depression and Childhood Development", ed. L. Murray & P. J. Cooper. *International Journal of Infant Observation, 2* (1): 112–116.

Lanyado, M. (2004). *The Presence of the Therapist.* Hove: Bruner-Routledge.

Lazar, R. (1998). Learning to be: On the observation of a premature baby. *International Journal of Infant Observation, 1* (2): 21–39.

Levenson, E. (1972). *The Fallacy of Understanding.* New York: Basic Books.

Lignos, E. (1997). "The Clinical Value of Training in Psychoanalytic Infant Observation for the Preventative Programme of a General Children's Hospital." Paper presented at Second International Tavistock Infant Observation Conference.

MacFarlane, A. (1974). The first hours and the first smile. In: R. Lewin (Ed.), *Child Alive.* London: Temple Smith.

MacFarlane, A. (1975). Olfaction in the development of social preferences in the human neonate. *Parent–Infant Interaction.* CIBA Foundation Symposium 33. New York: Elsevier.

Magagna, J. (1987). Three years of infant observation with Mrs Bick. *Journal of Child Psychotherapy, 13* (1): 19–39.

Maher, B. A. (1998). Stimulus sampling in clinical research: Representative design reviewed. In: A. Kazdin (Ed.), *Methodological Issues and Strategies in Clinical Research* (2nd edition, pp. 135–142). Washington, DC: American Psychological Association.

Maiello, S. (1997). Twinning phantasies in the mother–infant couple and the observer's counterpoint function. *International Journal of Infant Observation, 1* (1): 31–50.

Maiello, S. (2000). The cultural dimensions in early mother–infant interaction and psychic development: An infant observation in South Africa. *International Journal of Infant Observation, 3* (2): 80–92.

Martelli, M. P., & Pilo di Boyl, E. (1997). "Three Years' Work with a Group of Nursery School Workers through Participant Observer Method." Paper presented at Second International Tavistock Infant Observation Conference.

McDougall, J. (1986). *Theatres of the Mind*. London: Free Association Books.

McDougall, J. (1992). From the silence of the soma to the words of the psyche. *Journal of the British Association of Psychotherapists, 23*: 3–23.

McFadyen, A. (1991). Some thoughts on infant observation and its possible role in child psychiatry training. *Association for Child Psychology and Psychiatry Newsletter*: 10–14.

McFarland Solomon, H. (2002). Love: Paradox of self and other. In: D. Mann (Ed.), *Love and Hate*. London: Bruner-Routledge.

McGinley, E. (2000). The working through of an anorexic position at the breast. *International Journal of Infant Observation, 4* (1): 84–101.

Meissner, W. (1996). *The Therapeutic Alliance*. New Haven, CT/London: Yale University Press.

Meltzer, D. (1967). *The Psycho-Analytical Process*. Strath Tay: Clunie Press.

Meltzer, D. (1992). *The Claustrum: An Investigation of Claustrophobic Phenomena*. Strath Tay: Clunie Press.

Merton, R. K., Fiske, M., & Kendall, P. L. (1990). *The Focused Interview* (2nd edition). New York: Free Press.

Midgley, N. (2004). Sailing between Scylla and Charybdis: Incorporating qualitative approaches into child psychotherapy. *Journal of Child Psychotherapy, 30* (1): 89–111.

Miles, G., & Trowell, J. (1991). The contribution of observation training to professional development in social work. *Journal of Social Work Practice, 5* (1): 51–60.

Miller, L. (1992). The relation of infant observation to clinical practice in an under 5s counselling service. *Journal of Child Psychotherapy, 18*: 19–32.

Miller, L., Rustin, M., Rustin, M., & Shuttleworth, J. (Eds.). (1989). *Closely Observed Infants*. London: Duckworth.

Miller, L. R. (2001). "What is it that makes infant observation experience so valuable to the adult therapist?" Unpublished dissertation.

Mitchell, S. (1995). Interaction in the Kleinian and interpersonal tradition. *Contemporary Psychoanalysis, 31*: 65–91.

Molino, A. (Ed.) (1997). *Freely Associated: Encounters in Psychoanalysis.* London: Free Association Books.

Morgan, D. (1997). *Focus Groups as Qualitative Research* (2nd edition). London: Sage.

Morgan-Jones, R. (1995). Competencies, risks and developments. *British Journal of Psychotherapy, 11* (3): 436–447.

Muir, E., Lojkasek, M., & Cohen, N. (1999). Observant parents: Intervening through observation. *International Journal of Infant Observation, 3* (1): 11–23.

Murray, L., Fiori-Cowley, A., Hooper, R., & Cooper, P. (1996). The impact of postnatal depression and associated adversity on early mother–infant interaction and later infant outcome. *Child Development, 67*: 2512–2526.

Nacht, S. (1962). The curative factors in psychoanalysis. *International Journal of Psychoanalysis, 43*: 206–211.

Nelson-Jones, R. (1982). *The Theory and Practice of Counselling Psychology.* London: Cassell.

O'Brien, G. (1986). *Psychology of Work and Unemployment.* Chichester: John Wiley & Sons.

Ogden, T. (1997). *Reverie and Interpretation: Sensing Something Human.* Northvale, NJ: Jason Aronson.

Ogden, T. (2001). *Conversations at the Frontier of Dreaming.* Northvale, NJ: Jason Aronson.

Parr, M. (1999). Integrating infant observation skills into parent facilitator training. *International Journal of Infant Observation, 3* (1): 33–46.

Parrot, J. (1998). "Infant observation." Unpublished paper for BAP (British Association of Psychotherapists) training.

Parsons, M. (1984). Psychoanalysis as a vocation and martial art. *International Review of Psycho-Analysis, 11*: 453–462.

Parsons, M. (1986). Suddenly finding it really matters. *International Journal of Psychoanalysis, 67*: 475–488.

Phillips, A., & Sternberg, J. (2000). A compilation of early observations. *International Journal of Infant Observation, 3* (2): 93–100.

Pidgeon, N., & Henwood, K. (1996). Grounded theory: Practical implementation. In: J. Richardson (Ed.), *Handbook of Qualitative Research Methods for Psychology and the Social Sciences.* Leicester: British Psychological Society.

Pine, F. (1985). *Developmental Theory and Clinical Process:* New Haven, CT/London: Yale University Press.

Pozzi, M. (2003). The use of observation in the psychoanalytic treatment of a 12-year-old boy with Asperger's syndrome. *International Journal of Psychoanalysis, 84* (5): 1333–1349.

Rangell, L. (1975). Psychoanalysis and the process of change: An essay on the past, present and future. *International Journal of Psychoanalysis, 56* (1): 87–99.

Rayner, E. (1991). *The Independent Mind in British Psychoanalysis.* London: Free Association Books.

Reid, S. (1997). Introduction: Psychoanalytic infant observation. In: *Developments in Infant Observation: The Tavistock Model* (pp. 1–18). London: Routledge.

Renik, O. (1993). Countertransference enactment and the psychoanalytic process. In: M. Horowitz, O. Kernberg, & E. M. Weinshel (Eds.), *Psychic Structure and Psychic Change. Essays in Honor of Robert S. Wallerstein M.D.* Madison, CT: International Universities Press.

Rhode, E. (1997). First light: Knowing the infant as an actuality and as an idea. In: S. Reid (Ed.), *Developments in Infant Observation: The Tavistock Model* (pp. 89–97). London: Routledge.

Rhode, M. (2004). Sensory aspects of language development in relation to primitive anxieties. *International Journal of Infant Observation, 6* (2): 12–32.

Robinson, M. (1997). "Primitive mental states: Some commonalities between infant observation and adult psychoanalysis." Unpublished paper.

Robinson, R. (1992). "Minding the baby." Unpublished paper.

Root Fortini, L. (1997). "Reaching Insight through Observing in a Maternity Ward Work Group." Paper presented at Second International Tavistock Infant Observation Conference.

Rosenfeld, R. (1971). Contribution to the psychopathology of psychotic states: The importance of projective identification in the ego structure and the object relations of the psychotic patient. In: E. Spillius (Ed.), *Melanie Klein Today: Mainly Theory.* London: Routledge, 1988.

Roth, P. (2001). Mapping the landscape: Levels of transference interpretation. *International Journal of Psychoanalysis, 82* (3): 533–543.

Rustin, M. E. (1988). Encountering primitive anxieties: Some aspects of infant observation as a preparation for clinical work with children. *Journal of Child Psychotherapy, 14* (2): 15–28.

Rustin, M. E. (2000). "Creative Tensions: Child and Adolescent Psychotherapy as an Applied Psychoanalysis." Paper presented at EFPP Conference, Oxford, April.

Rustin, M. E. (2001). The therapist with her back against the wall. *Journal of Child Psychotherapy, 27* (3): 273–284.

Rustin, M. J. (1997a). The generation of psychoanalytic knowledge: Sociological and clinical perspectives, part one: "Give me a consulting room . . .". *British Journal of Psychotherapy, 13*: 527–543.

Rustin, M. J. (1997b). What do we see in the nursery? Infant observation as "laboratory work". *International Journal of Infant Observation, 1* (1): 93–110.

Rustin, M. J. (2002). Looking in the right place: Complexity theory, psychoanalysis and infant observation. *International Journal of Infant Observation, 5* (1): 122–144.

Salo, F., with Paul, C., Morgan, A., Jones, S., Jordan, B., Meehan, M., Morse, S., & Walker, A. (1999). "Free to be playful": Therapeutic work with infants. *International Journal of Infant Observation, 3* (1): 47–62.

Salzberger-Wittenberg, I., Henry, G., & Osborne, E. (1983). *The Emotional Experience of Learning and Teaching.* London: Routledge & Kegan Paul.

Sandelson, J. (1999). "Infant observation." Unpublished paper on infant observation for BAP (British Association of Psychotherapists) training.

Sander, L. (1974). Regulation and organization in the early infant-caretaker system. In: R. Robinson (Ed.), *Brains and Early Behaviour* (pp. 313–331). London: Academic Press.

Sandler, J. (1981). Character traits and object relationships. *Psychoanalytic Quarterly, 50*: 694–708.

Sandler, J. (1988). Psychoanalytic technique and "Analysis Terminable and Interminable". *International Journal of Psychoanalysis, 69* (3): 335–345.

Sandler, J., & Dreher, A. U. (1996). *What Do Psychoanalysts Want?* London: New Library of Psychoanalysis, Routledge.

Sandler, J., Kennedy, H., & Tyson, K. (1990). *The Technique of Child Psychoanalysis: Discussions with Anna Freud.* London: Karnac Books & The Institute of Psychoanalysis.

Sandler, J., Sandler, A.-M., & Davies, R. (Eds.) (2000). *Clinical and Observational Psychoanalytic Research: Roots of a Controversy. André Green and Daniel Stern.* London: Karnac.

Schafer, R. (1983). *The Analytic Attitude.* London: Hogarth Press.

Schlesinger, H. (1994). How the analyst listens: The pre-stages of interpretation. *International Journal of Psychoanalysis, 75*: 31–37.

Schore, A. (1994). *Affect Regulation and the Origin of the Self: The Neurobiology of Emotional Development.* Hillsdale, NJ: Erlbaum.

Schore, A. (2000). "The Neurobiology of Projective Identification." Lecture to Tavistock Society of Psychotherapists, 6 March.

Scott, A. (2002). "Group Relations as an Emotional Technology: September 11 in a Working Conference." Presented at Tavistock Institute Bi-

Annual Meeting of Heads of Organisations Running Group Relations Events, 6 September.

Sechrest, L. (1984). Reliability and validity. In: A. S. Bellack & M. Hersen (Eds.), *Research Methods in Clinical Psychology* (pp. 24–54). New York: Pergamon.

Segal, B. (2003). Anxieties, questions and technical issues in beginning observation. *International Journal of Infant Observation, 5* (3): 11–23.

Segal, H. (1962). The curative factors in psychoanalysis. *International Journal of Psychoanalysis, 43*: 212–217.

Sharpe, E. F. (1930). The technique of psychoanalysis. In: M. Brierley (Ed.), *Collected Papers on Psychoanalysis*. London: Hogarth Press, 1950.

Sharpe, E. F. (1947). The psychoanalyst. In: M. Brierley (Ed.), *Collected Papers on Psychoanalysis*. London: Hogarth Press, 1950.

Shengold, L., & McLaughlin, J. T. (1975). Plenary session on changes in psychoanalytic practice and experience: Theoretical, technical and social implications. *International Journal of Psychoanalysis, 57* (3): 261–274.

Shuttleworth, J. (1989). Psychoanalytic theory and infant development. In: L. Miller, M. Rustin, M. Rustin, & J. Shuttleworth (Eds.), *Closely Observed Infants* (pp. 22–51). London: Duckworth.

Silver, L. (1999). "Infant observation." Unpublished paper for British Association of Psychotherapists training.

Slade, A. (1994). Making meaning and making believe: Their role in the clinical process. In: A. Slade & D. P. Wolf (Eds.), *Children in Play: Clinical and Developmental Approaches to Meaning and Representation*. England: Oxford University Press.

Sorensen, P. (1997). Thoughts on the containing process from the perspective of infant/mother relations. In: S. Reid (Ed.), *Developments in Infant Observation: The Tavistock Model* (pp. 113–122). London: Routledge.

Sorensen, P., Foster, L., Jarrell, J., Mack, D., Presberg, J., & Weeks, R. (1997). The art of the ordinary: The role of observation in the study and treatment of young children and their families. *International Journal of Infant Observation, 1* (1): 9–30.

Steiner, J. (1993). *Psychic Retreats.* London/New York: Routledge.

Stern, D. (1985). *The Interpersonal World of the Infant.* New York: Basic Books.

Stern, D., Sander, L., Nahum, J., Harrison, A., Lyons-Ruth, K., Morgan, A., Bruschweiler-Stern, N., & Tronick, E. (1998). Non-interpretive mechanisms in psychoanalytic therapy: The "something more" than interpretation. *International Journal of Psychoanalysis, 79*: 903–918.

Sternberg, J. (1998). When too much is not enough. *International Journal of Infant Observation, 1* (3): 18–30.

Stewart, H. (1987). Varieties of transference. *International Journal of Psychoanalysis, 68*: 197–206.

Strachey, J. (1933). The nature of the therapeutic action of psychoanalysis. *International Journal of Psychoanalysis, 50*: 275–292 (reprinted from *International Journal of Psychoanalysis, 15*).

Strauss, A., & Corbin, J. (1998). *Basics of Qualitative Research* (2nd edition). Thousand Oaks, CA: London: Sage.

Strupp, H. (1973). *Psychotherapy: Clinical, Research and Theoretical Issues.* New York: Jason Aronson.

Sutton, A. (2001). Consent, latency and psychotherapy, or "What am I letting myself in for?" *Journal of Child Psychotherapy, 27* (3): 319–333.

Symington, N. (1983). The analyst's act of freedom as agent of therapeutic change. *International Journal of Psychoanalysis, 10*: 283–292.

Symington, N. (1996). *The Making of a Psychotherapist.* London: Karnac.

Tanner, K. (1999). Observation: A counter culture offensive. *International Journal of Infant Observation, 2* (2): 12–32.

Taylor, S. J., & Bogdan, R. (1998). *Introduction to Qualitative Research Methods* (3rd edition). New York: Wiley.

Trevarthen, C. (1998). When the beholder is beholden, the infant's psyche may be strong. *International Journal of Infant Observation, 1* (3): 105–116.

Trowell, J. (1999). Assessments and court work: The place of observation. *International Journal of Infant Observation, 2* (2): 91–101.

Trowell, J. (2002). The wider applications of infant observation. In: B. Kahr (Ed.), *The Legacy of Winnicott.* London: Karnac.

Trowell, J., & Rustin, M. (1991). Developing the internal observer in professionals in training. *Infant Mental Health Journal, 12*: 233–245.

Trowell, J., Paton, A., Davids, Z., & Miles, G. (1998). The importance of observational training: An evaluative study. *International Journal of Infant Observation, 2* (2): 101–111.

Truax, C. B. (1963). Effective ingredients in psychotherapy. *Journal of Consulting Psychology, 10*: 256–263.

Tuters, E. (1988). The relevance of infant observation to clinical training and practice: An interpretation. *Infant Mental Health Journal, 9* (1): 93–104.

Tyson, P. (1989). Two approaches to infant research: A review and integration. In: S. Dowling & A. Rothstein (Eds.), *The Significance of Infant Observation Research for Work with Children, Adolescents and Adults* (pp. 3–23). Workshop Series of The American Psychoanalytic Association, Monograph 5. Madison, CT: International Universities Press.

Waddell, M. (1988). Infantile development: Kleinian and post-Kleinian theory, infant observational practice. *British Journal of Psychotherapy, 4* (3): 313–328.

Waddell, M. (2002). The assessment of adolescents. *Journal of Child Psychotherapy, 28* (3): 365–382.

Warin, E. (1996). Infant observation. *Journal of the British Association of Psychotherapists, 30* (1): 85–102.

Wheelis, A. (1956). The vocational hazards of psychoanalysis. *International Journal of Psychoanalysis, 37*: 171–184.

White, C. (1994). Competencies. *British Journal of Psychotherapy, 10* (4): 568–569.

Winnicott, D. W. (1957). On the contribution of direct child observation to psychoanalysis. In: *Maturational Processes and the Facilitating Environment* (pp. 109–114). London: Karnac, 1990.

Winnicott, D. W. (1958a). The capacity to be alone. In: *The Maturational Processes and the Facilitating Environment* (pp. 29–36). London: Karnac, 1990.

Winnicott, D. W. (1958b). Child analysis in the latency period. In: *Maturational Processes and the Facilitating Environment* (pp. 115–123). London: Karnac, 1990.

Winnicott, D. W. (1960). Ego distortion in terms of true and false self. In: *Maturational Processes and the Facilitating Environment* (pp. 140–152). London: Karnac, 1990.

Wittenberg, I. (1993). "Beginnings: The Family, the Observer, and the Infant Observation Group." Paper presented at International Tavistock Infant Observation Conference, September. In: S. Reid (Ed.), *Developments in Infant Observation: The Tavistock Model* (pp. 19–32). London: Routledge.

Wittenberg, I. (1998). In: *Fifty Years of the ACP*. Film.

Wittenberg, I. (1999). What is psychoanalytic about the Tavistock model of studying infants? *International Journal of Infant Observation, 2* (3): 4–15.

Wolff, P. W. (1963). Observations on the early development of smiling. In: B. M. Foss (Ed.), *Determinants of Infant Behaviour* (pp. 113–138). London: Methuen.

Wolff, P. W. (1996). The irrelevance of infant observations for psychoanalysis. *Journal of the American Psychoanalytic Association, 44*: 369–392.

Youell, B. (1999). From observation to working with a child. *International Journal of Infant Observation, 2* (2): 78–90.

Youell, B. (2002). The child psychotherapist and multidisciplinary assessments for the family courts. *Journal of Child Psychotherapy, 28* (2): 201–216.